American Society for Training & Development

I N   A C T I O N

Developing High-Performance Work Teams

FOURTEEN

CASE STUDIES

FROM THE

REAL WORLD

OF TRAINING

ASTD

JACK J. PHILLIPS

SERIES EDITOR

STEVEN D. JONES

MICHAEL M. BEYERLEIN

EDITORS

Library of Congress Catalog Card Number: 97-78237
ISBN: 1-56286-079-8

Table of Contents

Introduction to the
In Action Series

As are most professionals, the people involved in human resource development (HRD) are eager to see practical applications of the models, techniques, theories, strategies, and issues the field comprises. In recent years, practitioners have developed an intense desire to learn about the success of other organizations when they implement HRD programs. The Publishing Review Committee of the American Society for Training & Development has established this series of casebooks to fill this need. Covering a variety of topics in HRD, the series should add significantly to the current literature in the field.

This series has the following objectives:

- *To provide real-world examples of HRD program application and implementation.* Each case will describe significant issues, events, actions, and activities. When possible, the actual names of the organizations and individuals involved will be used. In other cases, the names will be disguised, but the events are factual.

- *To focus on challenging and difficult issues confronting the HRD field.* These cases will explore areas where it is difficult to find information or where the processes or techniques are not standardized or fully developed. Also, emerging issues critical to success in the field will be covered in the series.

- *To recognize the work of professionals in the HRD field by presenting best practices.* Each book in the series will attempt to represent the most effective examples in the field. The most respected organizations, practitioners, authors, researchers, and consultants will be asked to provide cases.

- *To serve as a self-teaching tool for people learning about the HRD field.* As a stand-alone reference, each volume should be a very useful learning tool. Each case will contain many issues and fully explore several topics.

- To present a medium for teaching groups about the practical aspects of HRD. Each book should serve as a discussion guide to enhance learning in formal and informal settings. Each case will have questions for discussion. And each book will be useful as a supplement to general and specialized textbooks in HRD.

The topics for the volumes will be carefully selected to ensure that they represent important and timely issues in the HRD field. The editors for the individual volumes are experienced professionals in the field. The series will provide a high-quality product to fill a critical void in the literature. An ambitious schedule is planned.

If you have suggestions of ways to improve this series or an individual volume in the series, please respond directly to me. Your input is welcome.

Jack J. Phillips, Ph.D.
Series Editor
Performance Resources Organization
Box 380637
Birmingham, AL 35238-0637

Preface

This book is a compilation of case studies of teams that have become, or are in the process of becoming, high-performance teams. The purpose of this book is to provide a learning document on critical elements for team success. It provides an interior view of these teams to illuminate the essence of what made teams successful in a particular organization.

Target Audience

This book is designed for any practitioner interested in teams. Thus, it may be of interest to HRD professionals in organizations interested in teams; to managers and supervisors in these organizations; and to team members. Consultants also may find the book valuable because it covers a wide range of team issues and discusses specific interventions.

Lessons Learned

The authors of these case studies are passionate about their work with teams. They have all encountered obstacles in their efforts to develop high-performance teams. Not all obstacles can be successfully overcome, but the struggle provides a valuable learning opportunity. The authors, and their organizations, have very graciously agreed to share these lessons with us and give us the benefit of learning from their struggles.

Acknowledgments

We would like to thank the following people for their assistance with this casebook: Melanie Bullock, The Center for the Study of Work Teams; and Libby Morris, Performance Resources Organization.

Dedication

We dedicate this book to the ones who make it all worth it, our wives: Cathy Crooks (for Steve) and Susan Beyerlein (for Mike).

How to Use This Casebook

These cases present a variety of approaches to implementing teams in the workplace. Collectively, the cases offer a wide range of settings, methods, techniques, strategies, and approaches, representing manufacturing, service, and government organizations. Target groups for the programs vary from all employees to managers to technical specialists. As a group, these cases represent a rich source of information on the strategies of some of the best practitioners, consultants, and researchers in the field.

Each case does not necessarily represent the optimum or ideal approach for the specific situation. In every case, it is possible to identify areas that could benefit from refinement and improvement. That is part of the learning process—to build on the work of other people. Although the evaluation approach is contextual, these methods and techniques can be used in other organizations.

Table 1 presents basic descriptions of the cases in the order in which they appear in the book. This table can serve as a quick reference for readers who want to examine the evaluation approach for a particular type of program, audience, or industry.

Using the Cases

There are several ways to use this book. In essence, it will be helpful to anyone who wants to see real-life examples of team implementation. Specifically, four uses are recommended:

1. This book will be useful to HRD professionals as a basic reference for practical applications. A reader can analyze and dissect each of the cases to develop an understanding of the issues, approaches, and most of all, refinements or improvements that could be made.

2. This book will be useful in group discussions, where interested individuals can react to the material, offer different perspectives, and draw conclusions about approaches and techniques. The questions at the end of each case can serve as a beginning point for lively and entertaining discussions.

Table I. Overview of the case studies.

Case	Industry	Key Features	Target Audience
Eastman Chemical	Chemical	Supervisor transition to leader, leadership training, organizational strategy	Supervisors, managers, facilitators, design team and HRD staff
Marks & Spencer	Retail	Empowerment, redesign, work teams, sales teams, financial, design teams	Managers, supervisors, OD consultants, training managers, design teams
Harris Semiconductor	Manufacturing	Managing organizational change; socio-tech organization design; developing complex skills; synchronous flow manufacturing, total productive maintenance, business finance and strategy; team development	Managers, supervisors, design teams, OD consultants, training managers, and HRD professionals
Canadian Imperial Bank of Commerce (CIBC)	Financial services	Cultural change, a comprehensive change management plan, innovative lessons learned, key operating principles	Senior executives, project managers, design teams, team facilitators
Midwest Electronics	Manufacturing	Cross-functional production team goes to meet the customer	Team members, managers, design teams
BorgWarner Automotive	Manufacturing	Facilitator's role, facilitator skills, building commitment	Facilitators, supervisors, HRD staff

Table I. Overview of the case studies (continued).

Case	Industry	Key Features	Target Audience
Harris Methodist Health System	Health care	Organizational change, work team implementation steps, interpersonal development, leadership training	HRD staff, trainers, design teams, managers, supervisors
American Central Paper	Manufacturing	Team performance measurement, goal setting, problem solving, roles and responsibilities	Managers, supervisors, design teams, OD consultants
Middle Tennessee State University	Education	Strategic planning, team performance measurement, benchmarking	Managers, supervisors, design teams, OD consultants
The Internal Revenue Service	Government	Virtual team leadership issues, team development, communication	Managers, supervisors, design teams, OD consultants
Sapphire Electronics	Manufacturing—both production management and engineering/design	The use of management intervention in the development of self-managed work teams	Managers who have chosen, or have been assigned to, the task of personally developing empowered work teams
Imperial Manufacturing	Industry—strategic human resource systems consultants	Implementation of cross-functional support teams in all areas of a new facility	HR professionals, training system personnel
BE&K Construction	Construction	Team performance measurement, multicraft work teams, enhanced communication	HR professionals, training system personnel, project managers, team facilitators, design teams

Table I. Overview of the case studies (continued).

Case	Industry	Key Features	Target Audience
Hitachi and Texas Instruments	Semiconductor manufacturing	Merging cultures, international joint venture start-up, collaboration with international parent companies, and preparing a new workforce	Managers anticipating merging international cultures, starting a new company, OD consultants

3. This book will serve as an excellent supplement to other training and development or evaluation textbooks. It provides the extra dimensions of real-life cases that show the outcomes of team building and implementation.

4. Finally, this book will be extremely valuable for managers who do not have primary training responsibility. These managers provide support and assistance to the HRD staff, and it is helpful for them to understand the results that HRD programs can yield.

It is important to remember that each organization and its program implementation is unique. What works well for one may not work for another, even if they are in similar settings. The book offers a variety of approaches and provides an arsenal of tools from which to choose.

Follow-Up

Space limitations have resulted in some cases being shorter than both the author and the editor would prefer. Some information concerning background, assumptions, strategies, and results had to be omitted. If additional information on a case is needed, the lead author can be contacted directly. The address is listed at the end of each case.

Implementation of Work Teams: An Overview

Steven D. Jones and Michael M. Beyerlein

Introduction

"Work team" is a term that has become quite familiar in the past few years. The use of teams has expanded considerably since 1990 within the business sector. Teams have spread from their initial home in manufacturing to retail, sales, professional and technical, management, and even government and educational settings. The spread is not without problems, but the promise of teams continues to draw new enthusiasts. This chapter will provide an overview of what is involved in implementing teams, why people do it, and basic information about how to do it, so that success will be more likely than failure. This chapter also provides a general framework for reading the cases included in this book. The cases illustrate the principles described here and also answer the three questions: what, how, and why?

Work teams developed in a few companies in the industrial world almost randomly until the 1960s. Then the influence of a few publications and the publicity that some innovative companies received began to stimulate a pattern of accelerating growth. In the 1980s, teams were more widely recognized as a means of achieving competitive advantage and employee involvement. The total quality movement raised the awareness of managers and executives about the strategic value of teams in continuous improvement efforts. In 1987, Ed Lawler and his associates at the Center for Effective Organizations at the University of Southern California conducted their first survey of *Fortune* 500 companies to determine the extent to which teams were being utilized. They repeated this survey in 1990 and 1993. The survey results demonstrate a continual spread of team-based forms for organizing work. The latest survey found that more than 50 percent of the *Fortune* 500 firms are implementing teams, but that only 10 percent of the workforce was in teams as of 1993 (Lawler, Mohrman, and Ledford, 1995). Because of the well-documented growth rate and successes of teams, Manz and Sims (1993) estimate that 50 percent of the workforce will be in teams by the year 2000.

Creating high-performing, empowered work teams is at least as challenging and resource consuming as designing the next model of a complex, innovative product. Combine this complexity with the accelerating rates of team implementation, and we find a giant social experiment in the redistribution of power in the workplace. With the increased utilization of teams, we are beginning to detect patterns of success and failure from which we can learn. To learn, we will begin with the question "What are teams?"

What

The first issue to resolve concerns the meaning of the term *work team*. A number of definitions have been suggested. For example, in their watershed book of 1990, Orsburn, Moran, Musselwhite, and Zenger defined a self-directed work team as a trained group of employees, from six to 18, who were fully responsible for turning out a well-defined piece of finished work. More recently, Wilson and George (1991) defined a work team as a group of employees responsible for an entire segment of work or work process. Mohrman's (1995) definition of a team is similar: It requires interdependent tasks, shared goals, and collective accountability. While the definitions vary slightly, they have the following features in common:

- There is sufficient empowerment so that people believe they can make, or at least influence, the decisions that determine how the work gets done.
- Team members recognize that they need one another to achieve the work goals.
- Team members feel a sense of ownership of the work outcomes and for the work culture they all share.

Work teams come in many forms, with many specific purposes and many different names. We can view teams on a continuum with traditional work groups, characterized by hierarchical structures, minimal decision making, and job simplification, anchoring the left end. Anchoring the right end of the continuum are virtual teams characterized by the extremes of minimal hierarchy, large decision-making autonomy, and work with a whole task. Along the continuum are teams without coaches or supervisors, teams with coaches, cross-functional teams, and teams that cross organizational boundaries. Sundstrom, Demeuse, and Futrell (1990) suggested qualitative distinctions and classified teams as either management, project, production, service, action or performing (such as an orchestra), and parallel (such as an ad hoc committee).

If we examine the different attempts to answer the question "What is a team?" the answer is simply "a group of people who need each other." "Teamness" increases as the degree of task interdependence, decision-making autonomy, and wholeness of task increase. Some teams manifest their teamness in different ways, for instance, a management team vs. a parallel team. Finally, we recognize that teamness is not an all-or-nothing concept. We may function as a team part of the time and as separate workers who take orders at other times (Hackman, 1997). This notion of time leads us to the next question of when an organization is ready for teams.

When

Implementation of work teams requires some careful diagnosis of the business and the commitment that senior management is willing to maintain. Many implementation efforts fail because such prework was neglected. The basic conditions for implementing work teams, each of which is further described below, are as follows:
1. perceived need for change
2. interdependence
3. clarity of goals
4. commitment to goals
5. shared mental models
6. similar values
7. opportunity
8. protected space and time, free from interference
9. potential to contribute
10. norms of self-regulation
11. established boundary management
12. feedback
13. challenges from customers, competition, and changing work requirements

PERCEIVED NEED FOR CHANGE. From personal experience, we understand Mohrman and Cummings's point (1989) that real change only occurs when there is pain. There needs to be an awareness that something is not quite right. That discomfort usually has to reach a high threshold level before action is taken. First, senior management is often unaware of the pain at the level of the shop floor until it is too late to be proactive. Second, a long-term commitment by senior management must be fueled by a memory of that pain and the attraction of a proactive vision. First, identify the cause of the pain, then launch a change effort, such as the implementation of teams. Teams may not always be the appropriate medicine, however.

INTERDEPENDENCE. If the work people do does not require them to be interdependent, teams will flounder. Interdependence can be a function of the tasks, goals, feedback, or the customer needs. Organizing the teams around the key interdependencies identifies who belongs inside and who belongs outside of the team boundary.

CLARITY OF GOALS. The traditional approach for implementing teams is based on socio-technical systems theory. The steps for implementing that approach from the top down are well described in Mohrman and Cummings's book (1989). A crucial step is to clarify the goals of the implementation. Goal clarity comes from the framework established by creating mission, vision, and values statements. Where the goals are undefined, conflicting, uncommunicated, unbelievable, or ambiguous, the rest of the organization will not follow with their hearts.

COMMITMENT TO GOALS. Achieving the carefully defined goals depends on commitment at all levels. That is both extremely important and extremely difficult to achieve. Commitment depends on a sense of ownership. Since we care a lot more about our own things than those of others, commitment depends on seeing the implementation program as our own. Implementing teams, therefore, requires the best of two-way communication from top management and from the grass-roots level. This makes fully functioning steering committees essential for team implementation, and a recognition that time is required for quality communication.

SHARED MENTAL MODELS. Each of us brings a unique perspective to a situation, based on a lifetime of experience. Recent literature (for example, Senge, 1990) refers to that perspective as a mental model: our conceptual model of how the world, or some part of it, works. The uniqueness of the mental models in a group offers the value of diversity for problem solving, but coordination of effort requires some shared aspects of our mental models. Thus we need to share our models, appreciating the differences and resolving key discrepancies. We may even consider that we are not fully teaming unless we are sharing our mental models.

SIMILAR VALUES. Values drive our behaviors. Values that are compatible with work teams include: valuing what others have to offer, possibility thinking, involvement, fairness, equality, responsibility, and accountability. Some people prefer to work alone and never accept the idea that they can improve what they do; some people prefer to boss and consider themselves above the rest; some people dread being accountable. Such people seem unable to contribute in team environments; their values conflict with teaming and their teammates.

OPPORTUNITY. Teams emerge in organizations as a result of efforts by champions at the top, middle, or front line of the organization. Champions take initiative and create opportunities. Sometimes opportunity is created by a mandate from senior management; sometimes it is created by individuals taking risks. Isolated teams may have blossomed because one team member or team leader took risks and shared enough of the vision with the team to bring it along.

PROTECTED SPACE AND TIME, FREE FROM INTERFERENCE. Work teams do not spring full grown from a senior management mandate. They grow slowly, given enough resources. The most critical resource for team growth may be time. A team needs the time to meet, form its identity, and receive training, as well as time to experiment and learn from its failures and successes. Mature or advanced teams are rare; they are also impressive. Without time and space for growth, the organization will not reap the full benefits of teams.

NORMS OF SELF-REGULATION. The dynamics of a team are complex because of the number of team members and their interactions to accomplish a goal, which itself is typically complex. These complex dynamics need a controlling mechanism to replace the traditional command and control functions previously accomplished through supervision. The ideal controls seem to emerge when the team creates its own mechanisms to manage the behavior of team members, both formally and informally. The team members need to be able to expect something of one another. They also need a means of communicating those expectations and handling those situations when the expectations are not met.

ESTABLISHED BOUNDARY MANAGEMENT. Successful interaction within a team depends on solving several problems, including who is inside or outside the team, what kinds of decisions are within the purview of the team, how the team will cooperate with other teams, how the team will negotiate for resources from outside its boundaries, and how the team will contend with perceived threats from the "outside." Like any living system, a team seeks a boundary to define itself to itself and to the outside world. Teams are naturally sensitive to the defined group membership, changes in membership, and intrusions into their boundaries. Teams also require clearly defined boundaries for their responsibilities and decision-making authority. Teams cannot remain behind their boundaries, however; they need the capabilities to interface successfully with resource providers, other teams, steering committees, management teams, suppliers, and customers.

FEEDBACK. We cannot function well without feedback; we need feedback to know if we are on target. A team needs to know what needs to be improved, how successful its improvement efforts are, how to get what it needs, and how the big picture relates to its responsibilities. Team feedback systems reflect how well the team is executing its strategy. Without a feedback system based on strategy and performance measurement, the team will drift and lose its purpose for existence.

CHALLENGES FROM CUSTOMERS, COMPETITION, AND CHANGING WORK REQUIREMENTS. Having challenges from the customers, competition, and the work itself may seem like a point that could be taken for granted. These "crises of opportunity" are usually necessary to galvanize teams into action, however. Work that is merely routine and easily accomplished will not awaken the interest of teams.

SUPPORT. Mohrman (1995) found that 90 percent of what caused teams to fail was in their context. By context, she means the support systems in the organization that provide information and materials to the team. Support systems need to be aligned with the needs of the teams and include the systems for performance measurement, evaluation, and reward; systems for training and development, selection, and placement; the information and communication system; and the management system, which includes policies, vision, strategy, and goals.

Certainly an organization does not have to have all 13 of these conditions to successfully implement teams. If many of them are presently absent and not likely to occur, however, we wonder if now is the best time for teams. While considering the best timing for team implementation, we also find ourselves naturally wondering why it would be a good idea.

Why

In business today, the pace of technological change and the ferocity of competition exceed what we could imagine just five years ago. Most of us can't comprehend how severe it is today. Guess what! It will get more extreme in the future! Consequently, to borrow a phrase from Matsushito, founder of the giant electronics company by the same name, we need to "use every ounce of intelligence in every employee in the company."

Success begets success, and eventually failure. Ed Lawler (1988) describes Frederick Taylor, father of scientific management and modern industrial engineering, as reducing the role of the worker to that of a machine. Taylor stressed the advantages of machine pacing and limited job definitions. Authority and decision making were supposed to rest at the top of the organization while lower-level employees were to do, not think. Thinking, coordinating, and controlling were left to management. This resulted in the high-volume assembly line and its tremendous increases in productivity. The result was a formula for success that lasted most of the 20th century. That formula now has become a formula for failure.

Machines have replaced most of the lowest-skilled, nonthinking jobs— or those jobs have gone offshore. High-volume production is quickly becoming obsolete. Customer demand today is for customized production, short-order times, and "freshness dates" demanding quick changes and short production runs. The response to these demands requires giving control of the work to those closest to the work.

Of course management can't just give up control; it has to replace it with another form of control that stimulates rather than inhibits thinking. Teams provide a structured means of accomplishing this transition. The data shows that teams can work, although not always. Katzenbach and Smith (1993) summarized data from 50 cases of organizations using work teams. The results included improved customer satisfaction, increased profits and savings, and improved quality. Based on a survey, *Training Magazine* reported in 1992 that 90 percent of the companies that implemented teams experienced improved quality, 85 percent had improved customer service, 81 percent realized improved productivity, 80 percent increased profits, 76 percent improved employee morale, and 62 percent improved management morale. If we look at the business results of just a few companies, we find that teams reduced labor costs by 30 percent at Miller Brewing (Ohio); reduced claims backlog from 18,000 to 0 at Blue Cross/Blue Shield; reduced costs by 10 percent ($3 million annually) at LaRoche Industries; and decreased policy processing time by 20 percent at Milwaukee Mutual Insurance (Kricher and Golding, 1997).

The conversion from traditional organizations to work teams is not easy or quick; it takes time, effort, and risk. It is widely assumed that once a group is given the autonomy and responsibility of becoming a team, that it goes through several stages of development before it finally emerges as a fully functioning unit. Self-managing teams do not become self-managing overnight. A considerable period of training and development precedes complete self-management. Many teams never reach the advanced levels. It is a challenge that the writers of the cases in this book accepted and struggled with. Their struggles are enlightening, even though their team may have years of development ahead.

The Casebooks

We find numerous reports of team successes, and this casebook is full of them. We also know of team failures, and we suspect that many of these failures are the result of poor implementation. We want to stimulate more successful implementations. We now want to look behind the scenes of the successes and try to understand what makes them successful. We have asked the authors to provide an interior view so we can look into the heart of their team and learn from their experiences. The authors graciously shared their experiences with us because of their belief in teams. We hope that, in your interest in teams, you will honor their efforts by learning as much as possible from these cases. You may find that some of the case materials can be integrated into your training programs. To stimulate that effort, the authors provided case study questions at the end of each case.

In the spirit of learning, we invite the readers to give us their feedback and comments directed at making these casebooks even better learning experiences. We are interested in what you are interested in learning regarding teams. We are currently editing cases for volume 2 and planning future volumes. We welcome your help in improving the usefulness of these cases for the reader. If you have enlightening cases, please let us know.

Please send comments to either Steven D. Jones at Box X-105, Middle Tennessee State University, Murfreesboro, TN 37132 (e-mail: sdjones@acad1.mtsu.edu); or Michael M. Beyerlein at the Center for the Study of Work Teams, Box 13587, Denton, TX 76203 (e-mail: Beyerlei@facstaff.cas.unt.edu).

References

Hackman, J.R. "Teams That Work and Those That Don't." *Proceedings From the Best of Teams '97 Conference.* Lexington, MA: Linkage, 1997.

Katzenbach, J., and D. Smith. *The Wisdom of Teams: Creating the High Performance Organization.* Cambridge, MA: Harvard Business School Press, 1993.

Kricher, L., and J. Golding. "Measuring Team Performance." *Proceedings From the Best of Teams '97 Conference.* Lexington, MA: Linkage, 1997.

Lawler, E.E. III, S.A. Mohrman, and G.E. Ledford. *Creating High Performance Organizations: Practices and Results of Employee Involvement and Total Quality Management in Fortune 1000 Companies.* San Francisco: Jossey-Bass, 1995.

Orsburn, J.D., L. Moran, E. Musselwhite, and J.H. Zenger. *Self-Directed Work Teams: The New American Challenge.* Homewood, IL: Irwin, 1990.

Manz, C., and H. Sims Jr. *Business Without Bosses: How Self-Managing Teams Are Building High Performing Companies.* New York: Wiley, 1993.

Mohrman, S.A., S.G. Cohen, and A.M. Mohrman Jr. *Designing Team-based Organizations: New Forms for Knowledge Work.* San Francisco: Jossey-Bass, 1995.

Mohrman, S.A., and T.G. Cummings. *Self-Designing Organizations: Learning How to Create High Performance.* Reading, MA: Addison-Wesley, 1989.

Senge, P. *The Fifth Discipline: The Art and Practice of the Learning Organization*. New York: Currency Doubleday, 1990.

Sundstrom, E., K.P. Demeuse, and D. Futrell. "Work Teams: Applications and Effectiveness." *American Psychologist*, 45, 1990, 120-133.

Wilson, J., and J. George. "Aligning Your Performance Management System to Support Self-Managing Work Teams." In *Proceedings of the 1991 International Conference on Self-Managed Work Teams*, edited by M. Beyerlein, S. Flax, and R. Saiter. Denton, TX: Center for the Study of Work Teams, 1991.

From Supervisor to Team Manager

Eastman Chemical

Allen Ferguson, Amy Hicks, and Steven D. Jones

This case presents an interior view of how a traditional supervisor was transformed into a team leader. It describes the "agony behind the success" that we often don't get to hear. Supervisors experiencing this transition may recognize the stages of change, the critical training, and the insights into the new team leader role, as well as barriers that must be overcome. This case will provide useful landmarks for supervisors embarking on this journey. This case study reflects the opinions and experiences of Allen Ferguson as he made the successful transition from a traditional supervisor to a team manager, not necessarily those of Eastman Chemical.

Transition to Team Management

In the transition to teams, the crucial role of the frontline supervisor is often underestimated. Since employees take their cues from the supervisors, these people can make or break the team effort. On the surface, however, it appears that supervisors stand to gain the least from the transition to teams. In the transition, senior or upper management articulates the vision and reaps the benefits of the cost savings. Employees participate more and get to see their ideas for improvement implemented. But supervisors must radically change their management style, give up power, and patiently nurture the team development. Often this must occur in an environment where, at least initially, many employees do not want the additional responsibilities, and upper management maintains the traditional style. With apparently so little to gain, it is understandable that most supervisors have great difficulty making this transition. This case study

This case was prepared to serve as a basis for discussion rather than to illustrate either effective or ineffective administrative and management practices.

examines the ingredients of a successful transition from traditional supervisor to team manager at Eastman Chemical.

Background

Eastman manufactures more than 400 chemicals, fibers, and plastics in a global operation. In 1996, this company, headquartered in Kingsport, Tennessee, had 17,500 employees worldwide and sales of $4.8 billion. Prior to 1980, there were usually four levels of management, from the first-line supervisors to the division heads in the service organization. The management style of the company, similar to most organizations of that time, was very traditional, with a culture of command and control. Management took on the role of planning, while workers were responsible only for "doing." The assumption of management was that the workers had a good work ethic but must be closely supervised, since they could not be trusted to make decisions. Employees' ideas and suggestions for improvement were submitted primarily through a company suggestion system. Workers were "hands" carrying out management's plans, and this had been the approach to management since the founding of the organization in 1920.

In 1979, after considering statistical process control and total quality management (TQM) implementation, top management decided to pilot-test teams in one of its manufacturing divisions. Based on the lessons of this pilot, and driven by the vision of top management, Eastman began the journey to TQM and team management in late 1980.

At the time, American industry had ignored the world market and was losing sales, principally to their Japanese and European competitors. Edward Deming, the catalyst in the success of the Japanese industry, was hired by Eastman to evaluate its current system and recommend sweeping changes. One major responsibility of upper management was to reduce the levels of management to make the company more efficient. To support this change, the decision to move to team management at the Kingsport headquarters was made by the Plant Maintenance Division head in 1989. This decision was key to the Maintenance Division's organizational strategy for the 1990s.

The move to team management, however, posed a threat to the culture of the entire organization. Some managers, supervisors, and employees felt threatened by this transition to teams. The threat may have been greatest at the supervisory level, because the supervisors had to assume more responsibility and relinquish control after many years of operating in the traditional management style.

Allen Ferguson, one of the supervisors, had joined Eastman in 1955 and was soon accepted into a four-year apprenticeship program. In 1972, he became the maintenance foreman of the Tenite® Plastics Division. Then in 1983, he was made the chemicals maintenance supervisor. Ferguson became the training coordinator for the Plant Maintenance Division in 1987. While serving in this position, he acquired the needed interpersonal skills and computer skills that would become essential in his next role as a team manager in the Tenite® Plastics Division. Today, as principal team manager for this division, he is responsible for mechanical and electrical maintenance. During this time, Ferguson received training in statistics, seven-step problem solving, team leadership, and team management. Many of his skills were acquired through applying experience and training provided by Eastman's training department.

Even though Ferguson has worked for 40 years in a culture of traditional management, he describes himself today as a "transparent" manager. Before the transition to teams, he used the traditional approach to management, but he always had confidence that his workers could perform the daily activities without close supervision. Ferguson now believes that his function as a proactive and empowering team manager is to delegate responsibility and authority to his team, while furnishing the needed support and resources. This view has allowed him to become a successful team manager, though the transition was very difficult.

When the decision to change to teams was announced, there were mixed feelings within the organization, and reactions differed throughout the company. When Ferguson was reassigned to the Tenite® Plastics Division to manage a maintenance team, he, like most supervisors, did not believe a team-based approach would be successful in Eastman's culture. Because he had always been successful as a traditional supervisor, Ferguson felt personally threatened by the change and uncertain of his ability to make the transition. This new approach was unfamiliar to him, as was his new role in the organizational structure. He had always taken great pride in his work, but now his responsibilities were going to be drastically altered, and he did not have the proper training to accomplish this task. Ferguson was also fearful of losing his position of power. He now believes, however, that his years of experience as a traditional manager made possible his own transition to team manager. He even said: "I don't believe I could have made the transition if I had not been a good traditional supervisor. When people in authority over me tell me to do something, I do my best even though I don't agree." Although Ferguson's experience with traditional management facilitated his movement to teams, this same experience became a barrier for others.

Painful Transitions

Many of Ferguson's peer supervisors were not as willing to attempt the transition as he was. These supervisors also had been in positions of power and they were comfortable in the traditional role. Becoming team managers would require them to give power to their teams. Some supervisors understood management's vision and took to the change readily. Others who did not understand the vision, like Ferguson, followed management's orders anyway as a result of their traditional management role of obeying authority. But many supervisors were so wedded to the traditional management role that they did not want to manage in the new way. Many of them were reassigned to technical and staff positions. The supervisors with solid interpersonal skills began managing more teams. This reduced the Plant Maintenance Division first-line supervisors by 50 percent in the first three years. During this time, supervisors were being trained in team management. All of this change created more stress for the remaining supervisors, and many took early retirement. The introduction of computers into the workplace also contributed to the loss of supervisors, since many of them lacked computer skills. Throughout the entire change process, there has been a significant reduction in first-line supervisors to manage teams.

The crew members also had mixed reactions to the team concept. As a team, they would have to accept responsibility for their own work. Many were satisfied with carrying out their supervisor's orders without having to participate in the decision-making process, thereby avoiding accepting responsibility for their actions. Some teams got the impression that they could bypass their supervisor's directions by taking on the processes of team development. They believed they knew how their supervisors perceived managing teams and thought their supervisors would transfer or quit if the workers embraced this new idea. But they soon realized that, even though many supervisors were leaving, the transition to teams was not just a fad. Other workers were enthusiastic about being more involved in their work. Implementing teams demonstrated confidence in the workers by allowing them to have autonomy and to contribute ideas and suggestions.

The transition to team management has been a major turning point for Eastman. The sweeping alterations initiated a series of emotional stages that were a result of this major change in the lives of employees and supervisors. The initial stage was shock—a feeling of disbelief that the transition was actually occurring, and confusion about what each individual's role would now be. Facing an unfamiliar situation created an atmosphere of uneasiness. For instance, Ferguson was requested by his management not to give out work orders, which was the way he previously had managed what his work crews did. Shock would soon turn into anger and frustration, the second stage. Those affected by the change were very upset about it. They were angry that this team approach was going to affect their job responsibilities, since both supervisors and employees were content in their current roles. At this point, many supervisors retired, unable to let go of their anger.

Those who progressed entered into the third stage, denial. Both supervisors and workers viewed the transition to teams as just "another program of the month" that would soon pass. Many had the attitude that upper management would have to force them to change; so they continued to carry out their daily work in the same manner, while seeking reassurance that change was not taking place. Some supervisors provided confirmation by not changing their management style, and the team provided indirect reassurance by complaining and avoiding additional responsibilities. After realizing that change was inevitable, depression set in. This fourth stage was characterized by low morale and narrowed perspectives. The first-line supervisors felt trapped between management and their crews. Some managers thought the supervisors were not encouraging the teams to perform the processes necessary for change. The teams blamed their supervisors for enforcing the directions of top management. The first-line supervisors felt responsible for their team's behavior and for making the change work, yet they didn't know how to make the transition without their usual control mechanisms. This conflict caused depression for these supervisors.

Depression was followed by grieving, which resulted from the loss of a familiar, comfortable situation. Ferguson remembers the day he told his wife that he was no longer a supervisor. He felt the loss of his position and its accompanying power and prestige. Grieving was necessary to reach the final stage of acceptance. In the acceptance stage, the fear of change was no longer present. Changes no longer caused anger, because the benefits of change could be seen. Those who were able to reach this stage had a feeling of peace that change was the right step for the organization. When Ferguson finally accepted the transition, he began to understand the vision of top management. Even after acceptance, reverting to a previous stage is still possible, but those supervisors who made the transition became team managers.

Training

Eastman provided its employees with video-based training on these transitional stages. This training was one of the reasons that many of the supervisors and teams were able to make the changes required for the new system of management.

Management followed four phases in the transition at Eastman. The first phase was to focus on the Deming methods. These provided structure for the transition. The next phase involved training in a seven-step problem-solving process. These seven steps are (1) focus on and pinpoint the problem; (2) communicate, translate, and link the organization's objectives to each team's environment; (3) create a management plan; (4) improve processes (including work and interpersonal processes); (5) measure progress; (6) provide feedback; and (7) reinforce behaviors and celebrate results. In phase three, Eastman benchmarked with similar organizations that had made the shift from traditional to team management in order to monitor the organization's progress. The fourth phase, stabilization, required training for both management and teams in all phases of interpersonal team skills. The transition period is still in progress at Eastman. Some have not yet accepted the team approach. With management's continuing support, full compliance is expected by 1999, in Ferguson's opinion.

Eastman's management has provided support in many ways. In the beginning, a consulting firm was hired to provide instruction and training to both management and teams. This training empowered the employees by providing them the skills necessary to become fully functioning teams. Management has supported the actions of the team managers and has also made them accountable for these actions, which has increased team managers' feelings of personal responsibility for their teams' success. Upper management has provided direction and guidance through coaching and team meetings that are held to address the managers' and teams' concerns. One-on-one meetings also are held with individual managers when needed. The main support provided by management has been training. This along with other management support has been essential for the transition.

Eastman has provided training to all managers and employees throughout the transition process. Performance management training was given to all Plant Maintenance Division management, from first-line managers to the division head. The Maintenance Division developed training from these sessions and formed a group of consultants who worked with each crew and its team manager. Cost management, computer training, and workplace communication training were given, in addition to video training on essential elements of working in a team environment. For management, team training seminars were held. A week-long course called Leadership Involvement Facilitation Technology (LIFT) training, in which managers served as coaches, was required for all maintenance personnel. This was their first real experience working with teams. This training taught employees how to work in a cross-functional team and also taught them about types of leadership styles, such as demander, avoider, and engager. LIFT training and the building of interpersonal skills created the foundation for the transition. Training is an ongoing process at Eastman. Without training and other continuing support by management, the transition cannot continue.

Barriers to Change

Throughout the transition, the organization has had to overcome many barriers. Many traditional managers, who were present in all levels of management, have had to commit to this new style of management. As previously described, many supervisors retired or were transferred to positions where they did not manage teams. Without the support of supervisors, crews could not have accepted this new structure; so the supervisors' commitment has been vital. Another barrier has been the attitude of Eastman's traditional supervised crews. In the beginning, Ferguson's feeling that this style of management would not work was created by fear and lack of understanding. This fostered a resistance to the change. The transition to teams created a new culture that had to be able to work with the old one, since all divisions had not yet begun the transition. For example, the team-based Maintenance Division supported the very traditionally managed Manufacturing Division. Frequently this resulted in culture clash. Facilities, such as meeting rooms, that were needed to support the new culture also were not available. The diversity of the workforce created a barrier as well. Now that teams were communicating and participating more, they had to be trained in how to interact with others who had different values and attitudes. Interpersonal skills were imperative for overcoming these obstacles that Eastman faced.

In Ferguson's opinion some middle managers did not support the change. First-line managers had to address this issue by telling middle managers that their actions were inconsistent with the goals of the organization. The first-line supervisors also had to realize that some middle managers felt threatened by empowering the teams, just as the supervisors had. By empowering the teams, managers were not only relinquishing their own power, they also believed they were risking their job security. Since these new roles were perhaps the most difficult barrier to overcome, it took time for everyone to adjust.

New Roles

As first-line supervisors became team managers, their roles within the organizational structure changed. When they functioned as traditional managers, their role was that of decision maker. Traditional managers are like first sergeants in the army who bark out orders with no questions asked. With the teams participating in more of the decisions and having more authority, the team managers have become mentors and coaches. They support their teams with information on policies and processes that they need in order to make decisions for themselves. The supervisor's position of authority over the crew has developed into a position of responsibility to the team to support them by whatever means possible. The traditional first-line supervisors' narrow span of control enabled them to give orders and enforce them. As team managers, with a much larger span of control, they now have to provide the necessary information to their teams so that those teams can solve problems and carry out tasks. This has changed the role of managers from the owner of information to the facilitator of information. First-line supervisors were also task oriented. Their main duty was to plan the work and to ensure that it was done. Team managers now have to be process oriented. Their main duty now is to focus on projects and processes while allowing the team to focus on the daily tasks. Not only did the team managers have to adjust to these new roles, their teams did also.

One purpose of the transition to teams was to reduce the levels of management in the organization. Accordingly, the levels have been reduced from four to three in the Tenite® Plastics Division. These new levels are the team managers, area managers, and the division head. In the mid 1970s, six managers and one secretary were required to maintain the support maintenance for the Tenite Plastics Division. As a result of team-based management, the division now has one team manager and one area manager. The flatter hierarchy has forced team managers to transfer responsibilities to their teams. In Ferguson's case, he now has responsibility for what five other supervisors were formerly in charge of. Likewise, some of Ferguson's original responsibilities for daily tasks were transferred to his team, including managing voluntary overtime, time keeping, scheduling vacations, planning work orders, planning and scheduling team meetings, and scheduling visits to customers and suppliers. Duties are transferred by agreed-upon processes that are signed by both the team and Ferguson. By transferring these duties to his team, Ferguson is able to focus on the projects and processes of the Tenite® Plastics Division's maintenance area. This transfer of responsibilities was one of the first steps in the transition process for Ferguson's teams.

Within his own maintenance teams, Ferguson encouraged acceptance of not only his new role but the team's new role as well. For Ferguson, the next step in this transition was to develop trust between himself and the team. To create trust, he allowed the team to be responsible for tasks that were previously performed only by managers. Ferguson established boundaries for his team to operate within, which allowed them to have autonomy while still depending on him for "boundary" support. After the team began to trust Ferguson, they no longer saw him as a threat. Today they freely contribute ideas and ask for his opinion on improvement efforts. In the beginning, Ferguson sometimes had to meet legitimate demands of the team for resources, such as equipment or tools, to prove his willingness to support them. Both he and the team made concessions necessary to facilitate the change process. Ferguson explained the purpose of team management and how it would benefit the team. If at any time he made a mistake, he addressed the problem quickly with all of those involved. This has enabled him to gain respect and trust, while serving as a behavioral model to his team. All of these actions by Ferguson have created a norm of trust within his team.

Ferguson also has facilitated the transition process by positively reinforcing desired team behaviors. Commendations are given to team members for any work that adds value to the organization. These commendations are documented in the employees' personnel files. The team is also encouraged to document outstanding performance of its members to bring to Ferguson's attention. They even have been given digital and video cameras to record instances of good work or improvements in processes to later show to management. Ferguson also knows that praising the team members' accomplishments serves as reward in itself. Praise is not given unless it is deserved. Insincere praise, according to Ferguson, gives the team the impression that the manager is not being honest, resulting in diminishing trust, the backbone of team management. By providing positive reinforcement, the team has learned what behaviors are desired in their role in this new system.

Team meetings also have helped to clarify roles. As part of team management, Ferguson's teams meet every two weeks. These meetings primarily focus on problem-solving work processes and equipment-related problems, as well as other team concerns. The team leader function is shared by all team members by alternating leaders at each meeting. The team manager is considered part of the team and also has input in the meetings. Managers also are members of peer teams that meet twice a month. These meetings reinforce team manager roles and consistency among managers by allowing them to discuss processes and problems within the teams and to share ideas that may be useful to every manager. These meetings may address concerns within a team, or problems affecting other teams. Team meetings for workers and managers provide an avenue for communication and participation, which increases employee commitment to teams. This commitment results in successes not only for the team, but also for the entire organization as well.

Benefits

Since the transition to teams began in 1989, Ferguson's maintenance team has achieved three major accomplishments. The first involved multicraft teams. The team was allowed to make the decision to combine mechanical and electrical personnel into one team. This had never been attempted before at Eastman, since specialization had always been the norm. After making the decision to become a multicraft team, team members cross-trained one another on critical equipment tasks. The multicraft team was so successful that it changed the way maintenance operated plantwide. This program was adopted by all maintenance departments and has been a major source of cost savings to the organization. Ferguson's team was recognized by the president for its contributions to the company. This achievement by the team was followed by other successes.

The second success came as a result of Ferguson's vacation. Three years after teams were formed, he left for three weeks and allowed his team to manage itself. He gave complete authority to the team and accepted full responsibility for their actions. Not only did this show the confidence he had in his team, it also signified how far his team had come in three years. The team proved its competence by operating with no difficulties during Ferguson's absence. Another accomplishment was the promotion of five team members to higher-level positions. This demonstrated that successful team management increases human resource capacities for the company.

Team management has benefited Eastman in many ways. Nearly all employees are expected to be a member of, and contribute through, at least one team. Eastman has become a team-based organization of employees who think in terms of what teams can do to support the business. Employee motivation, efficiency, and productivity have increased. Sales have increased 84 percent in the past 11 years. Operating income had grown 14 percent since 1994. The maintenance organization has operated under budget for the past six years and has had a turnaround of several million dollars' profit. Process improvements ranging from 15 percent to 50 percent have resulted in cost savings for the organization. The primary benefit, which has made the aforementioned benefits possible, is an organizational culture that emphasizes honesty, integrity, trust, and teamwork.

Teams also have benefited from this transition. They now have autonomy in their work. They have a voice and participate in decisions that affect their jobs. Teams have received valuable training and acquired skills they might not have received under a traditional system. They now have a personal feeling of accomplishment from their work, which has helped to increase self-esteem and intrinsic motivation. Team members also know that they are part of an organization that values their time and their input.

Allen Ferguson has benefited as a manager and as a person from this experience. As a manager, he has stopped working for himself and started working for his team. He views team successes as his successes. He has learned to use positive reinforcement instead of punishment to shape his team's behavior. Ferguson approaches problems differently now, by listening to others and considering reasons for their actions before coming to conclusions. As a manager, he has learned the importance of consistency. When he reverts to traditional-style behaviors, his team does also. He believes "the consequences of being inconsistent are inconsistency." He has received valuable training and acquired interpersonal skills that have been useful in his everyday life. He now has a feeling of accomplishment from contributing to his organization and to his team. The most important benefit to Allen Ferguson may be the ability to be more open to new ideas. He once believed team management was impossible at Eastman. Now he believes "it does not matter what type of work you do, as a team you can do it better."

Questions for Discussion

1. How critical is the supervisor in the transition to teams? Why?
2. Why do so many supervisors have trouble with the transition to teams?
3. What do supervisors need in their transition to team manager?
4. What role changes are required on the part of upper managers, supervisors, and team members in the transition to teams?
5. What emotional reactions can supervisors expect to experience within themselves during the transition to teams?
6. What are the key differences between command and control management and team management?
7. What elements of command and control are retained or modified in team management?
8. What minimum skills and knowledge should a supervisor have before engaging in this transition?

9.   What rewards are there at the end of the transition for the supervisor who becomes a team manager?

10. List three key things you learned from this case. How would you incorporate them into your own change efforts?

The Authors

Allen Ferguson is retired from Eastman Chemical Company's Tenite® Plastics Division in Kingsport, Tennessee. He first came to work there in 1955 and has progressed from shop employee to principal team manager. Ferguson can be reached at 1113 Jackson Hollow Road, Kingsport, TN 37663; phone: 423.239.8979; e-mail: fergy@preferred.com.

Amy Hicks is a graduate student in industrial/organizational psychology at Middle Tennessee State University. She can be reached at 3034 John Bragg Highway, Woodbury, TN 37190.

Steven D. Jones is an associate professor at Middle Tennessee State University and a member of a self-directed work team with the industrial/organizational psychology program. He specializes in team performance measurement, leadership training, and team building. Jones can be contacted by writing to Box X-105, Middle Tennessee State University, Murfreesboro, TN 37132; phone: 615.898.5937; e-mail: sdjone@acad1.mtsu.edu.

How Self-Managed Sales Teams Led to Better Sales in a British Company

Marks & Spencer

Roger Woodgate, ABA Consultants
Niall Trafford and Angela Stephens, Marks & Spencer

Retail sales is a new frontier for teams. This case describes team implementation in a British retail firm as part of a change to an empowered work culture. It is encouraging that an organization that dominates its market niche would risk such a major change in pursuing a human resource strategy.

Introduction

Sales increases of 214 percent; 50 suit orders taken in one hour; an increase from $2,000 to $30,000 on one item within 30 days—impressive figures that most retailers can only dream about. These were all achieved through peer teams of sales assistants being encouraged to take ownership of the selling process. Peer teams have been the key to a radical change in the way Marks & Spencer, one of the United Kingdom's leading corporations and top retailers, has changed the way it does things.

What Is It?

It is an approach to creating a selling culture involving groups of frontline staff—sales assistants—generating and implementing their own ideas about how to improve sales and create a selling culture where every staff member is allowed to anticipate and respond to customer needs.

The peer teams of sales assistants, called Sales Improvement Teams, are unsupervised by management and are encouraged to implement

This case was prepared to serve as a basis for discussion rather than to illustrate either effective or ineffective administrative and management practices.

activities that will build on Marks & Spencer's unrivaled reputation for excellent service.

Background

The initiative was launched by Marks & Spencer in the summer of 1995. The challenge was that every staff member should be trained to sell by the year 2000. They wanted something sustainable and "lived" by every staff member. Not that Marks & Spencer was failing in the sales area. In May 1996, Marks & Spencer announced record profits of $1.5 million and was duly described in *The Independent Newspaper of London:* "Marks & Spencer confirmed its position as the Rolls Royce of the British High Street when it reported a strong increase in profits."

Marks & Spencer is the strongest brand name in the United Kingdom and is synonymous with quality. It is a company that pays its staff above-average wages; awards shares to staff along with annual pay raises; has a noncontributory pension scheme; and provides subsidized meals, a dentist, and a chiropodist on site in the head office.

Founded in 1894 as a market stall, Marks & Spencer has grown to be a $17 million giant with 284 stores in the United Kingdom. It owns stores in Canada; Brooks Brothers and Kings Supermarkets in the United States; and numerous stores throughout Europe and the Far East. The current chairman, Richard Greenbury, has worked solely at Marks & Spencer since joining the firm in 1953 as a management trainee. Most of his fellow directors also have worked their way up from the training level. Marks & Spencer's home-grown talent tells us something about the company's employees: They don't want to leave.

The continued expansion of Marks & Spencer abroad led to the opening of five new European stores and 12 Far Eastern stores in 1996. One thousand new jobs were created in 1995 and 1,500 more in 1996, yielding a total of more than 60,000 people employed by the company.

Why This Initiative?

Traditionally, responses to training initiatives are met with a top-down approach: The head office produces a training package that is distributed to stores; then employees complete the program and "check the box" to indicate they have completed the training.

This type of approach is not always effective because it fails to utilize the input, ideas, and experience of those on the receiving end, and it does not translate from intention to action. Therefore, it was decided to use peer teams to design and implement various ideas to create a selling culture. This approach was designed to ensure that the staff genuinely owned the initiative.

The decision to utilize self-managed peer teams to drive the process was made when Roger Woodgate of ABA Consultants returned from the United States after spending a year researching the effectiveness of self-managed teams in a changing workplace culture. At the time the initiative was being set up, Niall Trafford, Training Department, Marks & Spencer Head Office, heard the author's presentation to a team of senior training managers. "I was looking for an innovative approach that got away from a top-down, tell-them approach, believing that this was not the way to really change attitudes and help with buy-in," said Trafford.

The adopted approach involved inviting sales assistants to join Sales Improvement Teams in a number of pilot stores to generate ideas, involve other store colleagues in the generation of ideas, and evaluate the effectiveness of their new ideas. The eight pilot stores were selected from across the United Kingdom and Europe, including large and small stores. The trial period lasted from January to May 1996. The eight pilot stores were given an unstructured brief: "Try whatever you think will work, and break the rules if necessary." This caused some consternation at first as teams grappled with a blank canvas. After two or three weekly meetings, however, the teams realized they were genuinely empowered to generate and implement a variety of initiatives.

The company headquarters was eager to sponsor this approach because it also made a statement about their willingness to innovate. As with all of Marks & Spencer's product ranges, the Training Department prides itself on innovative approaches to improving business performance. Using peer teams to deliver this approach complemented their well-established management development strategy, which centers on continuous learning and self-development, both of which were central to this initiative. The approach was consistent with Marks & Spencer's management development strategy that employees take ownership for their development and ultimately their careers.

Getting Started

The initial design work for the approach was started in the summer of 1995. The design team was made up of three trainers from Head Office Training and an external consultant. The design meetings focused on the process, how the approach would look, what would be involved, and how it would be managed.

Some senior employees were concerned early in the process that because they were not using a traditional training approach (that is, preparation of a training manual and training courses), it would not be understood by some business colleagues. To counter this, it was decided to produce a briefing booklet, together with a series of meetings to help colleagues through the beginning of the process. Because trainers could not describe what the peer teams would actually be doing (on the basis that they would define their own brief and their own activities), it was important to brief the staff members verbally and deal with any anxieties.

The design team decided to run a pilot program first, using the eight stores drawn from across the business. This group would advise the design team on any problems they encountered. Each store was presented with a briefing booklet describing the objectives, key features, and the framework for the process (see table 1).

Table 1. Overview of pilot program.

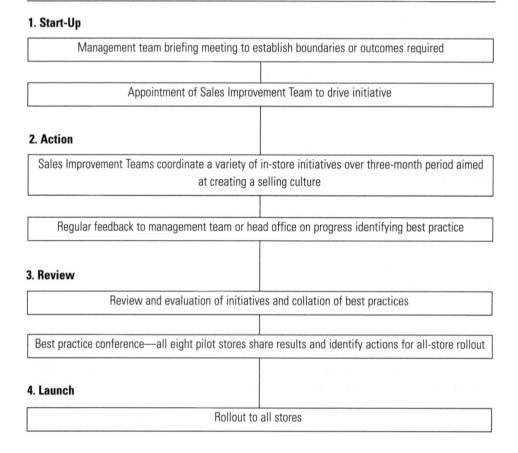

1. Start-Up

> Management team briefing meeting to establish boundaries or outcomes required

> Appointment of Sales Improvement Team to drive initiative

2. Action

> Sales Improvement Teams coordinate a variety of in-store initiatives over three-month period aimed at creating a selling culture

> Regular feedback to management team or head office on progress identifying best practice

3. Review

> Review and evaluation of initiatives and collation of best practices

> Best practice conference—all eight pilot stores share results and identify actions for all-store rollout

4. Launch

> Rollout to all stores

Introduction to Objectives

A major activity was initiated focusing on "selling as a way of working." The process is not about reinventing the wheel or a quick fix, but creating a sustained and consistent approach to selling, with everyone in the store seizing opportunities to sell. It is important to harness the existing skills, resources, and materials available to drive this initiative.

The strategy outlined here provides an opportunity to develop the appropriate attitudes and approaches to increasing sales through involving in-store staff rather than imposing a top-down solution. Approaches for knowing how to greet customers and when to sell will be developed within the store setting. In this way, the initiative will be owned by the individual store, and designed to meet their particular needs, whether it be in the United Kingdom or in Europe. The objectives of the strategy are to

- create a sales culture that permeates every store
- identify best practice in generating and developing a sales culture through the involvement of in-store staff
- encourage innovation and creativity in the selling practice
- involve the whole store in the process of owning and delivering the sales culture
- push ownership of the customer relationship to the point of delivery
- capitalize on existing knowledge, resources, and initiatives on selling within the business, not reinvent the wheel.

Key Features

The features of the strategy are as follows:

- Design and development of initiatives will be done in-store and not head-office imposed. The cornerstone of the initiative will be the setting up of Sales Improvement Teams (SITs) responsible for designing and developing innovations to improve sales performance.
- Specific selling challenges will be created to motivate in-store staff to improve sales.
- A best practice conference will be held to bring together the most innovative and practical ideas.
- A model and practical tool kit will be developed to support the roll-out throughout the United Kingdom and Europe. Ultimately this will become self-facilitated when rolled out.

The pilot stores had briefings for management and the SITs that were made up of eight to 10 sales assistants. The trial process would run from January to May 1996. When the trial process concluded, representatives from all eight stores would meet to identify key successes and failures, and provide program feedback. A smaller group (one person from each store) would meet to work with the design team to develop a resource guide to be used for introduction of the program to all stores.

How Did the "Say Wow!" Process Work?

The strategy, dubbed "Say Wow!" by the designers, was implemented as follows:

- To start the initiative, the store management team invited employees from the sales floor to join a SIT for a period of up to four months.
- A member of management acted as sponsor, but not leader, of the team. The team drove the process. The sponsor led negotiations with the team regarding the amount of time off the sales floor for meetings, budgets, how and when the team reported progress, and so forth.
- The brief given to the SIT was broad enough to encourage the team to generate its own ideas on ways to improve sales, and how to stimulate staff members to find opportunities to sell and take responsibility for the selling process. The team members were free to try whatever they wanted in pursuit of the above. There was no right way to sell.
- It was recognized that the teams might require help in the initial stages. A liaison person was suggested to join the meetings to act as an adviser, to help organize team building measures if necessary or to point out unrealistic activities. The person could be a supervisor or member of management but would attend meetings in an advisory capacity only.
- The SIT became responsible for informing other staff members in the store of their work (using bulletin boards, competitions, presentations, or training sessions).
- The SITs were also responsible for establishing miniteams from the store to work on their devised initiatives. The idea was that the SIT members would not do all the work themselves but would invite colleagues to join in initiating activities. This also drew other staff members into the process.
- The ideas were driven by the team, and over the four-month period, the team became involved in a wide variety of activities aimed at improving selling and service, and changing staff attitudes.
- It was suggested that the teams change every few months so that fresh ideas would be generated. That way, everyone had a chance to participate, and the initiative was sustained.

- When the team changed, two members of the existing team stayed with the new group to ensure continuity and avoid duplication.
- The teams were given broad guidelines to help them establish their process (see table 2) and then left to self-manage without any formal training input.

What Happened

Each one of the eight stores took a slightly different approach and experimented with different activities. Most took three to four weeks to get going, and they all followed a similar pattern. For many it was the first time they had not been told what to do. As one SIT member put it:

Table 2. Guidelines for establishing and running the sales improvement teams.

General

1. The role of the team is to generate innovative ways of improving the selling process and in so doing begin to create a sales culture that permeates the whole store.
2. During the pilot period, the team is encouraged to experiment with as wide a range of ideas as is practically possible, given financial and staffing constraints.
3. The team works with management but is not driven by it. The team is responsible for generating and evaluating its own ideas, but keeping management informed of activities.
4. The team should aim to involve as many people in the store as possible in the initiative. It is not the role of the team to do it all but to establish a number of miniteams drawn from across the store to initiate activity. The team, therefore, becomes an initiator and coordinator of actions.
5. The goal of the team should be to create a situation in which staff members throughout the store take ownership of the initiative so that selling as a way of working becomes a natural part of the working day.
6. The initiatives that are tried should fall broadly into any of three areas: attitude, approaching customers, and additional sales.
7. The outcome of the initiative should be the creation of a sales culture that all staff members buy into.

Setting Up the Team

It is suggested that after the briefing meeting the team meet soon to
- establish its own ground rules for how it is going to operate
- appoint a contact person
- identify a mechanism for communicating with management
- identify four to five activities to get the initiative off to a positive start
- identify in-store staff who would be useful members of miniteams
- begin the process of designing some measurements.

Table 2. Guidelines for establishing and running the sales improvement teams (continued).

Establishing Criteria

1. The team should establish criteria for the selection of activities so that some form of measurement can be undertaken. Examples are as follows:

   • Attitude. Does the activity encourage the sales staff to adopt a positive attitude toward customers?

   • Approaching customers. Does the activity help staff understand how and when customers want to be approached and how this should be achieved?

   • Additional sales. Does the activity help staff understand how to sell?

2. Using "attitude" as an example, defining some criteria will make it easier to measure success. The team might decide that an attitudinal goal to work toward might be "that every customer who comes into a store and is waiting for service is personally acknowledged within two minutes." By being specific, it is then possible to evaluate if this is happening by monitoring to what extent the goal is being achieved.

Learning From the Pilot

1. The reason for running a pilot program is to learn new ways of working with others. Therefore the team is encouraged to experiment and not constrain thinking to how things should be done. However, the pilot is not about making a series of demands of management (for example, "We need more staff"). Work is undertaken within the existing resource arrangements.

2. A log should be kept of all activities—what worked and what didn't—and the material faxed to each store to share learning experiences. Logging the material will also aid the process of putting together a resource directory ready for rollout.

"We struggled for three weeks not knowing what to do. It was very painful having to identify how to work together and what we were going to do, but the process was an important one to go through. We really learned how to work together and initiate action, and it has done wonders for self-confidence. We are now on a more equal footing with management and feel more comfortable about challenging the way things are done."

After overcoming the formative stage, the teams first identified three or four environmental issues to tackle. These included customer questionnaires, "drive-in" services, and staff questionnaires and quizzes to increase job awareness. The teams then moved on to more challenging work, which included changing attitudes toward selling and making an impact on sales figures. More than 70 initiatives were piloted and reviewed by the teams during the January to May period, and they fell into four broad areas of activity:

ATTITUDE. This included activities relating to attitudinal change in customer service and selling approaches. For example, one store initiated Stimulation Days for every member of the sales force. These days were aimed at stimulating staff members (not training personnel) to think about the selling process and involved visiting other nearby stores for comparative shopping and benchmarking.

CONFIDENCE BUILDING. This included anything related to building staff confidence toward selling. Actions in this area centered on product knowledge, increased awareness, job swaps, and special promotional activities.

COMMUNICATION. This centered on methods of communicating with the customers and obtaining their feedback on selling. Stores tried a variety of promotions, including competitions, special events, community activity, customer panels, and special days (for example, days for customers with special needs).

TARGETING SALES. These activities related to anything directly targeting sales, including special displays of coordinated goods, special promotions, and theme clothing days where staff would wear particular items. Spectacular results were achieved in bottom-line figures. It was not unusual for some clothing lines to have increased sales of more than 200 percent.

Summary of Outcomes

The main outcomes from the pilot program were identified as follows:

- increased staff enthusiasm—people wanted to be on the teams
- large sales increase in targeted areas
- increased awareness of what customers actually want and how they like to be sold
- increased knowledge regarding areas to exploit in the store
- more assertive, proactive sales staff with the ability to challenge, solve problems, and take action
- staff actively pursuing customers who have a need; not avoiding sales opportunities
- improved product knowledge and self-confidence to advise customers
- all staff generating ideas and seeing their ideas come to fruition
- using the talents and ideas of staff more effectively
- increased team spirit and understanding of other people's jobs
- a more positive attitude due to increased ownership for their work
- a chance to influence the business from the bottom up. (See tables 3 and 4 for reactions from pilot store teams.)

Table 3. One team's story.

This is the story of one of the Sales Improvement Teams and the process they went through.

Starting Up

"When we first got the briefing for Say Wow! it all seemed a bit vague. Now looking back, we had to go through the phase of working it out for ourselves. It was painful at times, but a very good development exercise. You could see us developing as we came to grips with it and work out for ourselves what to do. Now it's difficult to stop us!"

"People are not used to using all their skills, or ever knowing what they are. It takes some getting used to, using your head."

"The first few meetings are difficult because you are being asked to sort everything out. It also helps you recognize when you need to ask for help."

"It's surprising though how many ideas can be generated when you are free to brainstorm. In fact, we had so many ideas of things we wanted to try that we got lost in them. We needed to go back to basics and select two or three things to get going with. This, in turn, helped our confidence."

Management's Role

"At first you are nervous about your ideas because they might fly against what management thinks; so we learned it's important to partner with management and supervisors and involve them early on."

"The process has brought us closer to management. We're now on a level together. We worked out a role for management—they became advisers to us and alert us to the pitfalls."

Involving Other Colleagues

"We ran awareness sessions for colleagues on the sales floor as a way of getting their buy-in to what we were doing."

"The training sessions, which involved encouraging staff to air problems but also generate their own ideas about customer service and selling, worked well because they were delivered by ourselves (peers). Staff liked it because it wasn't a trainer or manager trying to force a view down our throats."

"It was important to let people have a 'moan' session as part of the training and then to deal with moans head-on. We dealt with moans up front which allowed the group to then move on."

A variety of measures were utilized by the pilot store to evaluate outcomes. These included

BOTTOM-LINE RESULTS. All stores were able to report improvements in sales directly related to SIT activity by analyzing sales figures before and after initiating an activity.

TESTING. Testing of sales staff on product knowledge was used to encourage learning about product lines.

Table 3. One team's story (continued).

"We also made the point that we acknowledged that staff members were probably already doing lots of good things, and had lots of good ideas, and that the training session would build on their contributions."

Making Things Happen

"It was important to get some early successes under our belts so we chose two or three actions that could be implemented quite speedily and raise our credibility."

"We wanted to raise our profile, so we had display boards put up, competitions established, and newsletters written to stimulate interest. But the best route was to get the staff involved in miniproject teams on some tasks, whether it be compiling customer questionnaires, or running promotions on certain lines in the store."

"Once we had some successes, we found that the staff wanted to come to the training sessions and wanted to know when they could join the Sales Improvement Team (SIT)—so the whole thing became self-perpetuating and created its own energy."

Keeping It Going

"It has been important for us to keep reminding ourselves that this is not a one-time occurrence. It is not a typical training program that has a start and finish; it is ongoing. Our aim has been to identify colleagues who can join an SIT, with new people joining every five to six months. In this way, new energy and ideas become harnessed."

"We are also holding regional best practice days where staff from other stores come together and share experiences. So there is always something to look forward to."

PERSONAL DEVELOPMENT REVIEWS. Each member of staff in stores has a personal development review, and the Say Wow! initiative was linked to each person's review session. In this way, staff could make a direct link between increased selling activity and their review of performance.

SELLING PERFORMANCE INDICATORS. SITs developed their own performance indicators to provide benchmarks of what might be expected of colleagues in the future regarding approaches to selling and service.

QUESTIONNAIRES. Extensive use of questionnaire feedback from both customers and staff ensured that changes resulting from initiatives could be monitored.

Sharing the Learning

The lessons learned from the eight pilot stores were shared at a best practice conference in May 1996. All participating SIT teams came together in London to learn from one another and discuss whether the

Table 4. Quotes.

- "One of the best team builds we could ever have done." Management team.
- "Being a member of the team has given me the confidence to try things, and this is the best development I have had." SIT member.
- "This has genuinely affected attitudinal change." Manager.
- "We tried an experiment with the challenge 'be seen with a customer at all times.' I spent a day on this and helped them spend an extra $7,500 in the process." SIT member.
- "We got the five most negative sales assistants to one of our sessions. It turned five negatives into positives. It worked because the training was run by one of their own." SIT member.
- "Through having a Sports Day focus on ladieswear, with us sporting a variety of leisurewear, we increased sales in ladieswear by 102 percent. Not bad for a first try." SIT member.
- "After our Mother's Day in-store competition, we hand-delivered two prizes to the mums on their doorsteps. We had mums crying. Maybe this didn't increase sales, but the goodwill it has created means our image is even higher in the town." SIT member.
- "We set up a ladieswear noniron shop—it generated $2,000 in the first week. By the fourth, we were pulling in $20,000. That's $18,000 more than we would have had. Tell us this doesn't work!" SIT member.
- "They all laughed at me, but for Pancake Day I said, "Let's take our stainless steel items relating to making pancakes down on foods." It's pulling in an extra $2,000 per week by doing this simple thing!" SIT member.
- "Through our innovations in the horticultural section, sales are up a modest 214 percent!" SIT member.
- "We got out and visited the local companies and asked if they knew about our suit-ordering service. It wasn't hard sell, but in one hour we took 50 suit orders." SIT member.

---

pilot should be introduced to all stores, and if so, what the package would look like. The participants recast the objectives, as they put it, "in their own language."

- Make selling and service part of everyday life at Marks & Spencer.
- Encourage motivation and creativity among staff.
- Make selling fun and exciting.
- Capitalize on the talent and knowledge existing within stores.
- Identify areas of poor sales performance and look at ways of improving it.
- Change the culture of Marks & Spencer by motivating staff to sell—not telling staff to sell.
- Increase sales and ultimately increase employees' paychecks.
- Understand how customers really like to be sold.

The conference participants also began to design the resource guide that would be distributed to all stores. One of the key selling points of the directory was that it was to be prepared by the SITs themselves; this would give it street credibility and avoid trainer jargon.

A smaller design team was drawn from the eight stores (one person from each store) and spent a day designing not only the framework for the directory but also cataloging examples of best practices. The design team emphasized that the materials and resources were to stimulate ideas only, not to be prescriptive in any way. One of the key lessons of the pilot had been to not define what the teams should do, and this philosophy was to be carried through to the resource guide. The final framework of the resource guide looked like this:

Part 1. Introductory Booklet: What Say Wow! is all about, how it works, and what you do to make it happen.

Part 2. Hints and Tips for Managers in Getting Started.

Part 3. Hints and Tips for Sales Assistants in Setting Up Teams.

Part 4. Summary of Projects Run by the Pilot Stores.

Part 5. The Resource Guide: A resource of ideas and suggestions you may wish to try.
Section titles would include:
• Attitude
• Confidence Building
• Communication
• Targeting Sales

Part 6. Main Outcomes You Can Expect.

Part 7. Key Lessons in Sustaining the Initiative.

The conference identified a plan for introduction to the business centered on divisional rollouts. The company was divided into regional divisions, and each division would have autonomy to introduce the process as they felt necessary. The guideline was to pick five to 10 stores in a division and utilize SIT members from the pilot stores as mentors; thus the process would continue to be driven from the bottom up. The SIT team members would also be involved in the divisional launch (see table 5).

The Problems

The problems identified during the pilot process relate mainly to issues about power: letting go, taking responsibility, empowerment, and involving others.

LETTING GO. This was the biggest challenge for management, allowing junior staff members to flex their muscles and possibly challenge the way things are done. Some managers found this more difficult to handle than others. However, as SITs gained confidence, they began to challenge some

Table 5. Launch of say wow!

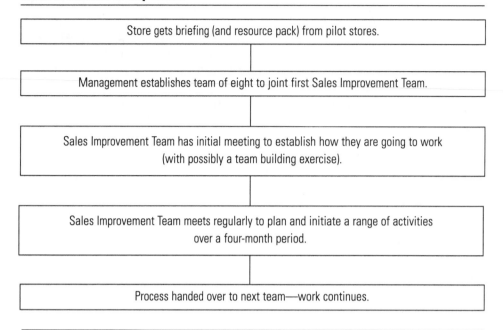

Store gets briefing (and resource pack) from pilot stores.

Management establishes team of eight to joint first Sales Improvement Team.

Sales Improvement Team has initial meeting to establish how they are going to work (with possibly a team building exercise).

Sales Improvement Team meets regularly to plan and initiate a range of activities over a four-month period.

Process handed over to next team—work continues.

of these areas. As time passed, managers gained confidence in their sales staff, and the culture genuinely began to change. The staff now had a say and, more important, a stake in how things were done.

TAKING RESPONSIBILITY. One of the biggest problems for SIT members was learning to take responsibility for their actions. This caused much angst in the first few weeks of the pilot. Teams were not sure how to initiate action, felt abandoned by those who had launched Say Wow!, and were not really convinced it was up to them.

EMPOWERMENT. Learning to work with and challenge peers, particularly regarding the areas of leadership, idea generation, and team management, proved more difficult for some teams than others. Asking for help from management (sometimes in terms of help in facilitating the team to function more effectively) was a major learning step for many SIT members. Although getting started was painful, all teams agreed it was an important step in their self-development. It was also an important stage in moving toward genuine empowerment.

INVOLVING OTHERS. While the initiative focused mainly on sales assistants, an important group felt disempowered by the process, the supervisors. They were not adequately involved in the briefing process and in some cases felt quite threatened by the initiative. The result of feeling excluded was a tendency to block the work of the SIT. This typically took the form of not allowing time off for an SIT meeting.

Once this problem was recognized, SIT members began briefing supervisors more fully. Supervisors also were included in the meetings, enabling them to have some ownership in the initiative as well. Everyone learned that the supervisor is a key player whose commitment is essential if SITs are to function effectively.

The Learning

The learning process focused on the following concepts:

- Every store approached the initiative differently. There was no standardized system. The success of the initiative rested on the fact that each store was able to interpret the guidelines in its own way and put its own mark on it. In this way, the approach has been unique as an intervention—no checking off boxes and no centrally imposed models.
- The whole initiative was driven by sales assistants, and this added credibility. All briefing sessions and training programs were designed and run by sales assistants.
- If staff members are given genuine responsibility for change, they will eventually rise to the challenge. It was important for management not to take back the reins—to support the team through difficult times, but not to bale them out.
- Even though the focus of the initiative is on frontline staff (sales assistants), everyone in the store needs to be briefed and involved in some way; otherwise they tend to sabotage (however innocently) the change effort.
- Management needs to hear from the organization that they have permission to let the SIT challenge the rules, policies, and procedures. This is the way real change occurs.
- Any training materials or resource guides that emerge from a pilot activity should be compiled directly by those involved in the experience. This adds credibility to the entire exercise.
- To keep the initiative sustained and energized, the SIT membership is changed every four to five months. This helps to generate new ideas. To avoid duplication and provide continuity, one member continues on the team.
- The importance of the teams being composed of peers cannot be overemphasized. This allows them the freedom to genuinely contribute without worrying that their ideas will be seen as stupid or not achievable.

Organizational Impact

The impact of the self-managed peer teams can be highlighted in three areas: personal development, organizational culture, and business outcomes.

PERSONAL DEVELOPMENT. The approach of throwing the teams into the deep end with no training has challenged the traditional view that people need training before they can become operational. Personal development became an outcome of the challenges that the team set for themselves. Team members learned to manage meetings, brainstorm, negotiate for resources, influence upward, and make presentations through task involvement.

All of the SIT members reported greater levels of self-confidence and belief in their ability to make change happen. Members of the staff previously regarded as cynical embraced the process and a positive change in attitude was reported from all stores.

ORGANIZATIONAL CULTURE. For a traditional top-down hierarchy, this leap of faith required to empower frontline staff was a major step. In the eight years preceding Say Wow! the Training Department had been laying the groundwork for a change in the organization's culture. Various management development and team building initiatives were already in place.

The department had already made a major impact on the way things were done. When the concept of self-managed peer teams was introduced by the consultant as a process to move selling forward, the approach was seen as a natural lead, and the organization was ready to buy in. This was the first time, however, that a human resource initiative was linked directly to commercial output, that is, improving the bottom line.

The impact on the ground has been to bring management and frontline staff together and enable dialogue to take place. This has helped the organization move away from a culture in which junior staff members tell senior staff members what they want to hear.

BUSINESS OUTCOMES. In any flourishing business, the hard question is "Has it improved business?" This process answers with an overwhelming "Yes." Stores have been able to provide evidence of bottom-line improvements so each activity can be seen in terms of more money. Being able to provide this evidence has ensured that Say Wow! is seen as a commercially important part of Marks & Spencer development.

Where Next?

At the time of writing, the initiative is being introduced to all stores in the United Kingdom and Europe. In the head office, the first pilot for administrative staff has been launched. The Postal Services Department (which handles the mail for all 4,000 head office staff members, 292 United Kingdom stores, and the company worldwide) has launched a peer team to examine service to the internal customer. This initiative, called "service as a way of working," will provide the blueprint for the next part of Marks & Spencer's cultural revolution.

Questions for Discussion

1. What are the implications, if any, for sales teams that are commission based as opposed to salary based?
2. What preparatory work might be required for the management and leadership of a store who have previously operated a top-down approach?
3. What actions might be needed to sustain the impetus of SITs after the first waves of activity?
4. What specialist training, if any, might be needed for sales associates who are going to facilitate the SITs?

The Authors

Roger Woodgate is cofounder and chairman of ABA Consultants, a leading consulting firm in the field of management development, leadership, and organization development, founded in 1985. Although based in the United Kingdom, Woodgate works extensively in the United States and the United Kingdom. In 1994, Woodgate was awarded a Harkness Fellowship and spent a year in the United States researching self-managed teams. Since then he has consulted widely in the field for both European and American corporations. He can be reached by writing to ABA Consultants Limited, 59 High Street, Royston, Hert SGS 9AW England; phone: 01763 248631; fax: 01763 242172; e-mail: 101625.3476 @compuserve.com.

Niall Trafford graduated in 1984 with a degree in English language and literature from the University of Wales. He joined Marks & Spencer in January of 1986 as a personnel management trainee working in London and Northern Ireland. He later moved into commercial management and worked in London and the West Country (Exeter). After this series of operational line management roles, he joined the Training Department as manager of operational and technological training. He can be reached at Marks & Spencer, Michael House, Baker Street, London W1A 1DN England; phone: 01719 354422.

Angela Stephens has worked for Marks & Spencer for 12 years, joining the Ladieswear Buying Department in their Baker Street head office in London. She has worked in the Training Department for two years and, until lately, managed commercial foods training for the company. In particular, she managed the development of selling skills for Marks & Spencer sales assistants. Stephens can be reached at Marks & Spencer, Michael House, Baker Street, London W1A 1DN England; phone: 01719 354422.

Organizational Transformation for Effectively Implementing a Team-Based Culture

Harris Semiconductor

Ed Rose, Steve Gilmore, and Ray D. Odom

A strategy for managing change builds a stable platform for team implementation. Harris Semiconductor presents a four-stage model that recognizes how psychological reaction to change can be managed through information sharing, training, team development guidelines, and management guidelines. Best practices, such as this one, set the standard for a proactive approach to change.

Abstract

Companies that want to be successful in the 1990s must develop organizational structures that utilize their human resources to the fullest potential. Employees must be empowered to make decisions that in the past were reserved for management. A focus on continuous improvement must be fostered. The challenge lies in developing effective strategies for change that mesh the technology of the industry with new and creative organizational structures.

Effective strategies for managing cultural transformation must start with a fundamental understanding of the conflict that exists between an organization's need for change and an individual's need for personal security. This paper addresses these issues by describing a successful strategy that has been developed and used by Harris Semiconductor in their implementation of self-directed work teams. Issues, such as rate of change

This case was prepared to serve as a basis for discussion rather than to illustrate either effective or ineffective administrative and management practices.

and psychological and social impacts of change, are addressed by a four-step process that has provided significant assistance in the cultural transformation to team-based management.

Introduction

Ben Franklin was quoted as stating there are only two things certain in life—death and taxes. Given the relatively relaxed pace of life in his time, it is understandable that he might have forgotten to add the concept of change to his list. Change has become an increasing part of everyone's life, with today's rate of change creating a situation of heightened anxiety for organizations and individuals alike.

Attempts at defining *change* must take into account whether the definition is driven from the perspective of an individual or of the organization. Alvin Toffler, in his book *Future Shock* (1971), defines change from an individual's perspective as "the process by which the future invades our lives." This invasive and somewhat threatening definition reflects a process that tends to be resisted out of natural instinct. On the other hand, an organizational perspective yields the definition: "any alteration initiated by management in an individual work situation or work environment." This perspective reflects the need for change faced by organizations as part of their survival process.

Organizational need for change is driven by many forces. Economic pressures in terms of competition are certainly primary forces. Legal and governmental considerations such as changing environmental and workplace regulations are also drivers in this process. Cultural forces, as reflected by changing youth and consumer values, as well as the need to be increasingly sensitive to multicultural and national values in today's global environment, exert a different set of pressures on the organization. Finally, the dizzying rate of technological innovation, knowledge explosion, and telecommunications capabilities forces a continuous reinventing of an organization's mission and objectives. The bottom line is that if an organization is to fulfill its needs, it must change!

Each person who works in an organization needs change for fulfillment. We must admit, however, that a basic need of individuals lies in maintaining their sense of security. This is increasingly more difficult in light of many of the changes facing today's corporate employees. Downsizing is almost everywhere, low-skilled manufacturing jobs are moving offshore, and employee empowerment movements are reducing the number of middle managers. The evolution to team-based management, with structure such as self-directed work teams, has resulted, at a minimum, in the reduction of the supervisor's role in the organization.

The pressures exerted on the corporation add new dimensions of change for employees to handle, new realities that are perceived as a threat to personal security. The need to manage change is driven by the basic conflict that arises between corporate and individual needs.

Rate of Change

The development of a strategy for managing change must start with a recognition of the demands placed by the rate of change on an individual's sense of security. Figure 1 illustrates the accelerating change of pace as reflected in man's evolution over about the last 46,000 years or 650 lifetimes (Toffler, 1971). Many of the forces that drive change today are products of recent lifetimes. In fact the overwhelming majority of all the material goods we use today were developed over the last 70 years. Similar examples can be provided for other elements of our lives, such as the speed of transportation and the exponential rate of increase in knowledge and information processing. With this in mind, the following thoughts offer important considerations in developing a change management strategy:

- Recognition of the demands placed on individuals by today's **rate of change** is an important step in understanding a person's response and resistance to change.
- The faster the rate of change, the greater the threat to an individual's sense of security. Management of change should strive to replace **fear of change** with a positive attitude toward change.
- Actions suggesting that change is under control will contribute toward the development of this positive attitude.

How Change Affects People

Most organizations dedicate significant resources to addressing the behavioral aspects associated with the change process. When introducing new technology, operating manuals and training sessions focused on the physical aspects of the change are routine and rigorous. Unfortunately the same level of attention is not given to the psychological and social impacts of organizational change.

Psychological considerations are those that cause people to alter the way they relate to and feel about what they are doing. Any change process will create doubts and questions in a person's mind. The severity of these doubts depends in part on the individual's personality and experience; it is likely, however, that many of these questions can be predicted. Social considerations refer more to alterations in the individual's established relationships with others in the work group and with the organization as a whole. Concerns about being cut off from fellow employees, being

Figure 1. Rate of change.

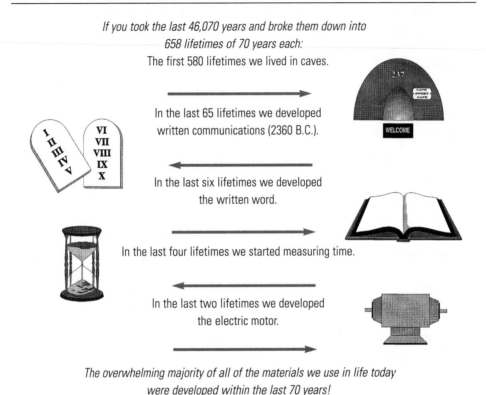

If you took the last 46,070 years and broke them down into
658 lifetimes of 70 years each:
The first 580 lifetimes we lived in caves.

In the last 65 lifetimes we developed
written communications (2360 B.C.).

In the last six lifetimes we developed
the written word.

In the last four lifetimes we started measuring time.

In the last two lifetimes we developed
the electric motor.

The overwhelming majority of all of the materials we use in life today
were developed within the last 70 years!

less informed, or one's self-esteem in a new peer group are examples of predictable questions that are driven by social considerations.

- Much attention and effort in managing change is devoted to behavioral effects. Yet equal or greater importance must be given to **psychological and social** effects if change is to be introduced and implemented successfully.
- Psychological and social effects stimulate **predictable questions** in the minds of those affected by change.
- Questions should and can be anticipated. The key lies in placing yourself, the manager, in the position of those to be affected by change.

Measuring Resistance to Change

Even though the general perception exists that it is human nature to resist change, many studies show that this is not necessarily true.

Individual attitudes toward change are a function of various factors, such as predisposed feelings about change of any kind, extent of personal security or insecurity, and cultural beliefs and norms. The attitude is also influenced by the individual's extent of trust in management and the work group, historical events relevant to the change, and apprehensions about change. Finally, the manner in which change is introduced and implemented in many cases is the determining factor in the degree of resistance to change.

Figure 2 summarizes these factors in the form of a "resistance" equation (Judson, 1964); for example, generally people assume that resistance is more intense with a larger numerator and a smaller denominator. Strong feelings of personal security and trust in management will tend to reduce resistance even when other factors in the numerator are large. Negative predisposed feelings about change will increase the influence of other factors that contribute to an increase in resistance.

The development of an effective management of change strategy starts by recognizing that at the moment of change, management has little control over predisposed feelings, sense of personal security, historical events, and cultural beliefs. Management does have full control, however, over the manner in which change is introduced and implemented and how many, and how effectively, questions about unknown futures are answered. Successful implementation of change will nurture those factors and reduce future resistance to change.

A Four-Step Process for Managing Change

The previous concepts were brought together at Harris Semiconductor to develop a four-step management of change process. This process was

Figure 2. A "resistance" equation.

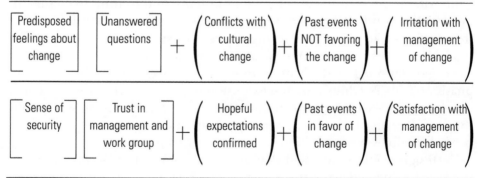

subsequently used to facilitate the transition to a team-based culture through implementation of SDWTs. This process is illustrated in figure 3.

Self-directed work teams can be described as small groups of people empowered to manage themselves and the work they do on a day-to-day basis (performing 85 to 90 percent of their day-to-day activities without outside resources). They are formal, permanent organizational structures or units, with members who carry out their normal operational responsibilities while also planning and scheduling their work, making production-related decisions, taking action to solve problems, and sharing leadership responsibilities. Self-directed work teams are based on the assumption that the only constant left in business today is change. Every organization and employee must adapt to the constant forces of change to keep up with and beat their competition. Involving employees in all aspects of the business helps an organization become flexible and highly competitive. The success of SDWTs can be tied to three key assumptions. First, those closest to the work know best how to perform and improve their job. Second, most employees want to feel that they own their jobs and are making meaningful contributions to the effectiveness of their organizations. Third, teams provide possibilities of empowerment that are not available to individual employees.

Step 1—Recognize the Effect of Rate of Change on Personal Security

This step requires an assessment of the organization before initiating change. This includes an assessment of rate of change, employee attitudes with respect to change, and other factors associated with resistance to change. This process reduces the negative effects associated with rate of change and its effect on personal security. The objective is to reduce the rate of change by determining if the implementation of a change will result in a desired outcome.

In 1989, Harris Semiconductor directed an assessment of various organizational initiatives that had been implemented to initiate change in operational production and engineering support areas. While some of these efforts had met with varying degrees of success, none provided a unified, concerted effort that would tie together all of the resources of the organization. The decision to move to a team-based culture with emphasis on SDWTs, while a natural extension of previous efforts, was deemed critical to achieving organizational objectives. This decision was within the overall goals of developing an organization and culture in which people habitually work toward continuous improvement.

Design teams, composed of employees from various levels and functions, were formed with the charter to assess the present system and

Figure 3. Managing change.

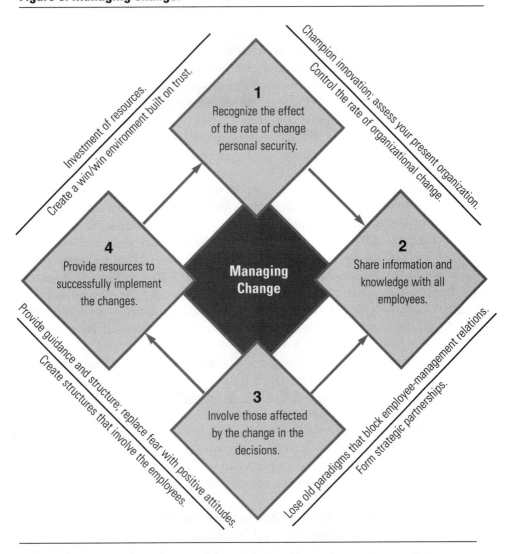

design a new organization. This process entailed a conscious effort to examine, evaluate, and redefine structural aspects of the organization, from
process and information flow to social systems and performance measures.

The objectives were to design a flexible organization, eliminate non-
value-added functions, and enhance efficiencies. Additional objectives
were to design an organization that focused on the customer and to create an environment that encouraged employee participation in the business. To ensure that the rate of change was not threatening to the employees'

personal security, Harris designed an implementation process that required two to five years to fully implement.

Step 2—Share Information and Knowledge With All Employees

This step is crucial in breaking with old paradigms that block effective employee-management relationships. The objective is to build a partnership with the employees based on trust. Information and knowledge are the fuel that drives change, and this step helps create an environment that anticipates questions related to organizational change. It also enhances the creation of two-way communication required to truly reap the benefits of the SDWT concept.

Implementation at Harris is carried out through an effective change management roadmap. First, a leadership team is formed to clearly define and communicate the organization's shared purpose for existing. This team generally consists of senior management, although at some sites it also includes senior employee representatives. This purpose statement generally defines target markets, products and services, and competitive strategy. This step serves to soundly anchor the organization's members on the playing field so everyone can participate in the game.

Next, the same team defines the organization's vision. How does it wish to be viewed by its stakeholders in two to three years? Three to five years? How is that different from today? How would the organization operate if it were already achieving its vision? What are the organization's core values, and do they need to change going forward? How would the organization behave if it were truly living those values?

This vision statement is then shared with all the employees throughout the organization. Each SDWT is encouraged to provide feedback to this process and is required to develop an internal operating vision statement in alignment with the organizational vision.

Step 3—Involve Those Affected by Change in the Decisions

This step allows those affected by change to provide input to the change process. In addition to the natural benefits that evolve from this empowering action, the objective is to replace fear of the unknown with a positive attitude toward change. As mentioned previously, one of the few factors that management can influence at the moment of change is the manner in which change is carried out. This approach also lays a solid foundation for enhancing trust and developing a more conducive environment for successful future changes.

This step was implemented at Harris Semiconductor through a partnership formed between human resources and plant operations. The role of human resources was to facilitate the change process; however, all decisions and investments were ultimately made by plant operations personnel. The design process involved the following phases:

1. An off-site workshop was implemented to expose middle management to SDWT concept and achieve management buy-in, also known as "singing from the same hymnal."

2. A steering committee was formed to support and guide the change process. Guidelines also were established for monitoring the implementation process. This committee included human resources and plant personnel.

3. Implementation teams were formed at the departmental level to coach department employees through the change process.

4. Middle management was given training to provide them with a strong knowledge base on SDWTs. This training also focused on the development and enhancement of interpersonal skills and the importance of these skills for effective leadership of the change process.

5. Local training resources and support in the form of facilities and training curriculum were established. Facilitators were identified to act as knowledge brokers to teams and management.

6. Both managers and employees need to demonstrate new competencies in order to succeed in the new organization. They must believe one another to be trustworthy, skilled, and personally accountable. Guidance in developing this mutual trust was provided through a structured approach to developing SDWTs. This six-part process is discussed in the next step.

Step 4—Provide Resources to Successfully Implement the Changes

The objective of this step is to ensure that sufficient investment in resources is provided to carry the change to successful implementation. This process also will enhance the trust factor and reduce the stress associated with a limited resource environment.

The primary resource investment at Harris Semiconductor was the establishment of a training department, devoted primarily to the cultural transformation to teams by providing support and facilitation. This training department provided facilitation services for all teams. Each team was given resources to assist in working through the following developmental steps:

1. **Purpose.** Why does the team exist?
2. **Vision.** What should the team look like in the future?
3. **Goals and Objectives.** What does the team need to accomplish?
4. **Strategy and Tactics.** How will the team accomplish its goals and objectives?

5. **Roles and Responsibilities.** What tasks need to be done? Who will do them? What responsibilities need to be transferred to the team? When will they be transferred?

6. **Standards, Norms and Expectations.** What rules guide team behaviors? How will the team handle conflicts?

Various team building exercises were developed to emphasize the role of relationship behavior to team performance. Training modules were also developed to introduce "habits of highly effective team members" to all participants. These five habits (modeled on concepts introduced by Covey, 1989) include

1. understanding the need for win-win interactions

2. mutual respect, including the development of an environment that will maintain and enhance team member self-esteem, and allow the team to focus on problems instead of personalities

3. the need to be proactive

4. the ability to listen with empathy

5. the ability to appreciate differences in personalities and opinions.

A survey of Harris Semiconductor teams (workforce of 1,200 employees at the Palm Bay site) was conducted in 1995, approximately four years after introduction of team-based management with SDWTs as a major focus. Based on the results, the four-step process was successful at Harris, while SDWTs appeared to provide a structure for the future:

- 87 percent of the workforce favored the SDWT structure.
- 96 percent of the workforce felt a need to contribute to the organizational goals, and they thought SDWTs provided the best structure for meeting their needs.
- 100 percent of the employees believed that SDWTs improved their self-esteem.
- 100 percent considered training as important to success as an SDWT.
- 95 percent stated that knowledge of where they were going and clear expectations were important to implementing the SDWT concept.
- 75 percent reported an improvement in attitude after implementing SDWTs.

The survey reflected a positive attitude on the part of employees. The key ingredient to successful implementation of SDWTs is how the change is managed. The four-step model (figure 3) for managing change is reflected in the survey results. Self-directed work teams can be a competitive advantage for American manufacturers by providing significant improvement, as supported by the survey data.

Once the team-based organization was put in place, management continued to provide a continuous stream of productivity and quality improvement tools, such as total productive maintenance, synchronous flow manufacturing, and statistical process control. Complementing these tools with a basic understanding of business finance, and a vision of where the company is headed, will enable teams to make knowledge-based decisions necessary to successfully achieve business objectives. Harris teamed up with Paradigm Communications of Tampa, Florida, to create an experimental business simulation game called Zodiak. This game allows participants to run their own company and make decisions that affect its profitability. Participants begin to appreciate and understand the reasoning behind management decisions, while preparing them to make decisions to help the company achieve business objectives.

Companies that implement SDWTs, de-layer management, and let employees make decisions without providing them with training and tools will find many pitfalls in their future. Real improvements in operational performance and competitiveness are key to a successful organization. Organizational change requires time and energy to be successful. The implementation must be nurtured and supported, as described in the four steps to management change (see figure 3, steps 2 and 3 specifically). These steps allow employees at all levels to participate in the decisions during the change process. Step 4 of the change model calls for management to create a win-win environment built on trust. A commitment was made by Harris management to invest both time and money to improve employees' skill levels, while increasing their basic business knowledge. A team, just like a mechanic, is only as good as the tools it uses. The following section will provide examples of tools and how they were used in the Harris journey to team-based management.

Creating a Win-Win Environment—Providing Quality Tools to the Teams

Like many companies, Harris Semiconductor manages its resources to improve productivity and lower manufacturing costs. One major initiative employed at Harris, theory of constraints (TOC), focuses on increased throughput, decreased inventory, and reduced operating expense. TOC is the central focus for individual, team, operational, and equipment improvements. Employees are involved in continuous improvement activities, such as total productive maintenance (TPM) and system improvement projects, to achieve TOC objectives as depicted in figure 4. Harris management creates a win-win environment by deploying and training employees in TOC and TPM, a subset of the total employee "toolbox" needed to be successful in today's very competitive environment.

As the initial step in the process, TOC and TPM site coordinators were selected and thoroughly trained. They then were given the goal of educating the entire workforce in these productivity and quality improvement tools.

The TOC coordinator received JONAH/licensee training from Avraham Y. Goldratt Institute, located in New Haven, Connecticut. The training included three weeks of JONAH training and an additional two weeks of licensee training (train-the-trainer). The JONAH segment teaches the use of thinking processes to answer three questions in getting a business on a rapid process of ongoing improvement:

1. What to change? (identifying the core problem)
2. What to change to? (constructing a solution)
3. How to cause the change? (devising the implementation plan)

Figure 4. Managing resources with TOC philosophy.

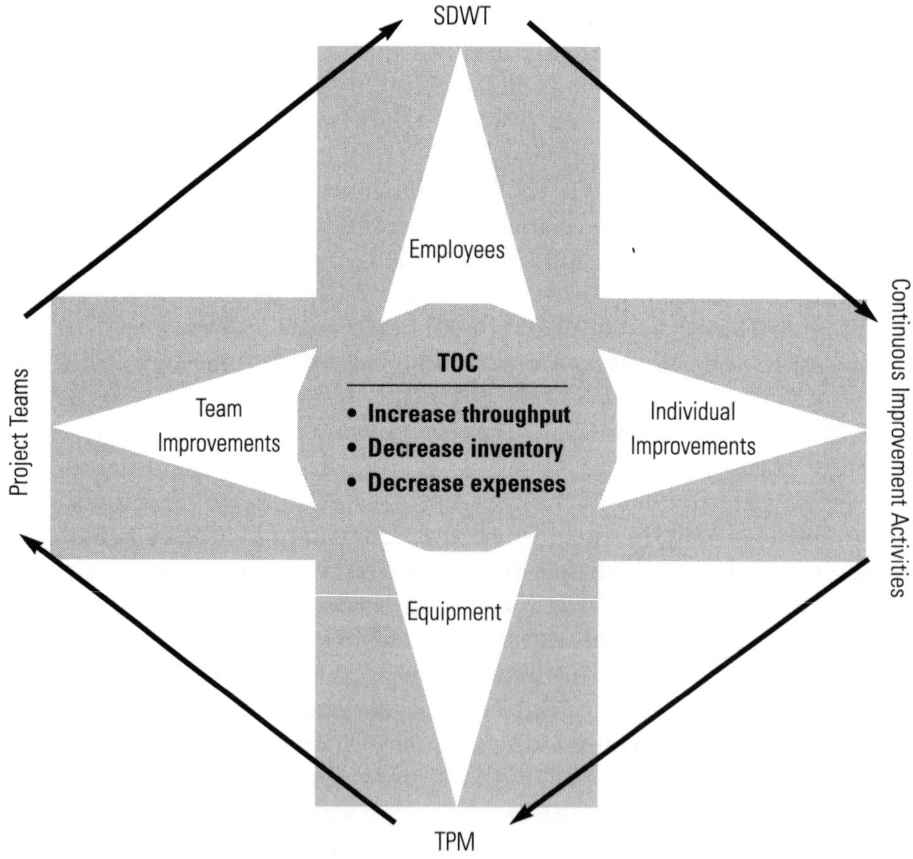

The licensee segment trains the JONAH how to teach the thinking processes to others, with the aid of Goldratt Institute materials and simulators.

Within the Harris Semiconductor factory, employees use a generic application, derived through the thinking processes, called the production application, or drum-buffer-rope (DBR). DBR allows employees to identify and manage the production pipeline in an imperfect world. DBR attempts to maximize pipeline throughput by effective bottleneck, or constraint, management. The fundamental principle is that the output of the production pipeline is limited by and can never be greater than the output of the primary constraint. This methodology aids in setting the priorities for addressing the most critical issues to be resolved with other improvement tools, such as TPM. This allows Harris, through integration, to increase its rate of progress in achieving its operational goals. This application also enhances management skills that assist in preparing the workforce for dealing with change and interrelationships among team members.

Statistical Process Control (SPC)

The heart of any continuous improvement activity must have statistical process control. SPC is the heart of all the quality tools because the process must be in control. Changes to the process must be monitored and corrected in a timely manner to provide the foundation for successfully using the other tools. Harris started SPC training in 1979 and continues to use it as a core training requirement for all employees.

Zodiak—Understanding Business Financial Decisions

Harris Semiconductor management believes that to improve employee understanding of the overall business and subsequently improve day-to-day business decisions on the factory floor, employees need business and financial knowledge. To this end, Harris and Paradigm Communications teamed to produce Zodiak, which is designed to give players a realistic experience in managing the business and finances of a publicly held, high-tech company. In the game, players work as a team to manage fictitious, financially troubled Zodiak Industries through three business years by making decisions based on cash flow, capital expenditures, and earnings statements. Zodiak simulates business situations, placing employees in the chief executive officer's position and showing them the consequences of their executive decisions. Using chips and chance cards, players guide Zodiak Industries from situation to situation and quarter to quarter. At one point, they run out of money but are saved in the nick of time by an accounts-receivable payment. This helps the players see quickly how important cash flow can be in managing a business.

Harris Semiconductor's goal in using Zodiak is to give employees a sense of how business finance and strategy will allow them to make knowledgeable business decisions while providing more understanding of business dynamics. To survive in the new workplace, organizations must encourage employees to think like business owners.

Conclusion

The Harris story is an example of how manufacturing companies can make significant improvements on the factory floor by implementing SDWTs. The key ingredient to successful implementation is how the change is managed. These teams can be the competitive edge for American manufacturers when implemented properly.

Companies moving from a traditional management structure to team-based management must realize that organizational changes require time and energy to be successful. Expecting overnight results will result in frustration and failure. The implementation must be nurtured and supported. Using the steps presented in this paper will improve the odds for effective cultural transformation.

Questions for Discussion

1. Why must management continue to provide teams with a continuous stream of productivity and quality improvement tools?
2. What are some productivity and improvement tools teams should receive from management?
3. How can social and psychological considerations affect employees after team implementation? Are these serious issues to consider?
4. What changes would you make to the four-step model used by Harris Semiconductor?
5. What is the importance of sharing information with team members? Make a list of what you consider to be the most effective ways of sharing information.

The Authors

Ed Rose is currently the training manager at Harris Semiconductor in Palm Bay, Florida. He graduated from Warner Southern College with honors in organizational management. He is the author of *Presenting and Training with Magic,* published by McGraw-Hill, and numerous team building exercises in resource books published by McGraw-Hill and HRD Press. Rose has 32 years' experience in manufacturing; has served as quality examiner for the state of Florida; and has published numerous papers on the subject of self-directed work teams. He is a corporate practice expert for SDWT with Harris Corporation. He is a frequent presenter at the ASTD and AWP national conferences, the University of North Texas International Conference on Work Teams, and other national organizations. Rose conducts workshops on team building at local colleges and high schools. He can be reached by writing Harris Semiconductor, Box 883, Melbourne, FL 32902-0883; phone: 407.724.7560; e-mail: erose@harris.com.

Steve Gilmore is the head of organization and management development at Harris Semiconductor. He has worked in the electronics industry for most of his professional career. He earned his B.A. from Mount Saint Mary's College. Gilmore has published several papers on the subject of cultural change and self-directed work teams (published in the *Quality Digest*). He has been an internal consultant in support of employee involvement and SDWT structures and educates managers in organizational design concepts, methods, and tools. He has presented at many conferences such as the ASTD International Conference, ASTD Quality Symposia, AQP National Conference, and Florida Governor's Sterling Awards Conference. Gilmore can be reached by writing Harris Semiconductor, Box 883, Melbourne, FL 32902-0883; phone: 407.724.7458; e-mail: sgilmore@harris.com.

Ray D. Odom is currently the plant manager, Palm Bay Operations, for Harris Semiconductor. Prior to his present assignment, Odom held positions of progressively increasing responsibility in both engineering and manufacturing. He holds a B.S. in electrical engineering from the University of Florida and is a graduate of the University of Florida graduate program in business. He has numerous publications on both technical and organizational topics. He has presented at the ASTD National Conference on SDWTs, as well as other technical and manufacturing conferences. Odom can be reached by writing Harris Semiconductor, Box 883, Melbourne, FL 32902-0883; phone: 407.724.7307; e-mail: rodom@harris.com.

References

Covey, S. *The Seven Habits of Highly Effective People.* New York: Simon & Schuster, 1989.

Judson, A. *A Manager's Guide to Managing Change.* John Wiley & Sons, 1964.

Martin-Vega, L. *Management of Change.* Gainesville, FL: University of Florida, 1988.

Rose, E., et al. *How TOC & TPM Work Together to Build the Quality Toolbox of SDWTs.* Palm Bay, FL: Harris Semiconductor, 1995.

———. "SDWT Requires Tools to be Successful." *In Proceedings of the 1995 Advanced Semiconductor Manufacturing Conference.* Boston: Harris Corporation, 1995.

Toffler, A. *Future Shock.* New York: Bantam Books, 1971.

Zodiak: *A Game of Business Finance.* Tampa, FL: Paradigm Communications, 1994.

Operational Excellence

Canadian Imperial Bank of Commerce (CIBC)

Berkeley J. Emmons

This best practices case offers a blueprint for team implementation viewed as a planned organizational change. This banking services center began teams during reorganization. The lessons learned address the delicate relationship between teams, continuous improvement, and downsizing.

Background

With assets of more than $C132 billion, the Canadian Imperial Bank of Commerce (CIBC) is Canada's second largest retail bank, with an employee base of 40,000 serving six million customers worldwide. Within CIBC, the Operations and Technology (O&T) group functions as an internal service organization, providing services related to items processing and information technology design, deployment, and maintenance to all bank divisions. Prior to 1992, processing services were provided by two autonomous functional organizations within O&T, each reporting to the division's senior operational officer. One organization provided check-processing services from regional operations centers located in Canada's major cities. The second organization performed branch banking functions, not related to direct customer sales and service, in regional "back office" centers. Although the two organizations maintained centers in the same cities (often in the same building), performed similar clerical and technical tasks that often involved handoffs from one to another, and were part of the same division, they were managed separately and were functionally independent.

In the fall of 1991, a decision was made to integrate the two organizations under a single executive in order to reduce personnel and

This case was prepared to serve as a basis for discussion rather than to illustrate either effective or ineffective administrative and management practices.

facilities costs and to improve work flow efficiencies. These new units would be called Processing Centers; the work of designing and implementing the change was called the Operational Excellence Project (OPEX).

Project Strategy, Goals, and Team Approach

As they embarked upon this restructuring project, senior O&T officers articulated a goal of "establishing a strategic partnership between customers, employees, and the bank." Prompted by a memo from a senior human resource executive, they identified employee empowerment and continuous improvement techniques as the primary means to achieve this objective and to produce truly breakthrough results. Support for this strategy grew from the belief that a traditional industrial engineering approach to the restructuring might achieve a 10 percent cost reduction, but the combination of employee empowerment and continuous process improvement offered the potential of making a significant contribution to a 40 percent unit-cost reduction over a three-year period, while simultaneously improving quality, customer satisfaction, and employee morale. The possibility of achieving these goals, often elusive in a traditional cost-reduction effort, built support for the OPEX initiative.

The 17 original centers, involving a total of 2,500 people, would be integrated into seven new centers, ranging in size from 90 to 460 employees. Redesign work at any given center was scheduled to be completed within 15 months after work began.

Because of this extended time frame, CIBC employed a phased approach to implementation that began in one center and subsequently moved to other regional centers (table 1). This phased approach allowed CIBC to develop and test new organization development tools, incorporate the learnings before rolling out to other locations, and avoid overextending its corporate resources.

Built into the project from the outset was the concept of employee involvement and empowerment, which translated into a commitment to high-performing work teams. In CIBC a team was defined as "an energetic group of people who are committed to achieving common objectives, who work well together and enjoy doing so, and who produce high-quality results." Although providing a useful framework, this did not adequately describe a high-performing team, so the following definition was developed: "A high-performing team is a group of eight to 15 employees who are responsible and accountable for planning, controlling, completing, and improving a well-defined piece of work, a whole product, process, or service." CIBC used table 2 to differentiate between a traditional work group and a high-performing team.

Table 1. Description of implementation activities.

Activity	Description
Selection process	Selection of people to fill project roles, including new center managers and newly created permanent positions for process and learning facilitators
Process integration design	Design of new processes that horizontally integrate the original functional organization
Cultural integration	Design of new cultural symbols and practices by special culture design team
Transitional organization design	Design of a new organization structure to optimally integrate and support new process designs; This structure called a "transitional organization" to convey that continued change should be expected
Process integration	Implementation of new process designs
Premises redesign	Concurrent redesign of the physical workplace as needed
Team formation	Formation of permanent self-managed work teams to operate newly designed work processes
Team training	Formal employee training related to interpersonal, team leadership, and administrative skills
Continuous improvement	Ongoing operation in a continuous improvement environment
Measures and standards	Development of baseline measures, implementation, and use of process performance measurement tools

Focus on Culture

Accordingly, with the strategy in place and the means to accomplish it selected, CIBC began the Operational Excellence Project in September 1991. The bank set out to reduce unit costs dramatically and improve labor productivity by transforming a functional, vertical organization into a self-managed work team environment using a process management methodology and socio-technical concepts.

Unlike some traditional reorganizations that developed a detailed blueprint for a new structure and a companywide implementation plan, the OPEX program designers focused on organizational culture. They believed that culture, not structure, would be the critical determining factor, either enabling or impeding the development of a continuous improvement organization within CIBC. They suggested that the right culture can result in a company making great strides; therefore, the wrong

Table 2. Traditional work group v. high-performing team.

A Traditional Work Group	A High-Performing Team
Information is available to and used by a select few.	Information sharing is everyone's need and responsibility.
What the boss thinks and says drives performance; the focus is on what goes on inside the company.	The requirements of internal and external customers drive performance.
Work is organized around functions and departments.	Work is highly cross-functional.
Managers control the work of others while making all key decisions.	Responsibility and leadership and decisions are shared with those closest to the work.
Jobs are narrowly defined.	Jobs are defined more broadly.
Quality control is the responsibility of management.	Quality improvement is built into everyday work.
Majority of work is done by individuals who have little control over their work methods and processes.	Majority of work gets done in teams that have a great deal of latitude in deciding how to do their jobs in the best way.
People's behavior and decisions are guided by rules, procedures, and policies.	Team behavior and decisions are guided by purposeful organizational vision, understood values, and accountability.

culture may greatly reduce the quality of decisions, the participation of employees, how well the technical tools are used, and the amount of progress made. In addition, they thought that for CIBC, one benefit of framing the restructuring in terms of culture was to encourage the organization to adopt a holistic perspective, thinking broadly about a full range of elements. To guide implementation, CIBC created a detailed OPEX change management plan.

Operational Excellence—Components

The OPEX change management plan was thoughtful, complex, and multifaceted, consisting of the 12 elements detailed below.

1. Organization Vision and Values

The first steps in OPEX for CIBC were establishing a mission for the new centers, a vision of how to achieve that mission, and the values governing both. These intangible elements were especially important because of the magnitude of change under consideration. Those employees involved explained the change as follows:

> We realized that we were mandating a change in the work and social culture for all employees across the country. We could not expect employees to have ownership and commitment toward an ill-defined future world. All of this needed a basic framework that defined the principles of our new world. To this end, the National Project Team developed a set of operating principles that would provide a national framework of ideals that established the boundaries within which each center would operate. Customization of local vision and values in support of the operating principles was encouraged.

An example of a vision and values statement developed by a local design team is provided in table 3; the full text of the corporate operating principles is included in table 4.

2. A High-Involvement Process

Overall, much of the work of implementing the Operational Excellence Project was carried out locally by a number of different types of dedicated teams. In addition to the National Project Team (see #5), center-specific implementation, design, study and action, and culture change teams were created, characterized by intensive engagement and involvement of all staff members. These are described more fully below.

Table 3. Calgary processing center.

Vision:	Together, as empowered employees, we will build an environment of trust and understanding, where continuous improvement leads to service that exceeds our customers' expectations.

Values:

Honesty:	To build our future on integrity and mutual trust.
Respect:	One must value and appreciate every individual equally.
Communication:	To communicate constructively in an open and honest way.
Initiative:	To be willing, able, and committed to continually improve.
Fellowship:	Through teamwork and support, we will participate as one to achieve common goals.
Commitment:	We do what we say we will do.

IMPLEMENTATION TEAM
- It is open to all center employees who declare an interest in being a part of the change.
- It forms the roster for selecting members of the design team, study teams, and other assignments and initiatives as needed.

DESIGN TEAM
- It spearheads the unique local design.
- For many this represents the first significant experience with teams and teamwork.
- It focuses initially on the following activities:
  — develop a team charter, including purpose, ground rules, and roles and responsibilities
  — develop a communication strategy
  — coordinate the development of a vision and values statement through a process that involves all center employees
  — identify needs and opportunities
  — create, assign tasks, provide assistance, and monitor progress of study teams.
- It involves a commitment of up to two days per week, for a period of 12 months.

STUDY AND ACTION TEAMS
- They fully define issue assigned.
- They carry out necessary detailed analysis, develop implementation strategy, and participate in communication to total organization.
- They are made up of two to 12 members.

Table 4. Operating principles of CIBC processing centers.

Meeting our Mission

Principles

- The organization and its employees will be adaptable to changing conditions and experiences.
- We will be flexible, professional, proactive, and cost-effective in providing products and services to our internal and external customers so that we constantly meet their needs and exceed their expectations.
- The CIBC Processing Centers are committed to service, quality, and continuous improvement. We will continually review, assess, and improve our processes, policies, and all other aspects of our operations.
- We will act with integrity, adhering to the highest ethical standards.

Meeting our Vision

Principles of Providing Superior Value to Customers

- We will be customer rather than transaction driven. Customer requirements will drive our processes, and where appropriate, customers will be involved in process redesign.
- We will be creative and responsive in satisfying our customers' needs.
- We will treat internal, as well as external, clients as customers.
- All decisions will be timely and responsive to the customer.
- We will strive to handle every transaction 100 percent correctly the first time, every time.

Principles of Contributing to CIBC

- We will reduce operating costs and improve productivity and effectiveness by providing efficient, timely, and accurate service.
- We will create a professional working environment that will help establish the Processing Center and CIBC as a recognized employer of choice.
- We will work in partnership with all areas of CIBC to establish the bank as the financial services supplier of choice for customers seeking the best value.

Principles of Creating a Positive Environment for Employees

A. General Principles

- Employees will be treated equitably with trust, dignity, and respect.
- We are committed to learning. Training, education, and development in technical, leadership, and interpersonal skills will be ongoing.
- Employees will be given the necessary training and education to perform their jobs effectively.
- Employees have the right and the responsibility to provide input to or have direct involvement in change processes and decision making.
- Diverse points of view will be valued and considered necessary for nonroutine, cross-functional decisions.
- We will ensure our employees have a clear understanding of how they contribute to the organization.

Table 4. Operating principles of CIBC processing centers (continued).

- Jobs will be designed to be challenging and rewarding and to empower employees, encouraging them to exercise initiative, discretion, risk taking, and accountability.
- Jobs will promote end-to-end responsibility for a product or service wherever possible.

B. Operating Principles

- Our actions will be guided by our five key values: respect for every individual, initiative and creativity, stewardship, excellence in everything we do, and teamwork.
- Communication will be open, two-way, and timely.
- Information, including operating data, will be shared with employees on a timely basis. Operating results will be shared daily. Financial and service or quality results will be shared at least monthly.
- Operating decisions will be made at the lowest possible level in the organization, to ensure that those affected by the decisions can provide input to, or make, the decisions.
- There will be minimal administrative functions, and these functions will support rather than control the activities of teams.

C. Teamwork Principles

- Employees will work together in teams to meet our short- and long-term business objectives.
- The teams or work groups will be organized to empower employees to take responsibility for whole job tasks and decision making, including traditional supervisory roles, such as work scheduling and assignment, cross-training, performance evaluation, and employee selection.
- Accountability and control of service or quality and cost-effectiveness will reside with the work teams.
- Work teams will be accountable for resolving and eliminating problems by continuous improvement and process redesign to prevent recurrence.
- Work team performance will be driven by customer expectations and measured on service or cost.
- Performance appraisal will be two-way between team members and their performance evaluators.
- Awards and rewards will be based on agreed performance results and will promote teamwork. Contributions to the success of the Processing Center will be recognized and rewarded.

D. Career Principles

- Employees who maintain satisfactory performance will not lose their employment as a result of work redesign.
- Career development choices and actions will be the responsibility of each individual. Managers will support the individual in identifying and pursuing career opportunities.
- To ensure effectiveness of work teams and to enhance personal career development options, employees will be flexible in accepting alternative opportunities in jobs, shifts, levels, and locations, and will be prepared to undertake necessary training, development, and relocation.

- It assesses work rules prevailing in the old organization and integrates or develops new ones consistent with the new environment.

3. Carefully Selected Senior Managers

Early in the Operational Excellence Project, the seven regional manager positions in the new organization were posted and individuals selected. Because the capabilities and attitudes of the center manager were considered a key factor influencing each center's success, great care was taken to select the best available candidates. Each candidate for the seven regional manager positions was required to

- complete a written application that included a paper on why he or she should be selected for the position and what his or her understanding of the of the new environment was
- undergo a half-day panel interview that included a presentation to the panel on the self-managed work teams, participation in role-playing exercises, and a behavioral interview designed to test for the characteristics and attributes required of a manager in a team environment
- undergo an intensive paper-based and clinical-interview psychological assessment, again to assess each candidate's ability to demonstrate the required behaviors
- undergo additional interviews with O&T senior officers.

Four of the 14 original regional managers were selected as new regional managers with expanded responsibilities. The three remaining positions were filled by individuals from outside the processing operations organization.

4. Dedicated Positions of Process Facilitators

A process facilitator position was created in each center to assist employees in moving toward a team-based environment. These individuals played a primary role in championing the initiative on a local basis, providing support to both technical and social processes, and in managing project activities, such as study team meetings. Reporting to the regional center manager, the process facilitators were a primary organizational development resource and the key contact of the National Project Team.

5. Support Provided by the National Project Team

While employees within the centers performed virtually all the design and implementation work, the National Project Team, essentially an internal consulting staff, structured and guided the overall project. The team was responsible for

- carrying out preliminary research of high-performing team concepts and organizations
- designing the overall project structure and guiding documents, and developing and communicating guiding philosophies, that is, the *Operating Principles of CIBC Processing Centers*
- assisting in planning and executing key human resource policies in support of a team-based environment, for example, management selection, training, performance management, and employment continuity policies
- developing a compensation system and reward and recognition program to support a team environment
- planning and executing a national communications strategy
- facilitating local working sessions on topics including
  — Vision and Values
  — Team Evolution
  — Process Assessment and Analysis
  — Cost-Benefit Analysis
  — Layout Planning
  — Transitional Organization Design
  — Transfer of Responsibilities
  — Measurement Culture
- developing and implementing new management systems on a national basis, that is, improvement register to track progress and team evolution tracking
- providing ongoing support on an as-needed basis, once center operations were self-sustaining.

6. Process Management Methodology

OPEX program designers considered a "reliable, systematic process improvement methodology" to be critically important. They believed that for a tool or methodology to be useful, it must be applicable anywhere, anytime, and by anyone. In choosing their particular methodology, they had to match the tools to the people who would be using them. Since most employees in the Processing Centers perform clerical tasks and have not been exposed to any previous training in process analysis, it became important to find a tool that was easy and effective to use. For continuous improvement efforts, they modified an existing process management methodology composed of three phases and 10 steps.

Specifically, the National Project Team stressed three phases: process assessment, process analysis, and process improvement. There was strong emphasis on getting input from customers and the people involved in the work, getting ideas through internal and external benchmarking, and ensuring buy-in to the changes by all stakeholders.

In the beginning, the project emphasis was on integration of processes to remove inefficiencies and redundancy in operation between the two units. In order to do that quickly, study teams were set up to study each process. The study teams had participation from all areas and levels within the center, and all members were given process management training. In effect, these teams were cross-functional problem-solving teams. As integration progressed, however, actual work teams were charged with responsibility for whole processes in terms of both performance and continuous improvement. These work teams formed the foundation for the subsequent organizational development.

The goal was to have 100 percent of the staff trained and using the methodology as part of their daily work duties. From past experience, project designers had learned that using a real process as part of the training is the best way for people to understand and apply the training. In other words, learn by doing. To determine if the methodology was being used consistently and if follow-up training was required, it was necessary to review the employees' documentation as part of the improvement process. In addition to the process management training, staff members have also been trained in measurements, cost-benefit analysis, writing improvement proposals, and risk assessment.

7. Common Performance Measurement Tools Used Companywide

Within boundaries, each center was allowed to do essentially as it liked in the design of their work processes, organization, management practices, and culture, as long as it was consistent with the operating principles. Through sharing of improvement initiatives, process standardization did occur. To facilitate ease of understanding and deployment, the measurement system focused on using the same measurement categories traditionally used by CIBC processing operations:

- Productivity (output per full-time equivalent [FTE])
- Cost (cost per unit of output)
- Accuracy (errors or complaints)
- Timeliness (service level attainment).

8. Challenging Performance Goals

To focus individual and collective attention, senior management established performance goals in the above-listed measurement categories. By any standards, these were a significant challenge to center management and staff. Over a three-year period, each center was expected to

- improve labor productivity by 30 percent
- make a significant contribution to a 40 percent unit-cost reduction
- improve customer satisfaction and employee morale by the same percentages.

9. Team Member, Leadership, and Other Training

Personal and leadership training to help employees function in this new, self-managed environment was an important part of the change program. CIBC committed to providing every employee at least 12 days of training annually. Some employees, such as design team members, received much more. Learning facilitator positions were established to deliver the following standard training courses as part of the new center operations:

- *Personal Leadership Skills Training:* A 12-module Zenger Miller training program required for all center employees, with each module requiring two to three hours of classroom instruction.
- *Team Leadership Training:* A six-module Zenger Miller training program, required for all employees before taking on the role of team leader, with each module requiring up to six hours of classroom instruction.
- *Administrative Skills Training:* With the manager's changing role, the team needs to learn how to deal with the rest of the organization, that is, purchasing, payroll, accounting, and so forth.
- *Job Skills Training:* The technical skills required for job performance. The team is trained on the actual tasks for which they are responsible. Team members continually add to their technical skills throughout the life of the team.
- *Problem-Solving Skills Training:* In order to successfully work at continuous improvement, teams need training in identifying opportunities and implementing improvements.

10. Commitment to Employment Continuity

Members of the National Project Team alleged: "It is fairly obvious that if employees lose their jobs as a result of identifying and making improvements, their willingness to participate dries up pretty quickly." To prevent this problem, CIBC made a commitment to employment continuity. This commitment was an extension of a general CIBC policy under which the bank promised to notify an employee three months in advance before eliminating a position and then to work with the affected employee for up to a further six months to identify job opportunities inside or outside the company. Employees whose jobs were affected by the Operational Excellence Project were exempt from the six-month limitation, and special efforts were made to provide training and other opportunities to make this a time of career renewal.

11. Challenging the Cultural Norms

Since the overall Operational Excellence Project focused on cultural changes, CIBC recognized the necessity of changing cultural symbols and signals to support the newly empowered organization. These "soft" considerations went along with the "hard" tools directed at costs, productivity, and so forth, to ensure a visibly new operating environment. By acknowledging the need for such symbolic changes, which could be directed and encouraged but not forced, the project designers hoped to ensure that the resulting transformation would be long-lasting and truly part of the organizational fabric of the bank. These symbols dealt with such matters as dress code, parking privileges, degrees of formality in the workplace, petty housekeeping rules—indeed all matters that could hark back to the old hierarchical organization and work against the concept of centers run by self-managed work teams.

12. Increased Communication

OPEX program directors maintained that "communication is the key to getting buy-in." They tried to create a management process in which everyone affected, both employees and customers, had the opportunity to influence the change proposals before they were implemented. Although getting buy-in can be the hardest part of continuous improvement, they believed that if dialogue was begun early and communication channels kept open, most employees would eventually accept and support changes, even when jobs were substantially changed or eliminated. One manager affirmed: "Having good communication with everyone affected decreases the chances of employee sabotage or malice (the subverting of new procedures by employees bent on proving the changes won't work)."

Results

Clearly, the key challenge of an initiative such as OPEX is not only to achieve the significant performance improvement targets but to do so with an accompanying increase in customer and employee satisfaction. So often improvements in one of these areas are offset by a corresponding decrease in another. The evolution to a team-based culture is the only effective way of driving all three of these objectives ahead in the same direction, at the same time.

The success of the OPEX initiative confirms this belief. At the end of the three-year project planning time horizon, actual improvement results were 109 percent of the targeted savings of a 30 percent productivity improvement. Only seven employees (of the approximately 750 eligible for redeployment) had failed to find alternative employment with the bank and were continuing to take advantage of the extended employment continuity provision.

To date, well over 300 fully documented process improvement proposals have been developed by center employees. Many have been implemented, while others, outside the boundary and control of center employees, have been passed to the appropriate department for attention.

Customers of the Processing Centers have responded very favorably to improved services, as the following sample testimonials confirm:

- "Our view of the Processing Center has changed 180 degrees over the past year. The big difference I have seen is their increasing focus on the customer."
- "You really are on the leading edge of employee involvement. Many companies talk about two-way open communication, but never really practice what they preach. Your team and department meetings and your fine newsletter are all concrete examples of your commitment."
- "With your vision statement and commitments posted throughout the center, the healthy buzz that one hears, it is clear to me that you have all made great headway, an achievement that anyone…would be very proud of. Truly a best practice team."

Employee reaction was equally positive as the following post-implementation review comments suggest:

- "Emphasizing the team's accomplishments, as 'our work' and not 'my work,' has brought out the best in us."
- "Nowadays there is a lot more involvement on the part of all employees in solving problems, making decisions, and getting information for themselves."
- "Employees are realizing that they can make decisions and changes; they can come up with their ideas, and the changes are being implemented and their ideas credited with some value. It's made a big difference in the morale of the staff."
- "The further you are along, the more you understand, and the more you realize that you will get something out of it and it truly can make a difference."
- "With self-managed teams, there will be more accountability, and with accountability, I believe you get improved performance and improved behavior. The bottom line is great customer service."

Lessons Learned

The Operational Excellence Project was begun in the fall of 1991 to undertake the integration of the eight data centers and the nine central operations service centers across Canada. At the same time, the project was mandated to introduce new work systems based upon the characteristics of high-performing teams. Work of this nature had never been attempted before within CIBC, and the challenges and opportunities facing the National Project Team resulted in a number of lessons being learned.

Different information sources were used in compiling the lessons learned. Initially, a postimplementation review was conducted by a random survey of approximately 15 percent of the Processing Center population. Also, interviews were conducted with more than 30 individuals who contributed their observations and perceptions. Finally, the project team compiled all of the comments and subsequently categorized them into nine headings. The following lessons learned provide a summary of the project team's interpretation of all the information received:

1. Business Focus
- Clearly understood and articulated business reasons for moving to a team-based environment are required before starting the initiative.
- Targets must be achievable and measurable.
- Avoid focusing on staff reductions and team implementation at the same time.
- The results of a strong client or customer focus are powerful motivators.

2. Leadership Support and Commitment
- We need earlier and more intensive engagement of leadership.
- We need a wide base of visible leadership to champion the initiative.
- We need high visibility of the team initiative with senior management.
- We need all levels of management to be fully committed to teams before starting.

3. Employee Involvement
- Most employees intrinsically buy into the principles of employee involvement.
- Most employees do not initially understand the full implications of the responsibility and accountability that come with increased involvement.
- Awareness heightening should be a continuous process, not merely an event.

- Buy-in, ownership, and sustainability of change are directly related to the level of employee involvement.

4. Learning and Education

- Training is more effective when delivered just-in-time rather than the conventional approach of training everyone in everything.
- Learning is more effective when the content is directly applied to a work situation.
- Learning requires reinforcement and ongoing support.
- We need a means of evaluating the effectiveness of interpersonal skills learning.

5. Communications

- No matter how much you communicate, it is never enough.
- Communication of a consistent message is most effective when different media are used.
- Communication of work in progress, as well as the final result, will increase buy-in and ownership of changes.
- Having a process to share information does not mean sharing will happen.

6. Continuous Improvement

- Expectations about results must be managed.
- Continuous improvement is a cultural change as much as it is a technological change.
- Do not underestimate the time needed to move people up the continuous improvement learning curve.
- Good data is critical to successful implementation of a continuous improvement culture.
- Avoid creating a situation that polarizes or disempowers management and staff.
- Baseline measures are a must if improvements are to be tracked.

7. New Roles to Support a Team Environment

- It's difficult to select leaders with the right attributes when the end state is unclear.
- Leadership evolution must precede team evolution.
- Strong facilitation skills are required on a local basis to spearhead the initiative.
- Need strong leadership role models to champion the initiative.
- Leadership must own the definition of their new roles and the resulting required change.

- Not everyone will want to change roles—expect casualties.

8. Team Evolution and Maturity
- There must be a balance between a structured approach and employee creativity within boundaries.
- A continuum for self-management is a better model than team evolution by stages.
- Any model for evolution must allow teams to start at any point, based on the team's maturity level.
- It takes a long time and requires patience by management and team members for teams to mature.
- For teams to become effective, there must be a balance between a focus on getting the work done, satisfying customers, and team relationships.

9. Implementation
- The process takes a great deal of patience and expectations must be managed.
- With the exception of some key underlying principles, any implementation must be customized.
- Leadership must not abdicate the responsibility of defining the "what"; teams must not refuse to accept responsibility for the "how."
- Key assumptions must be tested on an ongoing basis.
- Without external support mechanisms, you may create teams, but you will never create teamwork.

Questions for Discussion
1. Cultural change was a significantly important part of the Operational Excellence Project. How would you describe the culture within your organization and what unique challenges will you face in changing this culture as you move to a team-based organization?
2. The success of the project was due in large part to the involvement of employees in all phases of the work. What plans do you have to engage employees at all levels in your organization, and how will you harness their involvement?
3. If you were to pick the three most significant lessons learned for your organization, which would they be, and why?
4. The evolution of a team-based organization takes many years; indeed some would say it never ends. What are some of the events that can occur to derail the initiative, and what activities can be undertaken to ensure that momentum is not lost?

The Author

Berkeley J. Emmons is currently a senior human resources consultant with the Canadian Imperial Bank of Commerce (CIBC). He leads a team of internal consultants, responsible for the development, implementation, and support of teams and teamwork throughout the organization. He and his team have recently successfully completed a project in which they were responsible for process redesign, team implementation, and continuous improvement for more than 250 teams throughout Canada. Prior to joining CIBC, Emmons spent 12 years consulting to industry and business in the area of operational improvement. He is a graduate in industrial engineering from the University of Toronto and is a licensed professional engineer. Emmons can be reached by writing to Berkeley J. Emmons, P.Eng., Commerce Court North, 20th Floor c/o Commerce Court Postal Station, Toronto, Ontario M5L 1A2 Canada; phone: 416.861.5223; fax: 416.861.3887; e-mail: bemmons316@aol.com.

"Are Those Team Meetings Gonna Make You Money?"

Midwest Electronics

Stephen D. Hill

The title of this innovative case cuts to the chase. When times get tough, teams are often galvanized into action. This case describes how a cross-functional team went to the customer to increase sales following team building and training sessions. Results, including dollar value of sales, are reported. Show me the money!

Fear and inaction can paralyze an organization, even one fighting for its own survival. Like the venomous bite of a poisonous snake, the initial realization that a company is in trouble gives way to a numbing feeling that makes every movement slow and deliberate. Even if one does not talk about the fear, it still lurks in the deep recesses of the organization's culture.

When a company faces such a dilemma, opinions and solutions swirl, offering a dizzying array of promise and confusion. In one case, two men with contrasting opinions passed in the stairwell of a local hotel where a company was conducting a team building session. As the team development coordinator carried some visual aids into the meeting, the other skeptical man sneered, "Are those meetings gonna make you money?" The Bus Team would reply in time.

Confronted as they were by fear and indecision, the Bus Team would have been excused if they had decided not to try. Why should this cross-functional team of seven production employees and personnel from other departments think that they could convince customers to buy their products? In past years, manufacturing and sales would have remained safe behind their respective walls, rarely interacting. Unfortunately that approach had failed repeatedly, and jobs were at stake. Characterizing similar situations, Lippitt says that a turbulent environment seems to promote or even require high levels of intergroup dependence and cooperation (Lippitt, 1982). This paper will describe how the Bus Team expanded their narrow job descriptions and generated more than $1.5 million in annual sales. Through its efforts, this team provided an example of how a company can resolve cross-functional issues and improve its image in the marketplace.

Overview

For more than four decades, having a *Fortune* 500 company division nestled between the foothills and cornfields provided a small midwestern town with a sense of security. Like their parents before them, sons and daughters walked past the guardhouse, through the air lock of glass doors, and over to the time clocks that lined the entrances of this sprawling industrial complex. Old-timers still remember when the division was strategically important to its parent company.

By providing subassemblies used in the electronic circuit industry, the company prospered with the growing markets of computers, televisions, cars, and stereos. Consistently the company was a leading producer in a field of 20 to 30 competitors. As markets became global, international competition began offering quality products at lower selling prices. This forced the discontinuation of marginal product lines, squeezed by rising costs and lower prices. A proud factory that once employed more than 1,000 people now numbered about 400 and still fought to control costs and grow sales. Unfortunately the introduction of new technology and products failed to meet initial expectations, causing many starts, stops, and product recalls from the customers. The cold reality of a senior manager's comments should not have been a surprise. Still, his words to sell or close the plant, if it were not fixed, sent a chill throughout the community. The shock gave way to rising tensions, strained labor relations, and finger pointing, as the company and its employees struggled to redefine themselves. Besieged by these pressures, the company realized that technology improvements by themselves would not be enough. To meet the ever-increasing demands for higher quality at lower prices, the company would also need to improve the interaction between departments through interpersonal and team training. From this adversity, the seeds of a new idea developed in the minds of a few, dedicated employees.

Basic Training and Approach

Desperate and realizing that the plant was running out of time, four years ago the company launched a bold, systematic initiative to seek ideas from its employees. To lead this approach, the company promoted two people from within the company to coordinate the team building activities. They reported directly to the senior manager with the mission of creating an empowered environment to support business goals and objectives. A steering committee then formed to represent various divisions within the company to guide the effort. To provide a common language for the change initiative, the company conducted a series of three-day team building workshops for all 400 employees. Team building topics included

- principles of quality team management
- stages of team development
- effective communication skills
- conflict resolution techniques
- consensus building
- team roles and responsibilities.

Each session represented a cross section of the organization and typically included staff managers, production supervisors, employees, salespeople, and other support personnel. During team training, a comment sometimes heard is: "We are already a team and do not need training." One is wise to not to believe this siren. Assuming that "members already have all the competence they need to work well as a team" is a mistake (Hackman, 1990). Besides providing the basic team skills, each session was highly interactive and encouraged an open discussion concerning the issues facing the business. In support of the team training, the company trained more than 60 internal facilitators through an intensive three-day workshop to guide teams through the team process. This training covered facilitative roles, group dynamics and coaching styles, meeting effectiveness, facilitation process, facilitative behavior, interventions, values and beliefs, facilitation tools, video practice session, and other topics.

To give employees an opportunity to use these skills immediately, they conducted a two- to three-day problem-solving session. By learning total quality management tools, teams developed proposals around specific business issues. Management approved more than 90 percent of these ideas for implementation by the various teams. In all, 30 to 40 task force teams formed around specific issues to increase productivity, decrease spoilage, improve safety, and address other key initiatives. As these teams completed their missions, they celebrated their progress and disbanded. The objectives of other teams were ongoing improvement.

Bus Team Formed

To provide an in-depth understanding of the evolution of teams, this paper focuses specifically on the launching of the Bus Team from this process. During one of the above team building sessions, a group of individuals formed a grass-roots effort to improve an elusive high-technology product. This cross-functional team of 10 to 15 employees represented manufacturing, engineering, maintenance, customer service, product management, and sales. Sales personnel would call in on a speaker phone, sometimes at 4:30 a.m., to be part of the meeting. For two years, this team would meet for one to two hours per week to discuss ways to reduce spoilage and decrease cycle time. A facilitator worked with the team until they felt comfortable rotating the role. During these two years, the team successfully implemented approximately 50 ideas. Although the products were getting better, the market was slow to accept the new products because of previous product recalls. Falling sales caused additional layoffs, demoralized survivors, and a poor image in the marketplace.

At this critical juncture, the team attended the national sales meeting and listened to the sales force's concerns and issues. A few years back, it would have been unthinkable for production employees to attend a sales meeting. Team building had started to tear down the walls between manufacturing and sales and marketing. This continuous improvement team listened intently as salesperson after salesperson described the customer's reluctance to try the revised products. In concluding their presentations, the sales force requested updated specification sheets for distribution to the customers to "keep options open." To discuss the salesperson's plight, the cross-functional team called a voluntary meeting at 10 p.m. so that the late shifts could participate. Five members met in the cafeteria over coffee and doughnuts and discussed the issue until 1 a.m. With the help of a facilitator, the team reestablished ground rules and expectations for their interaction, thus reaffirming their commitment to one another. After lengthy discussion, the team collectively agreed that they had already addressed many product issues that still burned bright in the perceptions of their customers. Reaching a consensus, the team agreed its objective was to improve the company's image in the marketplace and thus increase sales and job security.

As team members brainstormed potential approaches, they narrowed the choices through a multivoting process. Developing data sheets, as requested by the sales force, led the list, followed by finding new ways to bring customers to the factory. The team feared that new data sheets would not address underlying customer fears and would end up in the waste-baskets. The second idea was intriguing but largely impractical because most of the new customers were on the West Coast. Few western customers currently took the time and expense to fly back to this midwestern company. Still, the second idea caught the attention of the team. If customers would visit the plant, a dedicated workforce could show off a long list of manufacturing improvements. In a moment of inspiration, someone suggested taking the "factory to the customer." The group spontaneously laughed at the notion of an industrial plant on wheels. In many organizations, an idea as far-fetched as this one would have been shot down immediately with killer comments like: "It will cost too much"; "We do not have the time"; "It will never work here"; or "We have already tried that one." Over the two years that the team worked together, they knew that many of their ideas had turned into small wins. The thought lingered: "How could we take the factory to the customer?" The idea quickly evolved into a bus full of people representing various processes, and thus the Bus Team formed.

Susan Koch and Stan Deetz (1981) argued that "metaphors literally anchor our understandings of experience" and "are at the heart of the interpretive process." The metaphor of a bus provided a sense of cooperation, solidarity, and action in troubled times. It represented a coming together, the basic premise of the team training, and a movement toward the end customer—the reason for their existence and excitement. "The best teams invest a tremendous amount of time and effort exploring, shaping, and agreeing on a purpose that belongs to them both collectively and individually" (Katzenbach and Smith, 1993). A cohesive symbol of this culminating effort would serve them well during the struggles ahead. With five people now believing in their idea, the team's attention now focused on convincing management, other production employees, and the customers. In an informal meeting, the senior manager encouraged the team to develop the idea further and to make a presentation to staff.

Needing to recruit more volunteers, they decided not to use the company newsletter. Instead, individuals solicited support one by one. The team owned the idea and wanted to explain it firsthand to fellow workers. Their walk and talk communicated an unmistakable sense of pride, belief, and conviction. From this experience, the company remembered a valuable lesson: Ownership and involvement go hand in hand. Over breaks and lunch, each team member personally interviewed fellow workers to develop interest. Through this approach, they recruited 14 more people to develop and deliver a presentation.

The final cross-functional team consisted of seven production workers, seven salaried people, and five salespeople. The five salespeople would supply customer contacts and coordinate logistical issues for the whole team. Production employees represented all three shifts and the four key manufacturing departments, because this team believed that with one committed member from each area of the factory, they could make a difference. Two production supervisors, two process engineers, one product manager, a customer service person, and a facilitator completed the team; seniority varied from 10 to 35 years. The results of taking the factory to the customer would later prove to pay for the training sessions for all employees.

Peer Pressure

The exhilaration of a new idea renewed the original team members' interest and provided a needed spark for new members looking to help. A high level of shared leadership would later characterize these teammates. The urgency of the situation was a two-edged sword. One edge, honed by the potential closing of the facility, was compelling and meaningful. On the other side, significant peer pressure developed from layoffs, high overtime, and strained union-management relations. Caught in the cross fire of these powerful forces, the team had to convince other employees, skeptical of management's intentions, that the idea was their own. One team member, who delayed his retirement to see the project through, caught the brunt of the conflict. A few negative individuals accused the team of trying to take the salespeople's jobs away. In his normal rapid fire of words, he acknowledged that the team was also concerned about this point, but that the Bus Team was just trying to help. He further elaborated that they did not want the salespeople's jobs anyway. Then the grapevine bristled with comments like, "When we are downsizing and losing money, why waste money on a bus trip?" This individual answered the question by joking that the company spent money on worse ideas than this one and expressed confidence that the plan would work. Finally, skeptical employees asked the team repeatedly, "Why should we support this team?" Again the response was simple and direct: "We can stand here and do nothing, or we can give it a shot. The choice is ours." This relentless pressure occurred not only at work but in the community as well, even at the local grocery store. Defending itself at every turn, the team was left on the brink of disbanding.

Teams can experience intergroup conflict and "polarization around interpersonal issues" characterized by storming (Tuckman, 1965). Mounting pressures caused them to slip into this turbulent stage. At a critical juncture, the team relied on four major strengths to remain intact, with the first being facilitation. The team got back together, shared their personal concerns, and vented their frustrations. When egos and emotions cloud rational thinking, the value of facilitation becomes clear. Often team members are unaware of their personal strain or the way that they are coming across to someone else. An objective, empathetic facilitator can aid understanding and suggest additional approaches to resolve the issues confronted. In this case, the facilitator led a discussion about past issues that individuals had faced. Next to each issue, they described the steps taken to overcome these obstacles and then listed their successes. When the team had completed this exercise, they realized that they had each overcome a long string of difficulties, some worse than the ones that the team now collectively faced. By sharing their concerns, the team grew closer together. Besides facilitation, another factor that helped the team remain together was the fact that several members had worked together at various stages of other continuous improvement initiatives. A series of small wins over time strengthens resolve for future issues.

A third strength for this team was the use of a common language of improvement, resulting from team building and problem-solving training. Through familiarity and practice, the use of tools like plan-do-check-act, brainstorming, nominal group process, and cause and effect become instinctive. Now, rather than focusing on the tool, the team could apply problem-solving techniques for results. Finally, the idea of a bus continued to provide a common identity that solidified the team and kept the dream alive.

The Presentation

The team then developed their presentation in subgroups and later shared their findings with one another in order to get buy-in and commitment. When these tasks were complete, one operator displayed his idea of employee involvement for the team: He modified a company slogan to include the special "team people" who manufactured the product. This slogan excluded the manufacturing people for more than five years, but when given the chance, he corrected it in a matter of minutes. With a colored flipchart illustration, he showed how the company had replaced the "wall syndrome" at the plant with wide doors that opened both ways. His drawing showed the factory as the "heart" of the operation—the team making the product. The heart connected customers to the sales force, engineering support, management, and suppliers.

After practicing their presentation with one another, the Bus Team walked into the staff meeting to seek funding for their project. In turn, team members relayed their beliefs to management. With 20 to 30 people present in a small, enclosed room, one participant, overcome by heat in the middle of the speech, began to faint. With a fellow team member sprawled on the floor, and people running to get water and a nurse, the atmosphere became very tense. After she recovered, someone on the team quipped that they were willing to die to make this trip happen. The tension in the room broke into needed laughter, but this team was clearly making personal sacrifices. Caught up in the excitement of carrying out the solution, the company did not anticipate the added strain for people unaccustomed to talking in front of large groups. Another participant later said that fear of speaking to an audience was an issue for almost everyone on the team. He said that he handled the fear because he believed in what they were doing. To remedy this issue for future teams, the company offered voluntary, public-speaking classes that met for two hours a week for three months. The senior manager, having heard their presentation, said that he could not turn down a team so dedicated. Staff members gave their full support for the team and suggested that they should "scrimmage first," by conducting a pilot presentation at two local accounts. The team heartily agreed, and the Bus Team was launched. One dedicated production worker later remarked that management thought "we were worth the money and effort to get us out there."

Customer Contact

The team continued to perform well through the pilot stage. They boarded an extended van and drove 90 minutes to the first account. In this short time, they realized that they would kill each other if they had to take a bus almost 2,000 miles to the West Coast. After considering all the logistics, the team found that it was cheaper to fly and rent vans than it was to charter a bus. Needing no other convincing, the team agreed to fly, but the enduring symbol of a bus remained in the hearts and minds of team members. Based on pilot feedback, the team included additional phone numbers and contacts of personnel at the factory to make it easier for customers to reach them. One customer liked the visit so much that they sent some of their production employees to visit the Bus Team's plant. Team members conducted the plant tour, answered questions, and involved other people from the plant. As a result, other employees volunteered to take customers on future tours, thus increasing employee involvement. One team member later remarked to a friend that 20 years earlier, management would have told the employees what to say. Now employees had the full confidence of management to lead the factory tours and to represent the company accordingly. After all, everyone had a stake in the successful outcome of these visits.

With management's support, the team prepared 55 letters to accounts on the West Coast that were not currently buying their products. Based on sales input, they addressed the letters to appropriate individuals at each account with titles such as president, vice president, manufacturing manager, and purchasing manager. After a week, team members began making phone calls to each account. The same group that feared public speaking was now calling major accounts. Based on the strength of their convictions and management's trust, the employees rose to the occasion. One person lined up three accounts immediately. Another unlucky individual called six straight companies, each of which said no. After being assured that his approach was sound, he later met with success and much relief. This experience further bonded the team together and helped them develop empathy for the sales group. Intrigued by the calls, 34 percent of the companies contacted agreed to a visit. Customers remarked that the sincerity of the people overwhelmed them. One Bus Team member later said that the "customers could not believe people from the floor were coming out and had something to sell." After this experience, the team members easily assured the rest of the factory that they had no desire to take the salespeople's jobs.

Dress Code

Though the team was making progress, the apprehension associated with trying something new in these difficult times caused the members to be edgy. One watershed incident involved a salesperson innocently suggesting that it would be nice if team members wore a dress shirt with khaki pants. Instead of personally sharing this request, a coordinator sent the message electronically along with other last minute details. Although e-mail systems can encourage communication, they can also distort meaning. The response was swift and angry. One reply said, "If what we normally wear is not good enough, then I am not going." Another member said he did not own any khaki pants because they wrinkled too easily. The company became aware that a dress code was a lingering symbol of status, rank, and position. Several years earlier, the company eliminated the wearing of ties as a sign of a more open and informal environment. As evidenced by this example, bitter emotions remained over this issue. The team member who forwarded the message electronically now personally explained to each person that the request was more a comment than a mandate. After a week of watching his colleague try to undo the damage, a perceptive observer composed a rap song. The lyrics ended with, "We don't care what you wear, just as long as you are on the bus." This humor, accompanied by apologies, helped ease tensions, and people were freed to wear what they wanted. As a continuing sign of the team's solidarity, several members came up with the idea of wearing matching red sports jackets, which management agreed to buy. Through these efforts, the team turned a negative situation into a positive display of team cohesion. The team later laughed about the incident, but this example serves as a reminder that even high-performing teams will go through turbulent times. Learning and team development are not always linear. Sometimes a team needs to regress before they can continue to grow. Incidentally, all participants wore dress clothes with their red jackets to the first account, without another word being spoken!

The Bus Trip

Before the "bus" left, a layoff occurred that caused management to reconsider if all team members should go on the trip. With increased cost pressures, all avenues were being considered to lower expenses. The team struggled with the idea and finally decided that if only some members could go, then it would be better to postpone the trip until sufficient resources could support the entire project. Management again saw the commitment, believed in the idea, and allowed the team to remain intact—a near miss avoided. The team then scheduled 19 account visits. In addition, they wanted to visit two distributors and three company warehouse locations to solidify existing relationships at those locations. To adapt to multiple customer schedules and the logistics of covering a thousand miles in less than a week, the team split into two groups. The teams flew to the West Coast, rented vans, and shared their story with customers who were not currently buying their product.

The typical presentation was 45 minutes long, followed by questions and answers for one to two hours. Customers sent three to 12 people to these meetings, including owners, presidents, vice presidents, and supervisors, as well as manufacturing, sales, quality, and production employees. Sensitive to their customer's 24-hour operations, the team offered to come in on the later shifts as well, but only one company took them up on this offer. Bus Team members shared personal insights on how they carried out the following initiatives for the customer's benefit: (1) empowerment and team building, (2) total quality management, (3) facilitation, (4) ISO, (5) customer support, and (6) technology.

Concerning empowerment and team building, a production supervisor spoke of how the role had changed from a traditional supervisor to that of a coach who removed obstacles and helped teams operate efficiently. Another person spoke of how the company had given the operators the authority to shut the line down over quality issues. One production worker also remarked that he felt involved only during the last four of his 16 years of experience, due to team building. He used to go home and not think about work at all. Now, because he is needed, he worries about the company. Another participant spoke of how his team helped a customer simplify the manufacture of their material, thus reducing its cycle time. Other team members shared how they worked with suppliers, operator to operator, to improve the supply chain. Some joint projects reduced spoilage at both the supplier and the company, resulting in better cost control. Another team building program discussed was one in which production employees "adopted" a customer. By using a special phone number, the customer could talk directly to an operator should the need arise. Typically this program added value in ensuring a smooth transition during specification changes. By being involved in the process, production personnel could start to anticipate the changes needed to ensure consistent products. One employee also related that leadership now invited production personnel to attend the manager's staff meetings to improve their knowledge of how the business operated. These experiences all helped to reinforce the point that the company's employees were working together to serve the customer.

The second part of the presentation focused on the use of total quality management tools to reduce spoilage, improve productivity, decrease cycle time, improve safety, and decrease "dumb" mistakes. Problem-solving techniques were shown to produce corrective actions for nonconformances that were focused on root causes, not symptoms. The third item on the agenda showed customers not only the value that the company experienced by using facilitators but also how this approach could benefit the customer. Facilitators acted as catalysts to improve the efficiencies of team meetings and to challenge teams to explore a wide range of options to optimize solutions. An outstanding example of how the first three items could work together was the implementation of an ISO9000 quality system. The company became registered in less than 18 months, using a team-based approach to develop and maintain the standards. Facilitated teams in each key area developed a flowchart for the key processes that were then used to develop documentation for each step. The people who worked the process wrote the procedures, thus helping to reduce communication issues regarding the meaning of various instructions. The fifth step in the presentation focused on customer support, which included customer service, stocking locations, distributor capabilities, and other matters directly related to servicing the customer. At one point, a customer expressed reservations about working with a midwestern company when their current suppliers were on the West Coast. One employee from a late shift spoke up and said that they could give the customer 24-hour coverage and handed him a list of phone numbers. The last point in the presentation focused on new technology being developed. Important to these discussions was the fact that customers could see for themselves how the company worked together. "Specific objectives have a leveling effect conducive to team behavior… titles, perks, and other stripes fade into the background" (Katzenbach and Smith, 1993). Titles blurred during the presentations as members helped one another define their mission.

The Bus Team tailored the question and answer session to the needs of each customer. Common questions included how the team got started, what struggles they faced, and how customers could use these initiatives. At the end of one session, the photography hound on the team told the customer's manager of quality: "This was our story. Management did not tell us what to say." Listening to his inspiring message, no one would have changed a word that he had to say. He owned the presentation and his sincerity and commitment were obvious.

To relax after several customer visits, one group visited a snowy peak for an impromptu, team building session. Unfortunately one of the most personable members of the team got sick and had to sit in the van the entire time. An occasional snowball landed on the van to include him. An incident occurred during this time that highlighted how team members enforced group norms. "Norms are shared expectations about how members of a group ought to behave" (Levine and Moreland, 1990). One team member made a flippant remark in response to a park ranger's comment that the thinner air on a mountain made objects expand. He took the opportunity to explain that his large, dear teammate really weighed only 100 pounds at sea level. That night, the team ate at a diner that displayed beautiful coconut creme pies in a rotating glass case. After ordering, he made the mistake of visiting the rest room before his pie arrived. When he returned, everyone was laughing and having a great time. As the sharp-tongued employee ate his pie, he commented that his stomach hurt, but he managed to finish the pie anyway. With each bite, the team roared with laughter. It was not until the following night that one member confided that they had sliced open the pie and spiced it with Tabasco sauce. After massaging his stomach and a bruised ego, the offender got the message to conform to the group norm of respecting others.

The Results

Of the 55 companies originally surveyed, 19 agreed to the Bus Team visit. The results of these visits are as follows:

1. Three companies placed new orders totaling more than $1.5 million in annualized sales at standard industry margin rates.
2. Another company approved the product for future usage.
3. One customer suggested changes in the product offering that would allow them to purchase material.
4. The presentations resulted in a follow-up ISO workshop conducted by the company as a value-added service to one account.
5. As a direct result of one production employee's suggestion, the company trained 116 people at 20 customer sites during a series of three-day facilitation workshops. Through these seminars, the company further developed customer relations, while the clients learned valuable team skills.
6. Out of 300 people present during these meetings, the average feedback rating for the team was 5.4 on a scale of one to six, with six being outstanding. Rating areas included knowledge, preparation, ability to relate to customer needs, and other topics. One company with nine employees present gave the team perfect sixes. Another company commented: "Perception is everything. Their message was clear. They have the products and services that we need."
7. Upon returning from their trip, each Bus Team member signed thank-you notes to each customer and followed up on action items.
8. One team member volunteered to write a communication for the company newsletter summarizing the team's success and its importance to the rest of the company.
9. To help other companies start the team process, the team went on to share its results on a radio show, at a chamber of commerce luncheon, and at a team conference.

Throughout the presentations, the Bus Team made it clear that their success was a direct result of the entire company and its support of this initiative. Because of their dedication and progress, the company has committed to support future bus trips, although turnover at top management positions may cause delays.

Potential Traps

Three potential traps can undermine the efforts of an organization to achieve results using the team process. One trap that companies and teams fall into is to give up prematurely. Even change that is healthy and needed can be threatening to other parts of the organization unfamiliar, or unwilling, to challenge their own beliefs. By being aware of these forces, a company can prepare itself in advance and redouble its efforts to support the team concept. Without a firm commitment from the company's leadership and to one another, the team could have bowed to a handful of negative individuals.

A second trap involves underestimating the potential of their people. "Out there in the settings with which we are all familiar are the unawakened leaders, feeling no overpowering call to lead and hardly aware of the potential within" (Gardner, 1990). During the team training conducted in this example, the company's leaders discovered that the laborers who punched the time clocks were also paramedics, nurses, church leaders, civic organization presidents, high school coaches, farmers, and small business owners. Leaders and followers in these other fields can make valuable contributions to improve organizational processes when encouraged.

Lastly, production supervisors need support and direction as they grapple with new expectations and realities. In the case presented, the company had promoted and rewarded traditional, autocratic leaders for decades and now needed participative coaches. Without their daily support, the best intentions of top leadership may go unnoticed by other employees. Charles Garfield (1986) highlights three major skills needed by these leaders: "Delegating to empower, stretching the abilities of others, and encouraging educated risk taking." To support this transition, the highlighted company offered a two-day training session specifically designed for the supervisors in addition to the three-day team building sessions. Also, the production supervisors formed roundtable meetings weekly to discuss ongoing issues.

Conclusions

The teamwork exhibited in this example required a consistent, long-term perspective. It should be viewed as a way to function, not another thing to do. The commitment among leading manufacturers to this approach is impressive. All *Industry Week* finalists for "America's Best Plants" in 1995 employed the practices of employee empowerment and employee problem-solving teams. In addition, 96 percent of these same companies used cross-functional teams (Sheridan, 1996).

To succeed, team members need a meaningful, compelling purpose to reach their full potential. Otherwise, "individuals may exert less effort when working collectively because they feel that their inputs are not essential to a high-quality group product." (Kerr and Bruun, 1983). Here the team knew that jobs and sales were at stake. By interacting with the customers, they designed approaches that could make meaningful contributions toward both causes.

The Bus Team was a peak team experience for many team members. Management, having a compelling need, trusted its employees and allowed them the freedom to flourish. As one production employee said, "Knowing that management would listen made all the difference." By visiting customers, employees at all levels within a company can experience a customer's needs firsthand. They can then translate these needs into actions free from the distortion caused by multiple channels and levels present in many organizations today. The Bus Team effectively showed that the road to success starts with a single idea, followed by patience and trust in the people who can affect the outcome. "When purposes and goals build on one another and are combined with team commitment, they become a powerful engine of performance" (Katzenbach and Smith, 1993). This experience may translate to your organization. Trust your people; they will not let you down. To answer the gentleman's question on the steps of the hotel, yes, these team meetings are going to make money.

Questions for Discussion

1. From your own experience, describe an outstanding team example.
   (a) What did it feel like to be associated with this team?
   (b) What obstacles did the team face?
   (c) How did the team overcome its difficulties?
   (d) How could you share your team success with other teams for their benefit?
2. Relate your experience with that of the Bus Team.
   (a) What characteristics are in common?
   (b) How do the teams differ?
3. Rather than using a team approach, what other options were available to management?
4. Should manufacturing "make," and sales just "sell"?
   (a) What are the pros and cons of cross-functional involvement?
   (b) Describe potential opportunities and risks associated with each option.
6. What specific initiatives developed cohesion among the team members?
7. How does your organization kill ideas? How can you address this issue?
8. Why was the dress code such a large issue? Did the team overreact? Why or why not?
9. What programs were created to involve production employees? Identify three additional programs to increase involvement.
10. What future awaits teams as we know them today? In five years? In 10 years?

The Author

Stephen D. Hill is the president of Key Learnings, a company dedicated to unlocking potential in organizations through education and training. He conducts workshops internationally in the fields of communication, conflict, customer service, facilitation, team building, and total quality management. Hill works with government, industry, and the service sector. Previously, he was the director of organization development at a liberal arts college. He also worked for 13 years with General Electric in the areas of team development, product support, marketing, sales, and customer service. Hill holds a master's degree in liberal learning with a major emphasis in organizational communication and leadership from Marietta College. He also has a bachelor's degree in electrical engineering and a cooperative education certificate from Auburn University. He is a G.E. Technical Marketing Program graduate and holds two organizational leadership awards for distinguished service. He can be reached c/o Key Learnings, Box 373, Harvest, AL 35749; phone: 256.830.0320.

References

Gardner, J. *On Leadership.* New York: Macmillan, 1990.

Garfield, C. *Peak Performers: The New Heroes of American Business.* New York: William Morrow, 1986.

Hackman, R. *Groups that Work (and those that don't): Creating Conditions for Effective Teamwork.* San Francisco: Jossey-Bass, 1990.

Katzenbach, J., and D. Smith. "The Discipline of Teams." *Harvard Business Review,* March-April, 1993, 111-126.

Kerr, N., and S. Bruun. "The Dispensability of Member Effort and Group Motivation Losses: Free Rider Effects." *Journal of Personality and Social Psychology,* 44, 1983, 78-94.

Koch, S., and S.A. Deetz. "Metaphor Analysis of Social Reality in Organizations." *Journal of Applied Communication Research,* 9, 1981, 1-15.

Levine, J., and R. Moreland. "Progress in Small Group Research." *Annual Review of Psychology,* 41, 1990, 585-634.

Lippitt, G.L. "Organization Renewal: A Holistic Approach to Organization Development" (2d edition). Englewood Cliffs, NJ: Prentice-Hall, 1982.

Sheridan, J. "Lessons from the Best." *Industry Week,* February 19, 1996, 13-20.

Tuckman, B.W. "Developmental Sequences in Small Groups." *Psychological Bulletin,* 63 (6), 1965, 384-399.

The Facilitator's Role in Team Breakthroughs

BorgWarner Automotive

R. Glenn Ray and Karen Stapleton

The facilitator role requires highly developed skills because this person promotes change without the luxury of power stemming from his or her position. In this case study, we can see the type and depth of skills that are needed and how those skills can be tested in team implementation. This facilitator was challenged to develop commitment in an organization that had previous failures in this area.

Facilitation at Work

Some teams have almost magical breakthroughs that move them rapidly toward high performance. One of the authors realized a team breakthrough early in his life. As a member of his high school football team, he experienced a dismal losing season his freshman year. The following two years were more successful, but there was always something that held them back. Halfway through the first game of his senior year, the spotty performance of the author's team seemed to be repeating itself. During the halftime intermission, the team lamented the 8-0 score in the opponents' favor. The coach helped them understand that they were not playing up to their potential and discussed the basics of administering the plays that they were missing. At the end of the intermission, they came out believing they could win, and they did just that. The score was 22-8, and the team had their first victory. They ended the season undefeated—the first time in the school's history. The coach had enabled a team

This case was prepared to serve as a basis for discussion rather than to illustrate either effective or ineffective administrative and management practices.

breakthrough that lasted the entire season. They were a different team after that halftime intermission of the first game.

This case study describes a team success involving small group facilitation. The organization involved is an automotive plant in Gallipolis, Ohio, that employees about 250 people. Like so many plants in the Midwest, this facility had been purchased in the preceding year. The plant culture is the composite of 27 years of highly traditional union-management interaction. After the acquisition, steps were taken to increase the supervisor-worker ratio to reduce autocratic management styles. Problem-solving teams for performance improvement in various areas were initiated. Early on in this organizational transition, historical trust issues clouded the probability for success.

This case describes the impact that facilitator training can have on organizational change. It is about how one facilitator internalized a three-day training program, practiced the skills and tools once back at the site, and realized significant results. While leading different groups, the facilitator built stronger teams. She enabled team member comments and struggled with team member commitment. As her comfort level increased, she even began teaching the skills she had gained.

Background of Site Teams

In years past, several teams had been constructed at this facility. Many disbanded for lack of interest, poor attendance, lack of structure, or slow progress. SMED (Single Minute Exchange Die) had been implemented in this plant on three separate occasions with some success. For some of the above-mentioned reasons, the teams had dissolved, which was devastating to the committed team members.

The facilitator in this case study had her first experience with teams as part of a successful glove cost-reduction team that met for approximately one and one-half years during 1992 and 1993. The members included two managers, the SPC (Statistical Process Control) technician, a maintenance man, a janitor, and two operators. The team went through various stages of development. They were untrained, but were able to work together and managed to reduce BorgWarner's glove costs by $50,000 a year. After a long debate, management finally agreed to terms that the team thought were important to be successful. Along with reducing glove costs, they added employee mailboxes for gloves, mail, and paychecks to be distributed.

The turning point for this site's team successes was the establishment of credibility between the workforce and management. Fact-based consensus decisions to improve the process were employed to focus on the superordinate goals of site productivity. Everyone was watching the progress of the first teams. They saw positive behavior changes, such as listening to one another, less explosive communication, and a willingness to work together.

Barriers to Implementation

One of the barriers to implementation of teams at this site was past history. Much of the frustration that employees felt was due to a lack of preparation, such as team development and facilitator training. This plant had a culture of mistrust, poor communication, lack of cohesion and commitment, favoritism for a small group of people, focusing on personal agendas rather than sitewide priorities, negativity, and avoidance of conflict at all costs. Many employees were skeptical and expressed the belief that new efforts would be in vain. Another barrier to consider in the implementation of this SMED team was the UAW (United Autoworkers) contract renewal that was coming up in only seven months. The team focused on overcoming these obstacles by staying positive, establishing credibility with success, and gaining trust and support from management, as well as from everyone in the plant. It was a constant battle, but the team persevered and worked diligently to improve the SMED process.

Developing the Facilitator

The facilitator featured in this instance, began as the executive secretary for the plant manager at the site. She then chose progressive roles as production control clerk, purchasing assistant, accounting clerk, and computer operator. This series of organizational roles enhanced her credibility once she demonstrated competent facilitator skills. She was provided an opportunity to attend several training programs. Three important programs included SMED, visual factory, and facilitator training. The last program proved to be a development catalyst for her and the team with which she worked in the plant. This story focuses on the results of the facilitator training program.

On November 7, 1995, the trainee arrived at the campus of Marietta College in Marietta, Ohio, to begin the three-day facilitator training program. The program was designed to lead the facilitator trainee through a series of techniques to build an effective work team. It defined specific facilitator behaviors and focused on providing several group problem-solving techniques.

Putting the Facilitator Skills to Use

The facilitator had been leading the SMED meeting prior to attending the facilitator training program. She began using the skills she had learned on her first day back at her workplace, including the use of flipcharts and colored markers. The SMED participants were very receptive and thought the different colors separated ideas on the flipchart, making the items visible and easy to refer to. Also, the facilitator rephrased the participant's ideas and watched for nonverbal signs that everyone was in consensus before writing the comments down. After the meeting, two operators told the facilitator that they thought the meeting went very well and had accomplished a lot. A critical factor enabling the transfer of the facilitator training to the workplace was the immediate practice of the newly acquired techniques.

Role Change With New Skill—Facilitator and Adviser Meeting

Next the facilitator began negotiating her new role with the managers on site. She discussed with her adviser the training techniques and how she would like to become an internal facilitator. The facilitator had very positive feedback, although her adviser was a little surprised at her desires. The adviser was supportive, however, and believed there was a great need in the plant for facilitation skills. While supportive of the facilitator's present responsibilities, the adviser did not agree to establish an internal facilitator position. A few days later, she discussed with the plant manager the excitement and success that the facilitator had experienced with her new skills.

Tools in Action—SMED Team Meeting

During the team meeting, the facilitator explained force field analysis. This technique, developed by Kurt Lewin, is used to determine the restraining and driving forces for improving a technical process. The technique involves brainstorming the driving forces (positive) and the restraining forces (negative) that create the present status quo of the current issue. Action planning is then performed on the greatest restraining force. During this session, the facilitator used the parking lot technique, which involves listing issues extraneous to the present agenda to be dealt with later. The parking lot technique pleased participants because it made them feel as if their ideas were important enough to address. Everyone wanted to meet the following week, even though it was a three-day week, because they wanted to continue the force field analysis and then move on to the multivote technique. The excitement of the team was building. Encouragement of the team members by the facilitator is similar to "blowing on the embers" because of the delicate nature of the first steps of a team. The initial team development sometimes takes a lot of energy. Other times the team will take off like dry kindling. At this time, the facilitator distributed evaluation forms to measure the team's progress and her facilitation skills to assist her improvement.

Problem Solving and Decision Making

The following SMED meeting continued to focus on force field analysis brainstorming concerning the duties involved with the operation of a particular piece of equipment. The team members enjoyed the technique because they thought everyone's ideas were captured on the flipchart. The team then progressed to multivoting, a prioritization technique. The decision rule for the technique is that the progression to the next vote depends on receiving votes that equal half the number of participants. In the first round, the team members may vote for each item they believe is a factor. In round two, the team members have three votes to distribute among the remaining items. In round three, each team member has only one vote to place on the items that received at least half of the participants' votes in the first two rounds. The votes are registered by placing adhesive dots on a flipcharted list.

All the participants enjoyed getting up and placing the dots on the chart, believing that it was a great way to get everyone's input and reach a consensus decision. The two most critical restraining forces were lack of manpower and lack of assignment of a particular position.

Team Actions and Support

Some of the SMED team observations indicated that there were communication problems on the afternoon and midnight shifts between the forge department and the tool room. Since the major problems existed on these shifts, a cross-functional, intershift team consisting of afternoon and midnight machine operators and toolmakers was designed. This team would get together for four to six meetings to resolve communication and procedure problems using a series of team building and problem solving techniques to arrive at a consensus decision. The production area's adviser and the tool room adviser agreed to this strategy. The team meetings were scheduled over the next few weeks.

During this same period, an adviser who was also a member of the SMED team stated in a half-joking way that he thought SMED was slowing down and losing momentum. Another adviser and an operator who were in the office at the same time came to the defense of the team, supporting its progress, and the facilitator. This support showed that progress and change are slow, but worth the effort.

Building a Team—Meetings of the Cross-Functional Team

On December 6, the cross-functional team was formed to work on resolving communication problems and procedure inconsistencies between the afternoon and evening shifts. One group's adviser suggested that a few of the team's difficult members should be involved for the purpose of developing ownership. This design had its problems, but it was a good way to further develop the facilitator's skills. The team consisted of eight operators representing the different groups and the facilitator.

During the first meeting, a mission statement and ground rules were developed by the team. Each ground rule was defined and discussed. Since this team would exist for a short time, they believed that the ground rules were fine without any additions or deletions. The one that everybody seemed to like and identify with was "no cheap shots." These meetings were difficult in the beginning. The two resistant members of the team appeared to be on the defensive. One individual questioned the facilitator's ability and her knowledge of the problem.

The facilitator explained that the closer a person is to the work, the more they know about the daily problems of getting the product produced. Several team members related well to this concept. She also explained the force field analysis and multivote technique. Then the facilitator started listing ideas that the participants had on the driving and restraining forces that created the status of communication between the represented groups. Finally, she added several items to the parking lot.

The facilitator noticed that the entire group was uncomfortable when one member questioned her on several items, sometimes monopolizing the conversation. There was a heated discussion between a couple of team members, and the team's communication deteriorated at this point. The individual's adviser later told the facilitator that this individual did not feel comfortable enough to continue serving as a team member. The actions of this individual were forms of resistance described in the facilitator training program.

The facilitator wrote an encouraging memo to the member who decided to leave the team. She told him that she hoped he would be involved with teams in the future. Even though she thought that she had done everything she could to make him comfortable, she apologized for any ill feelings he might have stemming from his team experience.

Building Commitment

The third meeting went very well. It was amazing how much more the team accomplished during this meeting than in the first two meetings. They decided to wrap up the meetings on December 20.

One day the facilitator walked into the lunch room where three operators were sitting at a table. She sat down with them, and one asked her what was going on with the cross-functional team. She told him he could ask the team member sitting at his table. So the operator asked the member, "What are they going to do to us?" He started to say something and caught himself. He gave the facilitator a puzzled look and said: "We, the team, have decided to work on ways to improve communication between the two departments. We are going to make the decision together." He struggled, but did say "we" are working on the problem as opposed to "they," referring to management. This change of thinking was a real struggle for the workers. To admit that they were team members, and that they helped make the decision and would live with it, proved that they were making choices to belong to rather than to fight the team concept. One reason why some employees do not want to be on teams is that they do not want to be blamed for wrong decisions. It is much easier to blame others than to admit a mistake.

Wrap Up—Final Cross-Functional Team Meeting

In the final meeting, the facilitator read off the items listed for the driving and restraining forces. When the group finished, there were one and a half pages on the flipchart listing parking lot items. Finally the group came to the multivote technique. The facilitator explained the technique to the group twice. One operator asked several questions. Two members of the team, who were also SMED team members, were asked to vote first to show the rest of the team how the technique works. Each team member took an active part in the voting. The consensus decision was finally established by way of the multivote technique. The restraining forces were narrowed to two items. Everyone was asked if they were in agreement, and they all gave verbal and nonverbal signs of agreement. Then the facilitator thanked everyone for being a member of the team and informed them that they would be brought back together after the results were discussed with the SMED team and management.

The two operators from the SMED team helped the facilitator collect the paraphernalia after the meeting. They both thought that progress had been made, and they told her not to be discouraged because one person had left the team.

Demonstrations of Resistance

The forge department meeting was the first one that the facilitator led since attending the facilitator training program. She began by preparing and distributing an agenda before the meeting. Everyone seemed pleased with receiving an agenda, and they were more prepared when the items were discussed. Each shift had a separate forge meeting.

The facilitator decided that even though this was a group and not a team, she would leave the team ground rules on the board. It was good to see everyone reading them when they came into the room, and they evoked interesting comments.

The forge midnight shift attended the first meeting. While discussing some of the items regarding SMED, one operator stated that he would not work with SMED. Then another operator across the room said he would not work with SMED. These statements were made in a half-joking manner, almost as if they wanted to receive a negative comment. The adviser told them that she had been in meetings with management in which they blamed the workers, and she had sat in meetings with the workers in which they blamed management. She thought that they should all try to work better together. Then the group discussed how they had observed individuals and departments fighting one another, prompting one team member to ask, "How can we have a divided house within our company and still stand up to the competition outside our walls?" Everyone was quiet at first, but the meeting improved and became more productive.

The second forge meeting was attended by the day shift. Everyone read the ground rules. Some chuckled. Some thought that this was the most productive one-hour meeting they had ever experienced. One operator did not show up for the meeting, saying he forgot. The adviser located him and reminded him of the meeting. The operator stated there were not enough chairs, so the adviser brought a chair to make sure this excuse was not valid. One operator spoke up and made a derogatory comment to another operator. Then a different operator stood up in the room and said: "Look at the board. See, no cheap shots." Everyone smiled and the cheap shots stopped.

There had been two different complainers within the group who normally dominated the conversation, talking about everything except the subject being discussed and arguing. That day they were less argumentative and as cooperative as the rest of the group. The facilitator put a parking lot sheet on the wall, and the group came up with a few items to address.

At the end of the meeting, the group still had 10 minutes left. The facilitator asked if anyone wanted to discuss items listed or ask any questions regarding SMED. A few operators left the room. One of the remaining operators asked a SMED team member, a forge operator, to elaborate on an item and asked questions about another item. The SMED member glanced at the facilitator with a surprised look. Not only did this operator ask him a question, but he asked it in a polite way. In the past, team members would have been scoffed at and given a tough time for volunteering to be on a team. After some team discussion, the operator who arrived late for the meeting walked over to the facilitator. In front of the remaining operators, he said he had never believed that programs or teams would work, but this time it was different. He thought that there was a sincere commitment from the team and management. He believed it would work and that the team was doing a great job. This observation by the operator was a major breakthrough, especially coming from this individual.

The afternoon shift meeting also went well. They asked a lot of questions, and they identified with the ground rules. One operator in this group, who was also a member of the cross-functional team, talked about the group's progress. The afternoon shift questioned the facilitator about management and their decisions. The group members said they trusted the facilitator and felt comfortable talking to her.

Positive Reinforcement

A maintenance man, who was not a member of the SMED team, was asked by the SMED team to design a diverter chute for the press. Not only did he devise a diverter chute, he also made and installed the chute. The facilitator wrote him a letter personally thanking him for the extra effort and for taking the initiative to install the diverter chute. His cooperation on this project was important to the team's success. A copy of the facilitator's letter was sent to the plant manager, personnel manager, the maintenance man's adviser, and the line manager.

The next day when the facilitator took a walk through the forge department, the maintenance man smiled and thanked her for the letter. He said for many years he had worked on projects for the forge department and had never been told thank you.

Teaching the Tools—SMED Team Meeting

A problem-solving analysis on the rail problems was completed. The rails conveyed parts and was redesigned by the SMED team to eliminate a mechanical bottleneck. A consensus decision was reached and it was decided to go from two meetings a week to one meeting a week. On December 19, there was a meeting with the plant manager and two line managers for an update on the SMED. The facilitator prepared an agenda, and the group went down the list. She shared with them the ground rules and the parking lot items from SMED, the cross-functional team, and the forge meetings. The facilitator also made use of the DESC scripting to make sure that her ideas were explained and understood. The DESC script is a feedback communication process described in figure 1. The facilitator's adviser informed her after the meeting that he and the plant manager had discussed the meeting and thought that she had done an excellent job facilitating it. The facilitator learned in this meeting that she was commonly referred to as the "mother of the plant."

What the Facilitator Learned

The SMED team celebrated Christmas at their December 21 meeting with a sausage breakfast. Most of the members of the team contributed an item to the breakfast. The plant manager sat down, ate with the team, thanked them, and talked about how well the team was progressing. They discussed the results of the cross-functional team meeting from the previous day and other agenda items. The facilitator told the team that it had been enjoyable working with them. She said that she had learned more this year about the plant than in all of her previous years of working there. She also expressed pride in the team's accomplishments. Each member was described as valuable, having made major contributions to the team.

A SMED team operator talked to the facilitator on December 22 before leaving work for the Christmas shutdown. He shook her hand, told her that he had learned a lot, and that it had been a pleasure to work with her. This comment made up for the many hardships she had endured in the preceding year.

Figure 1. The DESC feedback communication process.

D=	**Describes** and identifies the content and purpose of the feedback message.
E=	**Expresses** feelings. Basically this is an "I" message. When you do this, I feel pleased, sad, and so forth."
S=	**Specify.** In this part of the message, the future desired behaviors or activities are defined.
C=	Focuses on the expected **consequences** if the desired events occur or do not occur.

Positive Feedback

On January 4, 1996, a co-worker and team member at the plant told the facilitator that, during a meeting that day, the line manager whom he reports to praised her efforts and success with the SMED team, driving change, and building trust with the workforce. He also told her that he personally thought she displayed more self-confidence due to the facilitator training she received. Another adviser exclaimed, "She is a changed person since coming back from the facilitator training program." At another time, this adviser said that the facilitator had demonstrated effective problem-solving and brainstorming techniques, and that she had more confidence and a more relaxed manner. Another adviser explained that the facilitator had rebuilt the trust of the operators. This adviser described the operators as excited about the possibility of improving their changeover times.

Benchmarking and Team Member Commitment

The SMED team took a group trip to a forging company in Cleveland, Ohio, to look at a cassette system that would enable site operators to reduce their changeover time by 20 minutes. They toured a facility where team members learned how to
- measure machine uptime and downtime
- standardize and implement discipline to reduce changeover time
- pursue a common sense approach
- address the root cause of the problem.

One member of the SMED team chose to forego the trip to Cleveland to work at the plant. The plant's production schedule the day of the trip included the introduction of a new part. This particular operator had been working with engineering during the start-up phases of this new part. The manager, even though he needed the operator's expertise at the plant, gave him the choice to either stay at the plant and work with engineering or go on the trip. Even though the operator would have preferred to go on the trip, he decided that it was in the best interest of the plant that he stay. This entire decision-making process was unheard of in the plant. In the past, the operator would not have had the opportunity to make the decision, or the operator would have taken the trip instead of thinking of the best interest of the plant. This was a true breakthrough from the plant's traditional paradigm.

The Spread of Success

On January 12, the facilitator attended a management meeting as a participant. There she discovered a manager using an intervention, the parking lot technique, that he had seen the facilitator demonstrate earlier. She asked one person leaving the meeting, "How did the meeting go?" He stated that the parking lot was an effective tool for staying focused and keeping track of other important but unrelated issues.

As a result of a SMED team member's suggestion, management supplied free vending drinks to everyone in the plant due to a 70 percent reduction in changeover time in the forge department. Several employees questioned, "Why did the SMED team want to reward the entire plant?" The team members' answer was that many employees supported SMED and contributed to the team's success.

Some advisers had a meeting with the plant employees discussing breaks, lunches, and expectations. One of the SMED team operators told the facilitator that the meeting upset him because it was unproductive, with a lot of negative complaining. He stated that he used to have a bad attitude, and in the past would have been loud and complaining also. Since his involvement on the SMED team, however, he felt differently. He explained that the SMED team did not point fingers at fellow workers or management and that problems were solved constructively and positively to help the department and the plant. The team produced real accomplishments, and he felt good about them. He stated that he had been on other teams within the plant, but none were as positive or had produced consensus decisions like the SMED team. It was apparent that many organizational members were developing the ability to evaluate the quality of meetings and team interactions. This awareness was a critical step in spreading the success of site organization development.

Team Transitions

On February 21, three members were added to the SMED team. The facilitator led four hours of discussions to cover prior team agreements and processes. The purpose of this meeting was to bring the new team members up to speed quickly so that they could participate and take ownership of future team decisions. The topics of this meeting were ground rules, problem-solving techniques, team dynamics, and a general history of SMED. The facilitator chose to begin the session with the ice breaker "To Tell the Truth," which everyone enjoyed. This exercise has participants write down four statements about themselves, three true and one false. The statements can be as personal or impersonal as desired. An engineer wrote down that he liked his job. One operator laughed and suggested that his statement was a lie. The facilitator spoke up and said No, because anyone who works as hard and spends as much time at the plant as this engineer likes his job or he would not be there. The engineer, who is usually quiet, smiled to acknowledge that he appreciated the comment. The rest of the meeting was productive and contained no derogatory comments. At the end of the meeting, everyone seemed positive and excited to participate in SMED team endeavors.

Individual Breakthrough

During an afternoon shift on April 23, a coordinator asked the facilitator to talk to a forge operator regarding a checklist. The operator wanted to know why it was necessary for operators to fill out information on the checklists. The facilitator explained that this form enabled the team to construct a Pareto analysis to show improvements in changeover time. Also, the operator asked why it made a difference when one operator changed a press over in six hours as opposed to three hours for two operators. The facilitator explained to him that downtime cost associated with the forge press is important. Each hour a press is down is more costly than several employees' pay per hour. As the facilitator further explained this downtime issue, it was obvious that a breakthrough was occurring. The operator finally understood the basic concepts of SMED. Afterward he showed the facilitator some of his ideas for improvements and some safety concerns.

Even though several meetings had been held to explain the need for SMED, he had not previously grasped the need for more than one operator achieving quicker changeovers. The facilitator realized the importance of repeatedly explaining a concept. For some individuals. understanding sometimes requires one-on-one conversation as well as the opportunity to ask questions. Each of us learns differently, at different speeds, and with different communication mediums. We must use the language and approach by which each individual learns best. This experience is a valuable lesson in working with people and taking the time to address their individual needs.

Sharing the News

A manager from a BorgWarner plant in Germany visited the Gallipolis plant to learn about the kanban system and SMED. The facilitator described at length the SMED technique and team processes and structure. The manager listened intently, and when the descriptions were finished, he observed that the facilitator did more than talk about theory. The team examples and illustrations made the facilitator's points real and understandable. He was amazed at the success the teams had gained through working together. His intention was to reproduce these synergistic results in his German facility. Later on, he called the facilitator and explained he was trying to teach his department managers to work together as a team. The process was slow, but he was making progress.

During the month of May the facilitator was asked to present a summary of her site's successes to an international conference on SMED practices. She arranged to take an operator with her and delivered an hour-long presentation with a question and answer session following. She realized that the facilitator training she had attended enabled her to have the confidence and courage to speak to dozens of strangers.

The facilitator also has been tapped to assist other plants in Michigan. The Gallipolis plant hosted a supplier plant to discuss tooling issues. Plans are being made for a follow-up visit to the supplier plant. The facilitator and some team members will visit a BorgWarner plant in Romulus, Michigan, to explain facilitator techniques, group development, and SMED successes. Leveraging internal skills across a corporation is important in these days of limited resources.

Shaping Up the Place

The facilitator and the three shift coordinators had meetings with everyone in the plant on May 2 to explain a red tag strategy program in preparation for an ATS (Automatic Transmission Systems) Council visit to the plant. This council consisted of several divisional vice presidents, presidents, and plant managers who were having their quarterly meeting in Gallipolis. The group would tour the plant on May 23. A gathering of this type can have far-reaching effects on a plant because of the impact of perceptions on future decisions. Thinking about her training on the visual factory, the facilitator suggested that this was a good time to clean, organize, and paint the plant.

A red tag program was implemented throughout the plant. Every employee was given four red tags, which they could place on items in the plant that were unneeded or required relocation. The employees were enthusiastic and excited about removing unneeded items from their work areas. After two days, the smaller items were moved into a temporary red tag zone for disposition. The items were left in the disposition area for one week so that everyone would have the opportunity to retrieve any needed items. At the end of the week, the unneeded items were disposed of, needed items were relocated, and the organization, cleaning, and painting proceeded. In the end, three truckloads of items were removed.

On May 5, the facilitator and a few maintenance men loaded a scrap truck with unneeded items from the back pad of the plant. Once the truck was loaded using forklifts, the truck driver noticed that two pieces of scrap were hanging over the side of the truck. The pieces would have to be cut off before he could leave the plant. It was time for the maintenance men to eat lunch, so the facilitator explained to the truck driver that it would be at least 45 minutes before he could leave. While walking back into the plant, the facilitator discovered a maintenance man pushing a cutting torch cart onto the back pad. The facilitator asked him if he wouldn't be late for lunch. He explained that he thought he would cut off the hanging sections and just miss some of his lunch time. The facilitator thanked him for taking the extra time to finish up the job. Later the facilitator mentioned to the maintenance adviser what had happened, and he was shocked. In the past, this type of extra effort would have been a rare occurrence for a union employee at this facility. The scrap truck was loaded in approximately an hour rather than the usual two hours. Although this event may appear insignificant to some, it is important to celebrate the small successes. Small successes build the foundation to culture change breakthroughs.

Two-Way Listening

As the facilitator's reputation to motivate and solve problems with teams grew, she was asked to facilitate more decision-making sessions. One of these teams involved issues in the forge department. The first issue was where to add brushlon tables, a vibrating table with a chute to load parts into the press. Previously a brushlon table had been installed on one press. At the first meeting, the facilitator explained the force field analysis technique and listed the driving and restraining forces to installing brushlon tables. The operators wanted a table installed on forge line one because it was still hand-loaded and hot due to the draw location. They had repeatedly requested this change in the past. The engineers wanted to add a table on line three because it was down for maintenance work.

At first the engineers pushed their proposal. The facilitator urged both parties to listen to one another. The engineers learned of the day-to-day difficulties that an operator encounters. After the first meeting, the engineers listened more to the operators' concerns as opposed to forcing their ideas on the operators. There was a positive change in the engineers' view of the problem as they considered the workers' perspective. The meetings were a true learning experience for everyone.

A few weeks later, a major overhaul was implemented on forge line one. The managers listened to the operators' suggestions. The draw oven was moved, resulting in less heat and more space for the operators. Several other ideas were implemented, including the installation of a brushlon table. The operator who made the initial suggestion to move the draw oven told the facilitator that for the past 10 years he had made suggestions in meetings; this was the first time anyone ever listened, much less followed through. These sessions resulted in a breakthrough for management as well as for the entire forge department.

Getting Everyone Involved to Tell the Story

On May 20, the facilitator was asked to help with the operators who had volunteered to be tour guides for the ATS tour of the plant, some of whom were quiet, shy individuals (to the surprise of many employees). The facilitator suggested that brainstorming sessions—a free flow of any and all ideas—be held with each department to identify ideas that the operators thought were important enough to present during the tour. The operators came up with several subjects to cover.

The forge operators wanted background information typed up regarding SMED and WPO (Work Place Organization). One of the tour volunteers from the forge department was not a SMED team member; therefore, he was invited to attend a SMED meeting to discuss the tours. As the meeting began, he made a couple of jabbing comments about the team members. The facilitator referred to one of the ground rules, no cheap shots. The group was tense for a moment before everybody finally laughed. One operator suggested that a dunce cap should be made with "no cheap shots" written on it. Another operator said, "You'd better get two, because I will be wearing one all the time."

In a meeting held the next day with the shift coordinator and the facilitator, site managers informed them that new departments had been added to the tour. These additions created a couple of problems. The facilitator was unable to lead brainstorming sessions in two areas. Also the tour presenters had prepared 15- to 20-minute talks. The additional presentations left only about five minutes available to each person. The shift coordinator and the facilitator spent the rest of the day telling everyone about the five-minute time frame. The operators were disappointed, but they did the best they could and cut their material.

The facilitator and the tour presenters practiced a few dry runs of the presentation on May 22. The plan was that the operators would walk the groups to their destination and introduce them to the next guide. One forge operator struggled, and became very nervous and pale. The facilitator used the expectations check to clear the air. She asked the group to write down what they expected from the tour experience, including their hopes and fears. Then the tour presenters walked through the tour again. Each of the operators improved with the additional practice.

At about 11 a.m., after a final dry run, it was announced that an important ATS Council president would be touring at 1 p.m. that day—a day early. A manager from the Gallipolis plant was going to go on the tour with the president. The operators perceived this turn of events as a lack of trust. The tour lasted much longer than the designated hour. The president asked several questions, and he was impressed that the operators were the tour guides.

The site manager who went through the tour with the president was surprised and impressed by the operators' presentation, knowledge, and professional conduct. He complimented the operators on their wonderful job. The operator's role was critical for explaining the plant's potential for growth, continued performance improvement efforts, and teamwork. The facilitator explained to him that facilitator training was helpful in more than just meetings. The manager noted that everyone could see a positive difference in the facilitator. It was obvious that she enjoyed her work.

May 23, the morning of the tour, was exciting; everyone was well prepared and upbeat. Soon after 8 a.m., the council toured in groups of five to six people. The groups took longer than five minutes, but the operators fielded questions flexibly. The dignitaries seemed impressed with the plant. Some of the specific items with which they were impressed included the rolling cart with a kanban system to reorder forms, wire cabinets with items at point of use, the bulletin board displaying the Pareto analysis showing the reduction in changeover hours by quarter, and a dance chart. A dance chart depicts the press side and the hot-box side of a forge press. Every time an operator and an expediter (the person assisting the operator on a changeover) took steps to retrieve an item, they would draw a line on a chart to represent these steps. Soon the chart looked like spaghetti. They measured the steps taken during the five-hour changeover and discovered that the two operators walked 2.1 miles.

The tour presenter who was nervous the day before felt completely at ease. He said that all went well during his tour. As the third group was viewing the SMED bulletin board, one president was especially interested in asking a lot of questions. Another council member expressed concern that the time frame was being thrown off. The interested president explained that he had additional questions at this station and he would finish the tour in good time. The operator felt elated that the top council president was interested in his chart and information.

After the show was over, the tour guides, presenters, and other hourly workers were smiling, happy, motivated, and cohesive. There was a euphoric sense of pride and energy throughout the plant. The facilitator received thanks from several operators and most of the managers for her important role of organizing and coaching. The council made many excited and positive comments about the information that they learned during the tour.

As a follow-up, a meeting was held to show management's appreciation of the pride and ownership displayed by everyone on the floor. During the meeting, employees were thanked for the successful tours and presentations, the workforce's participation in the red tag program, and the cleanup. This meeting had the sweet taste of success. The facilitator had served as a catalyst of change. The culture was moved into the direction of a productive, warm, and friendly work environment. The pride, ownership, and satisfaction of a job well done were indescribable. A few weeks later, management rewarded all employees for their efforts with a free dinner.

Five years earlier, the management team would not have considered bringing an important council to this facility with an unsettled union contract less than a month away. Given this timing, the atmosphere would have been hostile, explosive, and negative. Definitely, this experience was another display of a breakthrough in the plant's culture.

Starting a New Team

The facilitator was asked to organize a new problem-solving team in the briquetting department. First the facilitator met with the entire department to explain the SMED technique and to ask for volunteer team members. Several individuals expressed doubt that any operators would volunteer. To their surprise, however, 10 employees stepped up to the plate.

The facilitator and two engineers conducted three meetings over two days with the briquetting department to reach a consensus on the type of kanban system that would be instituted: cards or racks. Since the engineers had preconceived notions, they relied on the facilitator's skills to achieve an objective outcome. The facilitator began with a discussion of the team ground rules. The meeting was quiet at first, but then the operators opened up and started talking. In this meeting, the facilitator also used a force field analysis and the parking lot technique. Everyone enjoyed their part in the decision making and information sharing. A manager who attended one of the meetings expressed surprise because one operator who seldom spoke in meetings offered his ideas. All three shifts arrived at the same decision and chose the racks.

The engineers noted the difference in interactions between the mature SMED team from the forge department and this new team from the briquetting department. The briquetting team members were quieter, less trusting, and more skeptical. It is important to realize that competent facilitation skills can enable a team to coalesce, but it takes time. There is no quick fix.

Respect for the Working Person

An operator approached the facilitator and told her how she motivated and inspired him to continuously improve and work toward meeting SMED team goals. He continued by saying that every day when the facilitator walked through the forge department with a smile and a "good morning," it made a difference to the operators. Simple courtesies are still meaningful in today's work environment.

A week or two later, the same operator and the facilitator were working on a SMED project together for approximately an hour. His assignment that day was to relieve the other operators. When the time came for his scheduled break, they had only 10 minutes of work to complete. The facilitator suggested that the work could be completed the next day or she could involve another operator. The operator volunteered to work through his break. After the task was completed, the facilitator went to his workstation and offered to buy him a cup of coffee. He said that he enjoyed finishing the task and that it was just like the facilitator to offer him something in return. This expression shows that everyone likes to be treated with respect, courtesy, and genuine appreciation.

Little Surprises

An operator approached the facilitator on June 10 stating that he needed a couple of sockets. The facilitator wrote down the sizes so she could order the sockets the following morning. A SMED team operator who was standing nearby heard the conversation. Early the next day before the start of the shift, the operator who had overheard them talking, handed the facilitator two new sockets. He had stopped at a store and purchased them. He wanted no reimbursement and asked that they be given to the operator who requested them without explaining who purchased them. One always hears negative stories about employees taking things away from the plant. This is an example of the opposite, in which an employee voluntarily supplied the plant's needs.

Personal Breakthrough

Approximately two weeks later, the facilitator was discussing with a SMED team operator the importance of listening to others during meetings, being objective, and working toward a win-win solution. He looked at the facilitator and told her that the training he had received through the SMED meetings had helped him in his personal life. It seems one of his sons had a problem that he discussed with his sibling. The advice-giving sibling suggested that it would be good to talk to Dad about this issue because Dad had changed. The son with the problem feared that if went to his father he would explode and not listen. Nevertheless, he cautiously proceeded to confront his father with the problem. The operator continued by saying that in the past he would have reacted just as his son expected. This time it was different. He listened to his son's situation and concerns, and he shared his own feelings. The results were that they worked out a solution they could both accept. His son was surprised and happy. This personal breakthrough began with his experiences at the plant and extended to the most important and intimate parts of this employee's life.

While the facilitator was discussing some plant problems with an operator on July 11, the operator expressed his surprise that a particular operator was willing to be a tour guide. Previously this operator had always become upset quickly. Now he stays calm and works well with others. He has made a remarkable, positive change in his personality.

Results

Some of the team results facilitated at this site were impressive. The SMED team achieved a 70 percent reduction in changeover time. Average site changeover times improved from 18.6 hours to 6.3 hours. A tracking system was instituted to measure changeover variables. Changeover items were located on wire cabinets at each press rather than scattered throughout the forge department. The kanban pull system allowed operators to make decisions on work in process rather than involving managers. Tooling was standardized. Supplies were integrated to the point of use, eliminating trips to the supply crib. The amount of waste produced during production was reduced.

Other employee developmental, cultural, and team process successes were realized. Resources were committed for a variety of training efforts. The plant advisers received facilitator and group development training. Credibility, attested to by members of all levels of the organization, has grown for the site facilitator and the facilitator role. The site facilitator has been asked increasingly to lead meetings objectively and to teach and facilitate problem-solving techniques. Interpersonal issues have been solved, and technical problems have been addressed creatively.

Conclusion

What are the prerequisites and qualities that a person needs to achieve the results described in this case study? Although doable for most people, the following prerequisites are necessary. First, one needs positive, supportive mentors for advice. Second, the appropriate skills must be developed. In the facilitator training program at Marietta College, the facilitator highlighted in this case study enhanced her communication skills, knowledge of problem-solving techniques, and teaching and coaching skills. The qualities needed to be an effective facilitator are

- respect for all employees
- persistence
- assertiveness
- desire to take risks
- a positive outlook
- caring for others
- a willingness to share information
- honesty
- integrity
- a willingness to deal with conflict.

Even with this combination of prerequisites and personal qualities, credibility and trust must be earned with every interaction.

There are several reasons why this case study describes a success. First, the facilitator was willing and able to practice the skills taught in the training program immediately upon returning to her workplace. Second, the company supported the facilitator as she practiced the skills. As the facilitator and the team demonstrated successes, the organization's managers increased their support. Third, the facilitator internalized the communication concepts involving nonverbal communication and small group processes.

Questions for Discussion

1. Why was the facilitator successful with a few new skills?
2. How did the use of facilitation skills and problem-solving tools create more team member commitment?
3. What was the approach that the facilitator took in dealing with resistant team members?
4. What are the different breakthroughs that are described in the case study? Explain.
5. How is the facilitator involved in the team development process?

The Authors

R. Glenn Ray is a professor of leadership and the director of the Institute of Education and Training for Business at Marietta College in the McDonough Center for Leadership and Business. He spent 16 years in industries such as chemical, mining, and manufacturing and eight years as an external consultant. Ray has authored more than 15 publications, including the book, *The Facilitative Leader*, to be published later this year. He has designed and administered training programs on small group facilitation techniques, team development, conflict management, managing change, and leadership. He teaches communication and leadership courses at Marietta College and can be reached by writing the Institute of Education and Training for Business, 204 McDonough Center, Marietta College, Marietta, OH 45750; e-mail: rayg@marietta.edu.

Karen Stapleton was the SMED/WPO coordinator for the Gallipolis, Ohio, BorgWarner Automotive plant. Since 1973, she was promoted through a variety of positions at this site, including SPC technician. Stapleton presented the successes described in this case study at the Second Annual Best Practices in Quick Changeover Conference in Danville, Illinois, in July 1996. She also worked with supplier sites and other BorgWarner facilities to assist in implementation of SMED and effective teams. Her present position is the training/purchasing/order processing manager at Peddinghaus Modern Technologies at Surgoinsville, Tennessee. Her responsibilities include training and developing teams, monitoring steel purchases and inventory levels, and managing customer orders. Stapleton is an active member of the East Tennessee ASTD Chapter, as well as the treasurer of the Hawkins County Personnel Association. She can be reached at Box 479, Surgoinsville, TN 37873; phone: 423.345.4500, ext. 2502.

Integrated Health-Care Support Teams

Harris Methodist Health System

Carrie McHale

Reorganization plans often call for the implementation of teams. This case describes restructuring efforts to eliminate "siloing" by integrating formerly separate hospital departments and by developing teams through redesign, skills training, survey feedback, and problem solving. A variety of training efforts were utilized, including team leadership, cross-training, interpersonal skills, and customer service. Implementation guidelines are provided, as well as an analysis of resistance to change.

As we move closer to the 21st century, members of the health-care field are revamping and upgrading their practices more than ever before. The focus is now on managed care, which allows the patient and the health-care practitioner to partner to ensure the best patient care possible. This requires health-care providers and hospitals to remain competitive in their use of technology and methods of medical practice. In order for health-care practitioners to remain effective in their service delivery within a hospital environment, efficient ancillary services also must be provided. The nonclinical services are now becoming a part of the health-care team. These services are responsible for creating a calming, efficiently running environment for hospital patients and family members. In order for nonclinical service departments to provide the best service possible, they too must run effectively.

Organizational Profile

A nonprofit hospital in a large metropolitan area had a growing concern about several issues ultimately affecting patient care, including cost-

This case was prepared to serve as a basis for discussion rather than to illustrate either effective or ineffective administrative and management practices.

containment, quality, response time, and the degree of customer satisfaction. Hospital administrators specifically focused on seven health-care support departments, including biomedical, food, grounds, power plant and maintenance, security, housekeeping, and the service center. Together, the departments totaled 150 employees, who represented almost every race and creed. The education level of the employees ranged from GED to college degree. The employees of these departments provided support to clinical staff and were typically among the lowest paid in the organization. Each of the seven departments had its own budget, which accounted for employee payroll, supplies, and daily business operating costs. These departments also had their own policies, procedures, and managers. The leaders of these departments worked independently of one another in a somewhat "silo" fashion. In fact these areas often competed against one another for budget dollars and resources.

The key players in this organizational redesign effort included those of the hospital as well as those of an outside consulting firm. The consulting firm signed a three-year agreement with the hospital organization to partner to improve the cost-effectiveness, service quality, response time, and the satisfaction issues mentioned above. A few executives from the consulting firm were asked to come in and initiate the change. The hospital management team they worked with were long-term employees (ranging from five to 20 years of service with the hospital). The seven departments were tied only by global organizational goals. These goals, however, were never understood or realized by the lower-level employees who provided the internal services. The history behind the departments reveals a definite competition for resources, especially between food service, housekeeping, and maintenance.

The goal of the change effort was to eliminate some of the competition between the seven departments in order to have an impact on wasted resources, duplication of effort, service delivery quality, and internal and external customer satisfaction.

Description of the Initiative

Originally the seven departments were divided between two directors, one of customer service and one of technical service. The two leaders did not communicate at all and came from very different management disciplines. After the consulting company arrived, the two directors began meeting to share their philosophies and coordinate their practices. The consultant offered a new management approach to the setting, and the directors brought the knowledge and understanding of the organization's goals, measurement systems, and policies. The consultant served as the general manager in charge of the whole operation. From that point, the general manager met separately with the directors and their respective leadership staffs on a weekly basis. This served as a bridge to move toward a work team implementation in the future. The seven departments were then integrated to operate from the same budget dollars.

A steering team and a design team were created to help the organization build work teams. Initially the steering team was composed of the customer and technical service directors and the general manager. The design team consisted of the steering team members and their leadership staffs. The design team meetings functioned much like a business operation meeting. Managers brought ideas from their staffs to be considered by this team. The steering team maintained the ultimate decision-making authority, however. Meanwhile the staffs in the seven departments still operated independently of one another and had little input to decisions.

After a year and a half of this traditional structure, a team development coordinator was hired. The team development coordinator worked closely with the steering team to create a work team design that incorporated the seven departments. As a result, the design team structure was substantially changed. The managers were asked to step down and invite a staff member to attend in their place. Two managers also served on the team as resource facilitators and rotated this role with other managers every quarter. At this point, there was no change in the steering team. The team development coordinator served on both teams and acted as a liaison between the two teams.

The next step the steering team took toward work team implementation was to develop a "core" and "customer" organization chart. The core half of the chart included such functions as power plant and maintenance; security; clinical dietitians; hospital cafeteria, including the cooks; and the groundskeepers. These areas were defined as core because their employees either required a special license or certificate to practice or could not be moved out of their area of expertise to cross-train in another. The customer half of the organization chart included the areas of housekeeping and patient food service delivery. The service center functioned as the hub of all the functions, as it handled payroll, customer requests and complaints, and coordinated resources for effective service delivery. All of these functions had two levels of management: a senior team leader (changed from manager), and a team leader (changed from supervisor). Biomedical services remained ancillary to the design because they were shared with the other hospitals in the health-care system.

Large communication meetings were held to share the plans of integration and to explain how the change would affect all employees. This round of meetings set the pace for similar quarterly communication meetings. At this point, however, there was still much confusion among staff members about the purpose and intent of the change. The general manager explained that this was just the first step to fully integrating the seven departments as one. Uniforms were purchased for employees, excluding management, dietitians, and service center representatives. This was not well received by employees, who tossed around terms like *clone* and *prisoner.* It was time to get some of the negativity out in the open as well as to prepare the employees for future changes.

Interpersonal Development

The team development coordinator, along with similar staff members from other hospital entities in the system, developed a training curriculum for staff members. The training program supported the organizational goal of employee development and the achievement of 20 interpersonal training hours per year for each full-time employee, and 10 hours per year for each part-timer. A more local goal of the training program was to help employees cope with the changes by equipping them with the necessary knowledge, skills, and tools. Each training year was kicked off by a huge Integrated Vision meeting, which explained the departmental goals and plans and drummed up excitement for the upcoming classes. These meetings also incorporated team building exercises to further integrate the seven departments and their leaders. The following first- and second-year training curriculum (see table 1) had a companion piece for the team leaders to use in developing their teams, entitled "Work Team Implementation Guidelines" (see table 2).

These courses ranged in length from three to four hours and were held at times that were convenient for the staff. The average cost for one employee to complete the six training modules was $200.00, including wages and course materials. All of the courses included skills practice, role play, and simulation. The team development coordinator also allowed a certain amount of discussion about the fears and concerns of the organizational change.

The team development coordinator soon became an employee advocate and informal counselor for the employees. Employee concerns were then brought to the steering team to address and solve. In fact many of the concerns revolved around management styles and abilities. This prompted the steering team to propose a training program designed specifically for leadership. First a leadership style survey, adapted from Harper and

Table 1. Training curriculum.

First-Year Foundation Courses	Second-Year Framing Courses
Introductory team building	A greater sense of worth (self-esteem)
Insight personality assessment (including discussion on flexing to work with those different from you)	Working through change (the stages) (personal and organizational)
Continuous work process improvement	Team dynamics (including leader and team member styles)
Basic listening skills	Meeting mechanics and decision making
Conflict management and resolution (using a five-step model)	Personal goal setting and time management
Identifying and serving your customers	Recovering a customer who has experienced bad service
	English as a Second Language (by request)

Harper (1992), was distributed to all employees to rate their manager on 20 different leadership characteristics. A multirater feedback approach was used, in which the leaders themselves, their peers, and managers rated their performance as well. This was not tied to pay incentives but was used solely for performance improvement.

Following the survey, the Walk the Talk leadership training program was developed. It was determined, however, that this training should have occurred much earlier in the redesign effort. During the kick off for the leadership training program, postsurvey feedback was delivered to the leaders. The feedback session gathered 25 leaders together to explain the survey results. Each leader received a report that delineated the top three areas of concern and suggested actions for improvement. Following feedback delivery, the leaders committed to action plans for performance improvement. During this first session, the leaders were also given the Work Team Implementation Guidelines, which identified each step required and each skill involved in implementing a work team. The guidelines also included a timeline for the leaders to follow. The leaders were to use the guidelines to facilitate the development of their teams.

Additional courses in the leadership curriculum were as follows:
- Team Building and Basic Knowledge of the Reorganization Process Toward Work Teams

Table 2. Work team implementation guidelines.

	Objective	Action	Facilitator	Timeline (Beginning)*	Evaluation
1.	Introductions/integration of team members.	Initiate the beginning stage by introduction of members. Repeated as new members join the team.	Senior team leader	1st meeting	With every new member
2.	Define team purpose: "Why do we exist?"	Discuss team purpose at first meeting.	Senior team leader	1st–4th meeting	As new members join the team
3.	Write a vision and mission statement.	Team identifies where they are headed in the future; creates a mission statement that actualizes their vision; communicates vision and mission to co-workers and leadership.	Senior team leader	1st–4th meeting	Review semiannually
4.	Team building/trust building exercises.	Team participates in facilitated activities that encourage open communication, accountability, and reliance on peers.	Senior team leader/ team development coordinator (TDC)	1st mtg–1st month. Continue Quarterly	Monthly (via direct observation/ questionnaires)
5.	Decide when/how often to have meetings.	Team members compare schedules to determine meeting schedule.	Senior team leader	1st–2nd meeting	Annually and as needed

* Indicates team development stage

Table 2. Work team implementation guidelines (continued).

	Objective	Action	Facilitator	Timeline (Beginning)*	Evaluation
6.	Learn meeting mechanics.	Practice such activities as setting and posting an agenda, identifying meeting ground rules, and writing action plans.	Senior team leader/TDC	1st–2nd month	Monthly
7.	Define meeting roles.	Elect the roles of team meeting leader, note taker, timekeeper, and process observer. Roles can be rotated every 3–6 months.	Senior team leader	1st month	When rotated
8.	Set ground rules of operation for behavior outside meetings.	Discuss and determine a code of ethics for daily operations.	TDC	1st month	Quarterly
9.	Communicate team member/leader expectations of each other.	Define levels of performance and individual contributions to the team; identify overall expectations of the team; convey team expectations to all employees.	TDC	1st month	Revisit in monthly meetings
10.	Determine decision-making boundaries.	Define the level of decision-making authority the team will be allowed; communicate this to all employees.	Director/senior team leader	1st month	Quarterly

* Indicates team development stage

Table 2. Work team implementation guidelines (continued).

Objective	Action	Facilitator	Timeline (Beginning)*	Evaluation
11. Role clarification (team member and leader(s).	List and define each team member's role and contribution to the team; establish role-specific performance expectations.	Senior team leader	Within 1st three months	Quarterly or sooner as team matures
12. Determine the decision-making style the team will use.	Discuss the different styles of decision making (authoritative, consultative, democratic, fully participative, consensus).	Senior team leader	1st–2nd month	Semiannually
13. Develop a communication plan with teammates, leaders, and other shareholders.	Post meeting minutes; create a communication tree or the "buddy" system to communicate happenings.	Senior team leader/TDC	Within 1st three months	Monthly
14. Discuss different personality types and how the team will handle them (via personality inventory).	Team learns what personality types exist on the team via an assessment; individuals learn how to "flex" their own behavior to work with others to meet the demands of the situation.	Senior team leader	Within 1st six months	Deal with problems daily; evaluate quarterly

* Indicates team development stage

Table 2. Work team implementation guidelines (continued).

Objective	Action	Facilitator	Timeline (Beginning)*	Evaluation
15. Use a conflict resolution model for team difficulties.	Use first-party communication to identify the problem situation; discuss each person's point of view and their needs in the situation; seek first to understand; focus on the problem, not on the person; discuss mutually beneficial solutions; follow a set model to resolve conflict.	Senior team leader or TDC	1st–6th month	Monthly or as needed
16. Troubleshoot team roadblocks.	Team members identify and deal with barriers to their success as a team, such as lack of communication, trust, or accountability.	Senior team leader	4th–6th month	As needed
17. Team members learn to facilitate meetings.	Team members learn how to keep meetings on track; allow everyone an opportunity to speak; disarm disruptive behaviors; bring the team to a decision point and revisit action items.	Senior team leader	6th month	Every meeting (via meeting feedback tool)

* Indicates team development stage

Table 2. Work team implementation guidelines (continued).

Objective	Action	Facilitator	Timeline (Intermediate)*	Evaluation
18. Learn and use a continuous improvement (CI) problem-solving model to solve work efficiency issues.	The team learns to identify needs for improvement and is able to analyze the problem, list potential improvements, suggest or put changes in place, and evaluate the solutions.	Senior team leader	6th month	Quarterly
19. Team time management and organization of work.	Prioritize tasks and maintain a proper workload balance; write action plans for projects with follow-up dates.	Senior team leader or TDC	6th month	Monthly
20. Awareness of internal/external customer service attitudes/actions.	Realize customer needs and proactively deliver services; disarm irate customers.	Senior team leader/TDC	1st–6th month	Daily
21. Establish internal customer contacts/determine customer needs.	Establish/maintain a rapport with customers; communicate regularly to meet expectations.	Senior team leader	2nd–6th month	Monitor progress monthly

* Indicates team development stage

Table 2. Work team implementation guidelines (continued).

Objective	Action	Facilitator	Timeline (Intermediate)*	Evaluation
22. Set performance goals; write action plans.	Determine team and customer needs/expectations; prioritize expectations; set goals that are specific and under the team's control; learn to put vital components into an action plan and follow through.	Senior team leader	6th–8th month	Monthly
23. Jointly work with other areas on projects.	Develop positive working relationships with other areas/units; maintain personal and team accountability; and communicate to all.	Senior team leader	1st year	Revisit in monthly meetings
24. Team members provide interpersonal behavior feedback to one another.	Team members are able to recognize the appropriate time to provide feedback; they use "I" statements and describe the purpose of the feedback; they allow the other person ample time to respond, and they and the other person plan for future behavior together.	Senior team leader/TDC	8th–12th month	Monthly

* Indicates team development stage

Table 2. Work team implementation guidelines (continued).

	Objective	Action	Facilitator	Timeline (Advanced)*	Evaluation
25.	Provide team rewards based on reaching team performance goals.	Team determines type of rewards given based on the magnitude of the achievement and the personal desires of the recipient; rewards are tied closely to performance and delivered immediately.	Director/senior team leader	6th–8th month	Monthly
26.	Recognize and organize team member training needs.	Team evaluates its own progress and devises a corresponding training schedule.	Senior team leader	1 and 1/2 years	Monthly
27.	Set up technical/CI training (if applicable).	Same as above.	Senior team leader	1 and 1/2 years	Monthly
28.	Selection input/team interview.	Team determines what knowledge and skills are desired for the team; team members may partake in writing the performance criteria and observe or interview potential candidates.	Senior team leader	1st year	Rotate selection team quarterly
29.	Coach peers through interpersonal skill practice.	Team members provide assistance to new or existing members in practicing interpersonal skills.	Senior team leader	1st year	Quarterly

* Indicates team development stage

Table 2. Work team implementation guidelines (continued).

Objective	Action	Facilitator	Timeline (Advanced)*	Evaluation
30. Measure/track team performance.	Team uses preset goals or standards and ground rules as a basis for measurement; team members can measure cost, quantity, quality, or timeliness of their outputs; measurements are tied to organizational goals and are easily understood by the team.	Senior team leader	1st–2nd year	Semiannually
31. Formal peer feedback/evaluations.	Based on preset and agreed-upon performance measures, team members actively participate in rating their peers' performance.	Senior team leader	2nd year	As needed
32. Team confronts troubled members/climate control.	Team members use appropriate communication, feedback, and conflict management techniques to handle troubled members; team uses preset performance standards as a means of discussion.	Senior team leader	2nd year	Monthly

* Indicates team development stage

- Skills Practice on How to Coach Your Employees Through Change
- Continuous Work Process Improvement
- Goal Setting and Time Management (Personal and Team Based)
- Conflict Resolution and Management
- How to Facilitate an Effective Meeting and Bring Your Team to a Decision Using Consensus Building
- Achieving Superior Customer Service

The average cost for one leader to complete the Walk the Talk program was $500.00, including salary and course materials. At the year-end of both the staff and leadership training programs, certificates of completion were distributed during a congratulatory celebration led by the general manager. The Walk the Talk program helped quell some of the employee negativity, as the leaders were better equipped to handle the problems. With this success, the steering team was determined to move a step closer to achieving a work team organization.

Like most hospitals, the one described in this case study was divided into separate units, all designed to provide specific care to patients (for example, Medical Surgical Unit, Labor and Delivery, and the Cancer Center). To help the clinical areas better meet their patient care goals, the steering team chose a design that was geographically structured. This design structure divided the hospital into the following geographical areas: Towers 2 and 3; Towers 4 and 5; Women's Health Care Center; Psychiatric Treatment Unit and the Rehabilitative Unit; and Ambulatory Care, Cancer Center, and the Emergency Department. Each senior team leader managed one geographic area. Each of the senior team leaders who managed a geographic area also managed one of the few existing core functions, which included security, clinical dietitians, catering, and the cafeteria. The power plant and maintenance, and grounds functions remained under the technical service leader, and the service center continued to serve the entire organization and report to the senior team leader (see figure 1).

The geographic teams on the hospital units consisted primarily of the housekeeping and nutrition disciplines. The housekeepers were required to clean patient rooms and unit hallways and rest rooms. The nutrition assistants took patient meal orders, assembled the food trays, and delivered the meals to patients. The ultimate goal was to have these two functions cross-trained with one another. Cross-training would increase the number of employees available to assist patients, thus decreasing service request turnaround time. Moreover, the design team created a plan to ensure that employees who were cross-trained were eligible to receive an increase in pay based on their performance in the acquired skills. In

Figure 1. Integrated department organization structure.

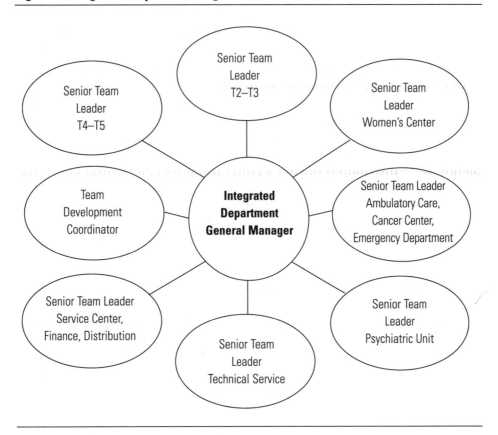

addition, the senior team leaders and some team leaders also cross-trained in areas outside of their experience.

The Psychiatric Unit was the first area to pilot the new design, chosen because of its small size (seven housekeepers and seven nutrition assistants). Another factor was that this smaller unit was separate from the hospital and was thus an easier area in which to manage such a change effort. The 14 employees began meeting as a group, since they were managed by one senior team leader. With the help of their leader and the team development coordinator, they followed the Work Team Implementation Guidelines to build their team. They formed as a team to construct their own mission statement, define meeting roles, such as note taker and timekeeper, and set meeting ground rules. This team elected their own team leader, who kept abreast of departmental and organizational changes and who organized and led the weekly team meetings. The team elected a new leader every six months. Because the team and their leader decided to have a high level of team decision-making authority in the beginning stages of their development, this team played a major part in the organization and decision making of their own cross-training effort. Their cross-training design required each of the housekeepers and nutrition assistants to train four hours a week with their counterparts (peer trainers). This training continued for six weeks, totaling 24 hours of hands-on training for each employee. More extensive training was not needed because when the employees were working in their newly cross-trained area, they could always rely on their co-workers for added assistance. Table 3 illustrates a sample skill competency assessment form that employees used while cross-training one another in the housekeeping function.

A second addition to this design was the maintenance function. Two maintenance assistants were assigned to all of the units to fulfill the light maintenance requests on the unit. A customer request logbook was put

Table 3. Skill competency assessment form.

Skill (Room Clean)	Verbal Understanding of Task (Date)	Practice Skill Ability (Dates)	Additional Training Needed (Yes/No and Dates)	Acceptable Performance? (Date)	Trainer
High dust					
Low dust					
Empty trash					
Clean mirrors					
Change bed linens					
Put soiled linens in linen bag					
Vacuum floor					
Clean baseboards					
Clean bedside table					

at each nursing station to provide a place for staff members to record service needs. Each maintenance assistant monitored the logbook at least four times a day and turned in a written work completion notice to the service center to track. It was the intent that the housekeepers and nutrition assistants also would cross-train to learn these duties, thus creating a team with multiskilled members. To begin incorporating the maintenance function into the cross-training design, the employees began carrying small tools, such as screwdrivers, on their cleaning carts. When employees came across a loose screw, they could tighten it. These employees also helped check the customer logbooks and performed other tasks such as changing regulation light bulbs.

After six months, the Psychiatric Unit team used the company's continuous improvement problem-solving model to troubleshoot areas of improvement. As the team began to share their ideas and make more decisions regarding the improvement of their work processes, team members' different opinions became more evident. To assist with the team conflicts that occurred, they practiced using the conflict resolution model noted in the guidelines, asking their senior team leader to help resolve their differences. The benefit of joint problem solving was pooling everyone's experience and knowledge, allowing the team to make more informed, thought-out decisions.

This team moved into the midstage of team development when they began to manage their work schedules and organize how their work was done. As the Work Team Implementation Guidelines reveal, the three stages of team development (beginning, middle, and advanced) have overlapping timelines. Different teams will move through the stages at different rates, depending on their level of cohesiveness. For example, the timeline for determining internal customer needs can occur between the second and sixth month. The Psychiatric Unit team achieved this action in the sixth month, as they met informally with their customers to determine expectations.

Team members on the Psychiatric Unit began providing informal positive and improvement-based feedback to one another in the 12th month of their formation, which brought them to the advanced stage of development. The team also recognized and requested from their leader interpersonal skills training, such as interviewing techniques. Shortly after one year, this team conducted panel interviews and had input toward selecting new members for their team.

The successful Psychiatric Unit team implementation plan was used as a model for the geographic teams on the other hospital units. The savings section of this document reveals the monetary success of this team. The impact of the success of this team reached far beyond cost savings. The relationship between the clinical staff and the support staff was greatly improved. Before the team was created, there was little communication about expectations between the nurses, housekeepers, and food service staff. The design of the team required members to regularly communicate with their customers, thus establishing a rapport with the clinical staff. In fact, the team began to invite some of the clinical staff and directors to their team meetings to jointly troubleshoot problem areas. The restructuring and cross-training also seemed to improve employee morale. Team members reported that they felt listened to by their leader and hospital personnel and took pride in owning the improvement of their work unit. Implementation on the other hospital units, however, was a slower and more painful process.

Resistance to Implementation

Employees in the larger hospital were very skeptical and often resistant toward the redesign for a variety of reasons. One factor may have been that some of the disciplines needed retraining in their own areas of expertise to ensure the consistency and success of the cross-training effort. At the time of the redesign, there was no consistent method of training newly hired staff members of the different functions; thus employees did not all perform the same job consistently. Employees reported feeling frustrated over the improper training and lack of support from some of their leaders.

Another factor in employee resistance to the redesign was the approach leaders took when communicating the changes to employees. First, many of the leaders did not communicate the redesign goals to their employees, or explain how the changes would affect them. Second, some of the key leaders were speaking pessimistically about the change process to their employees, causing a cascading effect of negativity. Also, based on the previous lack of support and communication from leaders, there were some serious trust issues. These feelings also occurred between upper-level management and the senior team leaders. Consequently all of this delayed the redesign effort about six to eight months. When the other geographic teams were finally formed, they each advanced through the three team development stages at a different pace, based on the level of trust among the members and the leader, the amount of time they were able to spend developing their team, and the amount of empowerment their leader allowed. On the other hand, the core teams such as security and the clinical dietitians were able to move through the team development stages with less difficulty.

Design Team

Meanwhile, the design team continued its redesign mission. As previously mentioned, the design team played a prominent role in the cross-training of team members. The design team was made up of one member from each of the seven disciplines in the integrated department. The team development coordinator facilitated the use of the Work Team Implementation Guidelines to form this team. First this team discussed its predefined purpose of providing a multidisciplinary approach to helping design and implement work teams across all seven departments. In order to create greater buy-in of the team's purpose, the team designed its own vision and mission statements in support of the purpose. To further facilitate the successful integration of the design team, the members learned how to hold an effective meeting and elected a team meeting leader, note taker, and a timekeeper. These roles rotated among members every quarter. During this initial formative stage, the team also determined its decision-making procedure, which was to discuss an issue in the first meeting, poll co-workers not on the team for input, and make the final decision at the next meeting.

Initially this team came together to set departmental improvement goals. The following are some of the design team's major focus areas:

- Establish a communication and coordination plan across all integrated department areas.
- Decide how the core teams (for example, maintenance, security) will support and communicate with the geographical teams.
- Determine how the service center will function to coordinate customer requests for the redesigned organization.
- Foster idea sharing between employees and the steering team.
- Initiate and monitor the success of the geographical work team implementation.
- Determine the need for and form additional employee committees to solve implementation problems.
- Help conduct a training needs assessment for multiskilling employees.
- Develop a plan for employee advancement through a cross-training effort.
- Write new job descriptions to complement employee multiskilling.

Based on the immediate need to begin the geographical teams, the design team initiated development of a cross-training approach for employees. The entire hospital organization had already condensed more than 60 job titles among the integrated department areas into six different levels. Employee job titles were put into one of the six levels based on salary ranges. The design team's task was to create a plan that would enable employees to move from one pay level to the next, by cross-training in a discipline outside of their own. The first step this team took was to list all of the tasks in each of the job titles (for example, housekeeper, nutrition assistant, groundskeeper, maintenance assistant). This task was achieved by obtaining all the job descriptions for the positions and bringing additional (other than the design team) subject matter experts in to recount their daily tasks. All of the tasks for any given function (for example, groundskeeper) were categorized into skill sets. The design team then developed a progression plan for a typical employee at the bottom level to advance by learning new skill sets. The Psychiatric Unit team skill competency assessment form was used as a model to ensure that proper cross-training occurred. The form illustrates the skill set in the housekeeping function (see table 3). The approach taken was to have peers train peers on technical abilities to help increase their skill base. A number of star performers were chosen to help cross-train their peers. The fact that these employees trained their peers in addition to their regular duties was heavily considered during their annual performance evaluation. There were two ways an employee could cross-train: personal desire to learn a new skill and be compensated for it, or an organizational need to help meet customer needs. As in the Psychiatric Unit case, the organizational need typically drove the cross-training effort.

The design team also created guidelines for leaders to follow when allowing their employees to cross-train. It was understood that an employee would have to spend at least 20 to 40 hours learning the new skill set. Consequently cross-training could take up to one year to complete for a single employee. In the Psychiatric Unit team's case, the organizational need to increase service response time drove the speedy cross-training of employees. The design team continued to evaluate the progress of this program and revamp it as needed, based on employee feedback. The design team further advanced through the team development stages as they began to investigate measures to track their team performance. They also talked about interpersonal skills they would need to enhance their performance, such as learning some of the measurement tools the organization used. Meanwhile they continued working to achieve their goals.

Due to the success of the design team, the senior team leaders took an even greater interest in the structure of the organization. Consequently the steering team began to rotate two senior team leaders on the steering team every quarter. The general manager continued to involve the hospital administrator and staff in the reorganization at hospital board meetings and specially called meetings.

Based on those employee concerns that the design team was privy to, a series of task teams were formed to address various employee issues. The first four task teams developed were the communications, rewards and recognition, food service improvement, and a housekeeping problem-solving team. The communications team was designed to be a permanent team, which would ensure that employee concerns were heard by management and that employees understood the rationale behind the new changes. There were five people on the team who spread out through the entire integrated department to hear employee issues. As a result, a monthly newsletter was published to answer questions, quell rumors, and share the interests of fellow employees.

The rewards and recognition team also was designed to be permanent. The main focus of this team was to foster a more positive attitude and increase the motivation of employees by recognizing their efforts. Some of the means this team created to achieve their goal were the Employee of the Month and Year award, the Pat on the Back for good performance, and the Integrated Department Follies (a week-long celebration that included a scavenger hunt, ice cream sundaes, and spin the wheel for prizes).

The food service improvement team was created to meet on an as-needed basis. Before the reorganization effort, there was a high level of dissatisfaction regarding the timeliness of food service delivery and the food temperature. Apparently food carts remained in the hospital corridors, waiting for busy staff members to deliver the food to the patients. This team was designed to address those issues. The nutrition assistants and housekeepers were not only cross-trained in each other's functions but also taught to personalize their food service delivery. Instead of picking up printed menu selections from the nurses station, the nutrition assistants or housekeepers began to take the patients' orders at their bedside. The employees then worked with the cooks to place the meals on the trays and personally deliver them to the patients. This whole process was called the Spoken Menu food service design.

The housekeeping problem-solving team also met on an as-needed basis. This team was created because of the concerns of housekeepers about fellow employee cooperation and teamwork. The five people on this team represented the housekeeping staff in determining methods to streamline work processes. A success they achieved was to have a check-in and check-out process for cleaning carts. Each cleaning cart (with its supplies) was labeled with a number that corresponded to a sign-in sheet. Every housekeeper had to check out a cart at the beginning of the shift and turn that same cart back in (with all supplies intact) at the close of their shift. The cart numbering helped to eliminate lost or stolen supplies, which in turn contributed to a cost savings. This change also helped increase employee satisfaction, knowing they could come to work and have all the supplies required to effectively perform their job. Some of the core teams held similar problem-solving meetings.

Costs

There were several factors of this reorganization that influenced the department budget. The main cost components included the addition of several employee team meetings, interpersonal skills training, cross-training the technical skills, newsletter publication, and the rewards program. From the beginning of this redesign initiative, the general manager required all senior team leaders to hold weekly employee team meetings to foster open communication. Those weekly meetings, along with those of the steering and design teams, amounted to approximately 13 one-hour meetings per week. Each meeting had an average of eight participants, who were paid an average wage of $10.00 per hour. Thus the average cost to hold these 13 weekly meetings was $1,040 per week ($4,160 per month). On the other hand, the task teams such as communication, rewards and recognition, and problem solving did not meet as frequently. There were five teams of five people who met for one hour on a biweekly basis. The average meeting cost for the five teams was $500.00 per month. In summary, the overall cost for the team meetings was $4,660.00 per month.

The cross-training cost was more difficult to compute than that of the meetings. The two factors taken into consideration for the cross-training cost were the wages of the trainer and the trainee. The average cost to cross-train one employee was $325.00, which posits an average wage of $13.00 per hour (combined trainer and trainee) and a 25-hour training period. The newsletter publication and the employee rewards costs were minimal, at approximately $50.00 a month.

Savings

The merging of the seven departments into one unit realized a few significant cost savings. The cross-training of employees in the housekeeping and nutrition areas allowed the organization to save money by decreasing the need for new hires in these disciplines. Because the team members were acquiring more skills and becoming more efficient in their jobs, less supervision was needed. Therefore six supervisory positions were eliminated, and approximately 10 vacant positions were not filled.

Another primary savings example occurred on the Psychiatric Unit. This first pilot team created methods to save money in that unit's cafeteria. Specifically the team identified a cost-savings opportunity on the salad bar. After six months of observation, the team realized that the patients were overusing the salad bar option. The patients were taking two or three oversized servings from the open salad bar for their visitors. The team decided to remove the salad bar and offer premade salads. This resulted in a 25 percent decrease in salad bar food costs. Consequently, this team was invited by hospital leadership boards to discuss their team approach and successes.

Data Analysis

Several methods were used to assess both employee and customer satisfaction. The entire health-care organization used the Gallup poll survey to determine quarterly patient satisfaction levels. As previously indicated, there was a high level of dissatisfaction among patients regarding food delivery times and correct food temperatures. Immediately after the Spoken Menu food service design was implemented, a slight decrease in patient satisfaction was noticed, due to an adjustment phase of the new program. Three months after the Spoken Menu implementation, however, patient satisfaction levels pertaining to food delivery time and food temperatures increased by about 30 percent from preimplementation levels. The food service team also distributed internal customer satisfaction questionnaires to the clinical staff of each hospital unit. The postreorganization findings indicated positive verbatim comments. The clinical staff reported that the Spoken Menu system enabled them to perform their clinical duties in a more timely manner because they no longer had to worry about monitoring food tray delivery or doing it themselves.

To assess the satisfaction levels of employees working in the integrated departments, the leadership styles survey discussed earlier was administered. The survey results revealed very high levels of dissatisfaction concerning the areas of open, honest communication; the satisfactory delivery of intangible rewards and recognition for performance; and listening skills pertaining to all levels of management.

The leadership survey was distributed again after six months and resulted in mixed findings. Employees rated their leaders much higher on their effectiveness pertaining to listening to employees and delivering open and honest communication. An increase in employee satisfaction was also found on the survey item that pertained to leaders communicating team happenings to others outside the team. More specifically, employees thought their leaders were sharing more information about their progress with staff in other areas of their department, an activity that would not have occurred unless the departments were integrated.

Unfortunately employees thought their leaders still needed improvement in recognizing achievements and acting on team suggestions for improvement. In addition to the survey, candid focus groups were held by the team development coordinator to determine progress. The focus groups revealed that employees thought they were communicating more effectively among themselves and working more as a team across the former department boundaries.

Conclusions and Recommendations

The overall strategy of reorganization was well thought out and planned by upper-level management, who composed the steering team, but the delay of obtaining support and involvement from the midlevel management (senior team leaders) was too great. The senior team leaders reported feeling excluded from the planning stages. This caused much frustration and consequently delayed team start-up and successful performance. In future redesign efforts, all levels of leadership should be involved in the design. Perhaps they will not have ultimate decision-making power about the direction the organization will take, but they definitely should have input. If the leaders in this case study had been more involved in the planning process, they could have helped troubleshoot obstacles to implementation that upper-level management was not privy to. The steering team should also ensure that the leaders themselves understand and be adequately prepared explain to employees the changes and their impact. The leaders also should communicate information consistently to all employees, so everyone involved hears the same information.

Obviously some resistance to change is expected. If the proper change management training and preparation had occurred earlier in the process, however, some of the resistance could have been minimized. First the organization must ensure that the appropriate leaders are chosen to lead the change initiative. A successful change management program requires strong, motivated leaders, which this program did not fully exemplify. Leaders should already be practicing basic management skills, such as time management, task prioritization, and handling difficult employees, before they are expected to lead a redesign effort. If these base skills are not evident, the change process is slowed down considerably.

A second factor that influences resistance among leaders is the fear of the unknown. As previously indicated, the leaders described in this case study were fearful and unsure about the change because they did not fully understand it or the rationale behind it. The in-house Walk the Talk leadership training program discussed in this case study had good intentions but did not occur early enough in the process and did not have the leaders' full participation. Future redesign efforts should require all leaders to participate in a change management workshop before the redesign ever begins. This should be followed up by similar sessions to help the leaders cope with the change and to coach them on how to assist their employees through the redesign. In many cases, leaders may need to be coached on the job by a colleague or facilitator to ensure skills learned in class are carried out effectively on the units. Finally, open discussions among all levels of leadership should occur regularly in order to work through the change process together. This will help increase the trust and cohesiveness of the leadership team, and thus present a more unified perspective to employees.

A more thorough analysis of the readiness to change at the employee level should have also occurred. For example, many of the housekeeping and food service employees lacked the basic skills to successfully and consistently perform their current jobs. These skill deficiencies contributed to the drastic delay in the cross-training initiative. Another barrier in the integration was the numerous changes to the design structure. The changes caused great confusion among the senior team leaders and their employees. More time should be given to test the true effectiveness of the design structure before trying alternative designs.

In the struggle toward work team implementation, many successes were realized, a few of which have already been noted. The integrated approach forced the once-thick boundaries between the seven departments to disintegrate. Because of this program, employees who never even knew one another or had competed with one another for resources were working together as a team to solve problems and address customer concerns. The increased employee involvement on the task teams and the design team had a significant positive impact on the quality of employee work life. As a result of the teams, employees were heard problem solving together in the hallways and on the nursing units.

The role of the team development coordinator is highly recommended and should be involved integrally in the initial planning and throughout the work team implementation. This role provided a successful bridge between employees and management and offered an objective viewpoint.

The final success noted was the constant effort made to communicate from the top level down to the staff level. The quarterly communication meetings that the general manager held helped to build employees' morale by involving them in the change program. These meetings and focus groups served to break the ice and begin the communication process, which according to the survey results, had a positive impact on the employees.

Overall, the integration of the seven health-care support departments to one functioning unit greatly affected the lives of the 150 employees involved. The redesign also had a positive effect on the entire hospital and the way in which it responded to the support service staff. There seemed to be a greater respect for the support service staff and their abilities. This new attitude allowed both clinical and nonclinical staff to join together to provide the most important service, patient care.

Questions for Discussion

1. What is the rationale behind the development of the design team? Describe the purpose it served and the ultimate impact it had on the organization.
2. Could the cross-training initiative have been planned and designed differently to have a quicker and more successful impact on the organization?
3. If you were the general manager, what approach would you have taken to allow the midlevel managers to have more involvement in the entire redesign initiative?
4. What additions would you have made to the interpersonal skills training programs so they would have a greater impact?
5. How could the transfer of training knowledge to the workplace have been tested? What would you have done to ensure that classroom skills were practiced in the workplace?

The Author

Carrie McHale is currently a performance consultant for Harris Methodist Health System in North Texas. At Harris Methodist she leads the design and development initiative of several clinical and support service work teams. She assists these teams in the identification, analysis, measurement, and solution development of problems involving workflow efficiency, productivity, and employee and customer satisfaction. McHale also provides interpersonal skills, management development, and continuous improvement training for the entire organization of more than 10,000 employees. She has more than five years of health-care experience and has previously worked as a team development coordinator to integrate support service and clinical teams to improve patient care effectiveness.

McHale has published articles on performance measurement, feedback, and goal setting, and is a regularly invited speaker on performance management and health-care teams at the International Conference on Work Teams in Dallas, Texas. She has an M.S. in behavior analysis from the University of North Texas and a B.S. in psychology from Texas Tech University. She is a charter member of the Center for the Study of Work

Teams at the University of North Texas, and served for five years as the editor-in-chief of the *Work Teams Newsletter,* a quarterly newsletter published internationally. She is a member of the American Society for Training & Development (ASTD), the Association for Behavior Analysis (ABA), and the Organizational Behavior Network (OBN). McHale can be reached at Harris Methodist Health System, Organization Development and Education Department, 601 Ryan Plaza Drive, Suite 140, Arlington, TX 76011; phone: 817.462.6179; fax: 817.462.6166; e-mail: carriemchale@hmhs.com.

Reference

Harper, A., and B. Harper. *Skill-Building for Self-Directed Team Members.* New York: MW
    Corporation, 1992.

Building a Team Measurement and Feedback System to Drive Performance

American Central Paper

Don Schilling

Teams can drift without a process to measure their performance that is aligned with company objectives. This case takes the reader on a step-by-step journey for developing team performance measures. The performance measures, in the form of team scorecards, become the vehicle for feedback, goal setting, and problem solving to drive performance improvements.

As the year 2000 approaches, it would be difficult to find an organization of any size or an industry that has not made a serious, formal effort to strengthen its competitive position. Organizations have employed one or more schools of thought to pursue their improvement vows. The concepts and techniques of total quality management, world-class manufacturing, organization design, and process engineering are perhaps the most popular paradigms of the past two to three decades. Although these models may differ in underlying principles and methodologies, a common set of performance improvement practices has seemingly emerged, among them increased information sharing.

In the 1990s, employees at all levels likely know more about their company than many higher-level managers knew just 10 years ago. It is not uncommon for employees to know their company's vision and business strategy, as well as sales and profits. Moreover they can usually cite their unit's primary customers, their requirements, and the plant's financial performance compared to major competitors. While more in-depth and frequent communication of general business information has apparently flourished, many employees are less informed about the contribution of their immediate work group.

Perhaps frequent reorganizations or the shift from more traditional functions to process-based team structures have contributed to the confusion. Regardless of the source, the same employees with the high business IQ often have noticeable difficulty stating the key objectives, measures, and current performance of their work group.

This case study describes how a medium-sized manufacturing facility designed, implemented, and enhanced an information system that has helped improve the performance of its core operating teams. It is organized as follows:

- Background
  — Organizational Profile
  — Establishing a Case for Team Performance Measurement
  — System Overview
- Design and Implementation
  — Selecting Measures
  — Setting Goals
  — Providing Feedback
  — Utilizing Performance Information for Problem Solving and Process Improvement
- Enhancements
- Results
- Conclusions and Recommendations

The study should prove helpful to team leaders and managers, as well as to internal and external organizational development specialists, who are responsible for developing high-performing work teams.

Background
Organizational Profile

There are well over 500 facilities in the United States that manufacture corrugated paperboard, known among the general population as cardboard, and convert it into packaging containers (that is, boxes). Competition is strong within this sector of the forest products and paper industries to sell this commodity product. This case involves one such facility located in a large metropolitan area in the Southeast. It is one of nearly four dozen corrugated container plants operated by its parent company, a *Fortune* 100 firm.

The plant is a P&L center, containing its own salesforce and employing a total of 210 people (170 hourly and 40 salaried). A perennial high performer, the plant has achieved top 10 percent financial earnings and excellent operating results among its sister plants since the early 1980s. It is consistently perceived by competitors to be a leader in its local market. The union-free environment is characterized by a high degree of trust between management and labor. As a result, the so-called flagship plant frequently has been considered fertile ground for innovative practices. So if it's not broken, why fix it?

Establishing a Case for Team Performance Measurement

The plant's mindset that "getting an A was not good enough" was championed by the production manager and shared by the entire management team. He noted that, although the unit performed well in comparison with other plants within the company, improvement in critical plantwide indexes had been slowing. Productivity or capacity increases and waste reduction had been leveling since the mid 1980s. Sales pointed to price pressure, as competitors took aim at dethroning the king of the market. Couldn't costs be further reduced? Moreover, given the deceleration in the rate of continuous improvement, inquiries began to surface concerning the unit's incentive plan. Did the plan add value, or had it become simply an entitlement?

There were technological bottlenecks or constraints, of course, but the availability of capital was questionable, particularly as the market became less predictable. The challenge was straightforward: improve performance with the existing resources—the strategy: more widespread involvement.

The plant had a successful track record of applying basic problem-solving techniques and project management skills in cross-functional teams. Significant improvements had been achieved in on-time delivery, inventory optimization, process capability, and a host of other strategic objectives. Yet to date, hourly production employees had only limited involvement in these initiatives. The top management team reasoned that engaging all employees in structured problem solving and process improvement would extend these benefits. Such high involvement also had become a corporate expectation. All that remained was to figure out how.

Borrowing on his previous experience as an external consultant, the human resource/organizational development (HR/OD) manager suggested that progressing from an A to an A+ required a different approach to employee involvement (that is, different from that required to go from a D to a B, for instance). His following two recommendations were accepted:

1. Natural work teams should be formed in which participation would be required, as opposed to creating voluntary task forces. Although their boundaries might change, these teams would be perpetual in nature.

2. Each team's improvement efforts should be driven by ongoing measurement and feedback of key performance indicators.

System Overview

The Performance Measurement and Feedback System (PMFS) was initiated in early 1991 with the core operating or production teams for two primary reasons: (1) the long history of measurement in the manufacturing and converting operations would enable a quick start to the initiative; and (2) the cumulative impact of improvement across these teams was a critical success factor in the plant's strategy. A total of 14 core operating teams were involved in the initial intervention. The Accounting Department was chosen as a knowledge work group to pilot test the development of performance indicators for a team with no history of measurement. Other teams became active in the performance-driven involvement effort by pursuing measurable improvement projects, but they did not participate in the PMFS per se.

Over the past several years numerous people have been involved in developing and supporting the PMFS besides the team members. Despite the breadth of this involvement, the primary roles and responsibilities have remained relatively stable (see table 1).

Two points are particularly important to understand about the key players in the system. First, the quality engineer originally involved possessed exceptional programming skills that enabled automation of the system at a time when suitable off-the-shelf software could not be found. One also should note that the unit employed management-directed work teams in which supervisors served as team leaders. Although this did not necessarily inhibit team member involvement, it did serve to accelerate implementation in comparison with the author's experience with self-regulated teams.

Design and Implementation
Selecting Measures

As previously mentioned, the core operating teams had never known a time when their performance was not measured, a common trait of manufacturing functions. In fact there was an oversupply of data, most of which the operating teams never saw, or found to be so overwhelming that it had not proved useful in managing and improving performance. It was a proverbial case of data rich and information poor.

The HR/OD manager and quality engineer started the effort to prune the performance indicators to the vital few by inventorying the measures currently available. They applied three rules born out of the literature

Table 1. Roles and responsibilities.

Position	Role	Primary Responsibilities
Production manager	Process champion/sponsor	• Establish the need for the process. • Mobilize commitment and resources to support the process.
Human resource/organizational development manager	Process facilitator	• Guide the initial development and implementation. • Assist process owner and others to apply process improvement tools and team skills to continuously improve the process.
Quality engineer	Process owner	• Identify and develop process to meet internal customer or user needs. • Manage the process to maximize process efficiency, effectiveness, and flexibility. • Maintain the central database.
Human resource/administration assistant	Process coordinator	• Assist the process owner primarily by compiling source documents and entering data.
Supervisors	Team leaders	• Review performance data with team members and direct problem-solving activities.

and previous experience to their list: (1) the total number of performance measures should be limited to five to 10 for each team; (2) the measures should span the four focus areas of the unit (productivity, quality, cost, and safety); and (3) the measures should meet the maximum number of criteria for good team measures.

The proposed list was presented to the production manager (process champion), the supervisors or team leaders, and finally the team members for review, modification, and approval. Rather than test the measures against all the criteria (see table 2), these sessions focused on three key questions: Can the team have a significant impact on the measure (influ-

Table 2. Criteria for good performance measures.

1. Results Based
   Does this measure represent a team accomplishment rather than an activity or behavior?
2. Team Oriented
   Does the measure represent a result accomplished by the team as opposed to an individual or small number of team members?
3. Global
   Does the measure reflect an overall goal of the team v. a subgoal?
4. Influenceable (control)
   Can the team have a significant impact on the measure?
5. Corruption Resistant
   Is the measure resistant to tampering and falsification?
6. Accessible
   Does the data required by the measure already exist or easily accessible?
7. Frequent Feedback
   Can performance on the measure be reported at least monthly?
8. Measurement Family
   Do the measures collectively span the scope of the team's responsibility?
9. Customer Perspective
   Do one or more measures reflect the customer's view of the team's performance?

---

ence)? Is the team interested in improving the number? Is the team willing to accept judgments about its performance based on the measure?

Naturally, the pilot test development of measures for the accounting team proceeded differently. The team did not, however, reach agreement on a family of measures. Therefore only a brief review of its process steps is presented (see table 3). A discussion of this aspect of the intervention appears in later sections (see Results, and Conclusions and Recommendations).

Setting Goals

Historical data were collected and calculated on all measures selected. Facilitated by the HR/OD manager and quality engineer, supervisors were asked to submit a "minimum/maximum" performance level and a long-term target for each indicator, using a guide based on simple descriptive statistics.

Performance worse than the minimum/maximum for a predetermined period of time was used to signal problem solving or other interventions

Table 3. Developing new performance measures.

Application to Knowledge Work Teams

Step	Activity
1	Provide basic education in measurement. —Role in improving performance —Fundamental units of measurement (frequency, ratios) —The need for evidence or permanent record
2	Identify the primary products or services supplied by the team. —Option: List the three to seven major functions performed.
3	Determine the business and customer requirements for each product, service, or function. —Quantity? (volume, rate) —Quality? (accuracy, usefulness) —Cost? (efficiency, budget) —Timeliness?
4	Identify evidence of performance to each requirement. —Observable events or records Note: This step frequently may cause confusion and proceeding to step 5 may be preferable unless step 5 is generating few measures.
5	Brainstorm potential indicators. —Review units or types of measurements. —Review sample measures.
6	Select five to 10 measures for team scorecard. —Test against criteria.

(see next section on providing feedback). The long-term target was considered attainable in one to one-and-a-half years. Team members were asked to set short-term targets using the historical data and the guide (see figure 1). This expectation was considered attainable in six months to a year.

The historical data served as a starting point for developing the range of performance expectations. Minimums and maximums and short- and long-term targets were adjusted by the production manager, team lead-

Figure 1. Performance standards guide.*

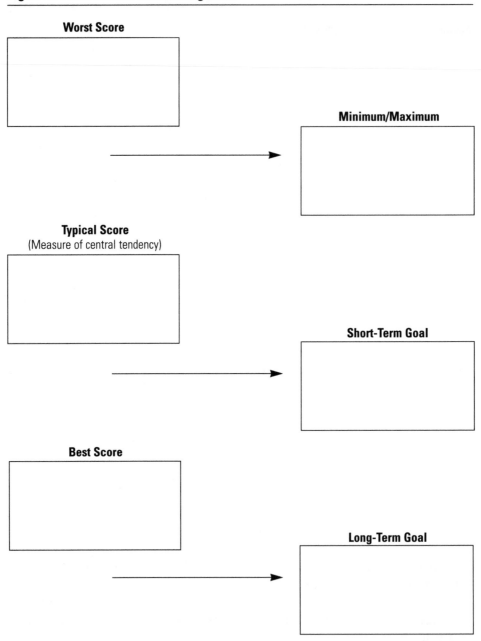

*Adapted from guide developed by Tarkenton Conn and Company. In *Maximum Performance Management: How to Manage and Compensate People to Meet World Competition* by Joseph H. Boyett and Henry P. Conn. Macomb, IL: Glenbridge Publishing, 1988.

ers, or members based on their knowledge of the process (strong hunches regarding cause-effect relationships); planned modifications or upgrades to equipment; and anticipated changes in product mix.

Providing Feedback

Performance measures may be the heart of the PMFS, and various standards of performance add meaning to these measures. Yet all the effort devoted to identifying select measures and collecting the associated data would be wasted if the information is not presented in a user-friendly fashion. The feedback format of the PMFS had three components: the one-page scorecard, standard run charts (line graphs), and the exception report.

The one-page scorecard was a simple table showing the team's performance on the various measures in relation to performance expectations (see figure 2). It consisted of one or more columns for each of the following:

- the performance indicator
- the score for the most recent reporting period (current performance level)
- year-to-date performance
- standards or benchmarks for referencing current performance, including baseline (usually the previous year-end or year-to-date performance) and the expectations described in the previous section (minimum/maximum and goals)
- the trend, which was labeled positive, negative, or neutral. The trend was based on a line of best-fit calculated over a predetermined minimum number of data points. The slope of the line considered to be positive or negative, depending on desired direction, was specified by the quality engineer. It was adjusted based on team input.

A run chart was constructed for each performance indicator to facilitate identification of trends or other patterns of performance (see figure 3). Where possible, scales were standardized to permit team comparisons by overlaying transparencies. Graphs typically presented a run line of current performance and horizontal lines representing baseline, year-to-date average, and either short-term or long-term goals, whichever was most relevant to the current level of performance.

Due to availability and the need to smooth out weekly variability in some of the data, all performance indicators were initially reviewed monthly in team meetings. The team leader distributed and reviewed the one-page scorecard. A line graph for each indicator was presented using an overhead projector. The teams discussed any patterns or other note-

Figure 2. Team performance scorecard.

Team: Corrugator—Second Shift
Leader: John Smith   Report Date: July 5, 1996
Period: June 1996

Category/Performance Measure	Current Performance	Y.T.D. Score	Baseline	Short-Term Goal	Long-Term Goal	Min./Max.	Trend
Productivity							
1. Lineal foot/minute							
2. Downtime frequency/day							
3. Downtime minute/day							
Quality							
4. No. of complaints							
5. Cost of complaints							
6. Product audit %							
Cost							
7. Wet-End waste %							
8. Dry-End waste %							
Safety							
9. Consecutive days without incident							
10. Housekeeping %							

Figure 3. Run chart with key reference lines.

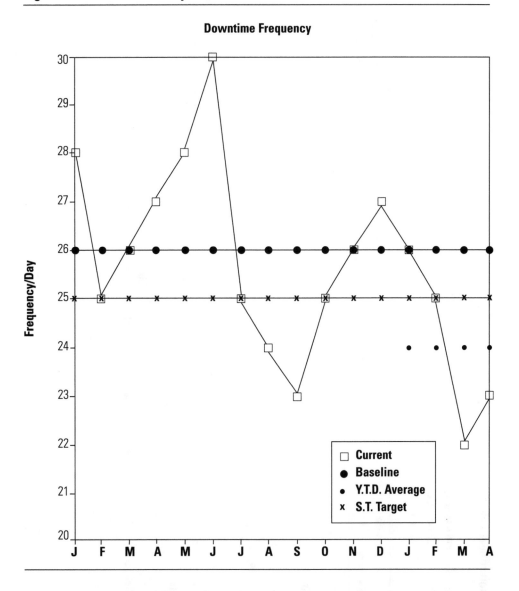

Downtime Frequency

worthy aspects of the performance data. Following the performance review, the team engaged in problem solving or other activities directed at improving targeted performance as described in the next section. Performance graphs were posted on team bulletin boards following the team meeting.

The exception report was the remaining component of the feedback delivery (see figure 4). The production manager and team leaders re-

Figure 4. Exception report.

Management Level:	Production Manager, George Bell
Current Period:	June 1996
Report Date:	July 5, 1996

Performance Measure	Team	Leader	Current Level	Short-Term Goal	Consecutive Performance	Long-Term Goal	Consecutive Performance
Lineal foot/minute							
Downtime frequency/day							
Housekeeping %							
Housekeeping %							
Housekeeping %							
Housekeeping %							
Set up time (minute)							

Negative Exceptions

Performance Measure	Team	Leader	Current Level	Short-Term Goal	Consecutive Performance
Wet-End waste %					
Complaints					
Housekeeping					

ceived a one-page summary of the performance information from all of the teams for which they were responsible. It was formatted to highlight performance worthy of recognition (positive exceptions), as well as those areas requiring urgent attention (negative exceptions). Positive exceptions represent current performance at or above goals, while negative exceptions represent performance below predetermined minimums or above predetermined maximums. The report showed the number of consecutive reporting periods in which the exceptions had occurred.

Utilizing Performance Information for Problem Solving and Process

While some performance measures improve from feedback alone, generally speaking most meaningful measures require more active intervention. Therefore each team was required to pursue a measurable performance improvement project at all times. Team leaders and members received training in the steps, tools, and skills of the parent company's standardized problem-solving process. Each team's progress was tracked and publicly displayed across the nine steps of the process, starting with step 1—identify the problem.

To increase the likelihood that a team would identify a worthy improvement target, three basic sources of direction were utilized (see figure 5).

Management priorities were identified by simply asking key managers what improvement opportunities came to mind when they thought of a particular team. These priorities were not shared with the team until af-

Figure 5. Selecting worthy improvement targets.

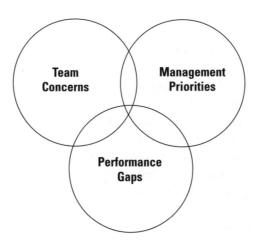

ter they had independently brainstormed their own concerns, headaches, and opportunities for improvement. Teams were also asked to "look at the numbers" with a watchful eye on the size of the gap between current performance and the expectations reflected by short- and long-term goals. Not surprisingly, there was a rather high correlation among management priorities, team concerns, and performance gaps resulting in a well-defined problem or improvement objective. In some instances, a performance measure included in the PMFS was the direct target of the intervention (for example, waste percentage). In other cases, the target was a component of a performance measure on the team's scorecard (for example, a particular type of waste). As previously mentioned, the teams that did not participate in ongoing performance measurement and feedback using a family of measures did at least pursue a measurable improvement project as described above.

In summary, the initial design and deployment of the Performance Measurement and Feedback System across 14 teams required about three months. This included the selection of five to 10 performance measures for each team (though many teams shared the same measures); the setting of minimums and maximums as well as short- and long-term goals; the development of the feedback process; the use of the data to help select performance improvement projects; and the initial programming required to automate the process. Over the past five years, the system has continued to evolve.

Enhancements

The core of the PMFS has remained relatively unchanged over the nearly six-year life of the system. Teams have changed boundaries, driven by the addition of new manufacturing and converting processes. With the exception of a few interruptions, teams have reviewed their performance via the scorecards and graphs, set goals, and conducted regular problem-solving sessions—and they continue to do so. But several changes have been made, both expected and unexpected, to improve and keep the process alive.

SOME OF THE MEASURES HAVE BEEN CHANGED. It's like looking for fingerprints on a glass—if measures don't change, the system is likely not utilized. They're expected to change. The most significant change was in a unit of measurement. Team members pointed out that throughput was better measured as number of feeds per hour than as square footage per hour. It was less influenced by the product mix and more sensitive to the behaviors of the operators.

TEAM GOALS OR TARGETS ARE NOW PRIMARILY DRIVEN BY PLANTWIDE OBJECTIVES. The standards of performance required of the team are extrapolated from the measurable objectives that need to be achieved in accordance with the plant's strategic plan. For example, if the strategy calls for a 10 percent increase in capacity, team productivity targets are set to reflect their needed contribution to this objective. These "nested" goals improve team alignment with the unit's strategy. Historical team performance data is used to check the reasonableness of these expectations rather than to dictate the targets. It is interesting that the strategic needs and the historically based feasibility are perceived to usually match up. This reportedly strengthens the credibility of the strategy and the meaningfulness of the goals.

TEAMS SET ONE GOAL. Although the data-based guide was relatively easy to use (see figure 1), the distinction between short-term and long-term goals became increasingly blurry. Teams sometimes flew directly to the long-term goal without any stops at the short-term goal. Fluctuations between short-term and long-term standards were often considered normal variations unworthy of any recognition. In any event, the difference between short-term and long-term goals outlived its usefulness.

TEAMS ESTABLISH A GOAL ON ONLY ONE "GLOBAL" INDICATOR. The team's problem-solving efforts had moved some numbers, but it also had revealed that some of the most critical numbers didn't substantially improve as a result of these smaller victories. It seemed that the success of the structured employee involvement (that is, each team had a measurable improvement project) had inadvertently created some tunnel vision. The practice of reducing improvement opportunities to highly controllable components of performance had actually diverted attention away from the biggest bottlenecks. To counter this development, a policy was established to set a goal on only one performance measure that was the best overall indicator related to the unit's critical success factors. And even though measurement and feedback continued on all the other measures, it also eliminated the tedious setting of goals on indicators of limited relevancy to strategic business needs.

DAILY FEEDBACK IS PROVIDED WHERE POSSIBLE. Persistent tracking and review of performance led to more frequent inquiries about how well the team was doing. Many employees had taken the initiative to seek out daily and weekly scores even before PMFS. Consequently, more formal means were developed to provide feedback for daily performance. This enabled operators to better detect special sources of performance variability. Scorecards and graphs continued to report monthly and year-to-date performance to help identify more common, persistent variables affecting performance.

Results

It has been said often that it is tougher to remain on top than it is to get there. The plant had accepted the challenge to further improve an already enviable track record, maintain its status as a perennial high performer, and reinforce its position as a market leader. It has succeeded.

The unit ranks in the top or next quartile on seven of nine macro performance indexes among its nearly four dozen sibling plants. It continues to achieve earnings in the top 10 percent of its peers. The effort to accelerate the stagnating rate of improvement on some key indicators, which had driven the overall change initiative, has had mixed results. Volume or throughput has again tapered following an increase fueled by expansion. Waste, on the other hand, has steadily decreased by nearly 20 percent over the past six years.

Obviously, it is difficult to determine the contribution of any one process or intervention to the unit's performance. The plant undertook numerous initiatives from 1991 to 1996. To what extent can the performance be attributed to capital infusion, revisions in the incentive plan, or team problem solving? The relative contribution of the PMFS can perhaps be summarized best through anecdotal evidence.

The most frequently cited benefit of the PMFS has been that it establishes accountability. The consistent tracking and reviewing of the same or similar indicators year after year has conveyed that performance matters at the team, and in turn, individual levels. The use of team meetings to analyze and problem solve performance gaps revealed by the PMFS has fostered a positive form of ownership as opposed to a less desirable approach in which someone else hands out consequences for not meeting expectations.

The exception report is considered an effective means for triggering proper management action. Managers do not have to fumble through volumes of reports to realize when recognition or process improvement support is warranted. When the exception report was discontinued for a period of time, the production manager requested that it be resurrected.

In the early stages, the scorecard and graphs helped teams identify improvement projects. The low hanging fruit has been gobbled up, however, and the system has only recently been modified to better detect barriers to performance whose removal would yield the greatest potential value. The verdict is still out on the effectiveness of setting a goal only on the global indicator with the most strategic relevance (see Enhancements).

On the downside, the vision of developing one-page scorecards for five to seven management and support teams barely got off the ground. The pilot test with the Accounting Department was initiated but faded during the transition of some of the key players to new roles. The measurement of knowledge work teams is discussed in the final section of this case study.

Overall, the perceived value of the system is probably best manifested by the diffusion of the system throughout other corrugated container plants. Intentional efforts to share learning among units fostered several versions of the PMFS in different locations. Eventually the division published a series of manuals detailing best practices desired across all units. One of the reliable methods included in this comprehensive prescription for improvement was the PMFS.

Conclusions and Recommendations

The organizational behavior management literature has long maintained that knowledge of results is one of the most powerful sources of gratification and motivation experienced by workers. The deployment of the PMFS at this high-performing manufacturing facility verifies that there are numerous benefits when employees at all levels "know the score." While general business knowledge is important to the improvement process, measurement and feedback seemingly play a comparatively greater role at the team and performer levels than visions, missions, and strategies. As the current HR/OD manager said, "People focus on what is measured." And in this era of information overload, focus is often difficult to achieve. Several specific observations are also worthy of mention.

The author is somewhat surprised by the new practices of setting one goal and the exclusive use of goal setting on only one strategically important measure. Setting short-term and long-term goals has been used in other organizations to operationalize the concept of continuous improvement without risking deficiencies in motivation due to excessive delays in goal achievement. Short-term goals are employed to increase the probability that noteworthy accomplishments can be reinforced in a reasonable period of time (for example, within six months). Long-term goals are used to establish "stretch" targets that challenge performers and help create competitive advantage. Setting more than one goal also affords a means for management to communicate their expectations via the long-term goal while providing an opportunity for participative goal setting by the team via the short-term goal. Possibly the high trust environment and the existing high levels of performance diminished the need for the two-goal approach.

With respect to setting a goal on only one measure, the rationale was clear: Establish strategic alignment and worthy improvement targets. Organizations clearly cannot afford to have teams devoting limited resources to reducing performance gaps of little importance. Avoiding goal setting on multiple measures would likely serve to focus attention on the measure for which a quantitative expectation has been specified. Expectations for the other measures have not been eliminated, however, merely not communicated. Several alternatives might be considered.

First of all, continue to set goals on all measures, but develop a more formal process for directing and approving structured problem-solving efforts. One organization with whom the author worked was losing $250,000 per month in scrap. Although they established multiple measures with goals for each team, team improvement projects were required to target scrap reduction either directly or indirectly (in the case of support teams).

A second approach used by some organizations is to differentiate key business indicators and strategic improvement indicators. The former are measures that reflect performance of the fundamental management system (for example, variance to budget, timeliness of product or service delivery). They are relatively constant. The latter usually change every one to three years consistent with critical success factors for the business. Structured improvement efforts are typically reserved for performance gaps on these strategic measures. Measures can exchange categories as business needs change.

A third alternative is to expand the type of measures included in the PMFS. Results measures, which we have emphasized, can fail to reveal the most significant performance barriers, especially in continuous process operations. The addition of key process measures will often direct attention to the most valuable interventions.

Knowledge work is on the rise, yet difficulty in measuring such work remains widespread. One obstacle is the overt and covert resistance to measuring white collar teams. Many believe that such work is too creative or lacks the repetition required for measurement. A little education and the opportunity to discuss concerns can be very effective in breaking down this wall. Another problem is that we often form groups of knowledge workers who are not actually a team. They don't share a common purpose, operate within or across the same processes, or depend on one another to accomplish common results. The ability to identify team performance measures is an excellent test of team formation. If they are not a team, it will be difficult to make them behave like one. Finally, creating new measures requires highly skilled guidance. Processes such as that presented in this study (see table 3) are necessary but not sufficient. Organizations should consider building this skill base internally or obtaining external expertise.

In conclusion—if it's measured, it's managed! The Performance Measurement and Feedback System has played an integral part in maintaining and enhancing the competitive position of a high-performing manufacturing unit.

"In the end, it's the numbers that really matter." (Author unknown)

Questions for Discussion

1. Who and what triggered the development and implementation of the performance information system?
2. Clarify the two initial recommendations made by the HR/OD manager. Why do you think these recommendations were made? What might have been some alternatives, and why do you think they were not suggested?
3. Based on the role descriptions of the key players, what do you think their working relationships might have been like?
4. How were the performance measures for the core teams reduced to the vital few?
5. Using the performance standards guide (see figure 1), identify minimum and maximum short-term and long-term goals for a measure for which you have historical data. What are your reactions to these quantitative expectations? What do you like and dislike about the tool?
6. What are the three components of the feedback delivery process? Explain the major features and purposes of each.
7. How were performance measures used to identify improvement targets for team problem solving? What other perspectives were used to select an improvement target?
8. Describe the five modifications to the original PMFS. Which one do you think is the most significant enhancement? Why?
9. On a scale of one to 10 (with 10 being extremely valuable) how valuable do you think the PMFS is to the organization based on the results presented? Why?
10. List three to five key learnings you gleaned from the case study. How would you incorporate these if you were to build a measurement and feedback system?

The Author

Don Schilling is a human resource and organization development manager for a *Fortune* 100 firm in the forest products industry. Previously he has held positions as quality director for a market leader in outdoor cooking appliances and senior consultant for a consulting firm promoting innovative management practices. His 17 years of experience span a wide range of high involvement and quality improvement initiatives. Schilling is the author of a number of articles on improving human performance. He earned a master's of science in behavior analysis from Southern Illinois University and a bachelor of arts from the University of Cincinnati. Schilling may be contacted by writing Box 188, Longview, WA 98632; phone: 360.576.4898.

Strategic Planning and Performance Measurement in an Academic Team

Middle Tennessee State University

Beverly G. Burke, Sharon L. Wagner, and Judith L. Van Hein

Written by team members, this case describes how a team developed its own set of performance measures based on their strategic plan. It describes efforts and results over a four-year period that began with a flush of success and later encountered more challenging problems. With this case, we find it is easier to start teams than it is to maintain their success.

Three principles of navigation are: (1) know where you are; (2) know where you are going; and (3) plan how to get there. Navigating a team to high performance follows the same principles. Any successful team must have a planning process for setting goals and for devising actions to reach the goal, and it must have a method for evaluating current status. The evaluation is necessary at the beginning in order to know the start point, and it is necessary as an ongoing process to guide efforts and keep the team on track.

This case describes the development of a team in a university setting and focuses on these principles of navigating a team toward high performance. The team used a visioning process to set a goal, a strategic planning process to plan movement toward the goal, and evaluation procedures for ongoing measurement of the team's performance. The evaluation procedures included benchmarking with a few of the best programs nationwide; developing and using a quantitative performance measurement system; and developing a skills taxonomy to systematically evaluate the educational program and to develop student evaluation methods. All

This case was prepared to serve as a basis for discussion rather than to illustrate either effective or ineffective administrative and management practices.

of the evaluation procedures reflected the team's value that feedback needs to be objective and quantitative in order to be genuinely useful.

This is an unusual case in several ways. One feature that sets it apart from most teams is that team development was initiated by the team members themselves. A group of faculty, with no external pressure, decided that they wanted to function as a team and acted with autonomy to transform themselves into a team. The university administration had no knowledge of the transition until the team requested support of the effort.

Two factors were critical for success of the self-created team, one within the team and one external to the team. Within the team, progress was often a result of questioning assumptions. Many times the team responded to "You can't do that" with "We'll find a way." This proactive approach resulted in significant breakthroughs. External to the team, the main concern was the direction of the university as a whole. The team could succeed only if the team goal was congruent with the overall goals of the university.

The academic setting is unusual for team development because traditionally it has been a place where faculty members work independently and where rewards and recognition are based on individual achievement. Thus team functioning is contrary to the individual achievement culture. Also, academia typically has functioned with little planning or accountability, so this team's focus on strategic planning and performance measurement and its group orientation has established it as an anomaly in a university setting.

Another unusual aspect of this case is that, as professors of industrial/organizational psychology, the team members brought with them knowledge of team concepts, as well as other organizational expertise. They were able to become a high-performance team without training or team facilitation from outside the team.

In other ways this case shares similarities with many other teams. The evolution into team functioning was gradual, and the transition had begun by the time the term *team* was used by the team members. Team development was facilitated by a participative and empowered atmosphere resulting, in part, from the leadership styles of the program coordinator and the department chairperson and, in part, from the recent addition of a large number of new faculty members due to rapid growth of the university.

Like many other teams, a difficult aspect of the process for the team members is that earlier efforts attacked easier problems that had a quicker payoff. Current efforts are directed toward more complex problems with long-term payoffs, and team members are frustrated by slower progress.

An encouraging aspect, however, is that a large initial time investment created systems that currently require less time for ongoing maintenance, so the team has effected a redirection of priorities and effort.

Organizational Context

Middle Tennessee State University (MTSU) is a public, regional university, and the Psychology Department has offered master's degrees in several areas, including industrial/organizational (I/O) psychology, for many years. MTSU grew dramatically during the late 1980s and early 1990s. The university viewed this growth as a positive trend, but existing systems were strained under the new demands. The history of the university as a small regional teachers college with relatively open admissions and top-down management was changing.

The growth of the university coupled with high faculty turnover resulted in a largely new staff for the I/O program. Only two members of the current team of eight faculty members were at MTSU before 1990. Four new faculty members were hired in two years, none of whom had experience as full-time university faculty. Their initial impression of MTSU's I/O discipline was that it offered a good collection of courses but no real "program." That is, there was no sequence of classes for students to follow and no information about student enrollment or graduation rate. However, both the department chairperson and the I/O program director had very participative leadership styles. Input from junior faculty was welcomed, and the I/O faculty met often to discuss and plan course offerings and student admissions.

Because of the similarity in their graduate training, the four new faculty members found they shared a common vision of what the I/O program should look like. With recent graduate school experiences themselves, they wanted to create a student-oriented atmosphere. The faculty wanted to create a supportive environment for the students while providing them useful skills. There were moves to make the course content more practical and to gain better internship opportunities for the students. To achieve this goal, everyone took on added duties to try to build the program. An orientation program, student database, and recommended sequence of courses were developed. The faculty worked to build an ongoing relationship with the Society for Human Resource Management (SHRM), the primary professional organization in the field, and with local industry. These efforts not only provided students with internships but also helped build the reputation of the MTSU I/O program. In addition, members of the team socialized together, which provided further opportunities to develop a shared set of values and ideals.

One of the factors that increased interaction among the I/O faculty was the decision to request to have most of their offices near one another. Although the location was, perhaps, some of the less desirable office space, it has provided the team the opportunity to meet informally in the hallway. These casual interactions have greatly enhanced the team spirit and enabled the team to address issues quickly.

When again faced with the task of replacing a member of the group, the faculty were concerned about finding someone who would fit in with the group—someone who shared the commitment to students and had a program orientation. With four new and relatively inexperienced faculty members already on staff, the group decided to look for someone with prior university experience who also might be a strong researcher. Fortunately the group was able to find someone who not only fit these criteria but also had expertise in teams. As a team expert, he played a large role in the team development activities. The next new hire and most recent addition to the team brought with her several years of experience with a large consulting firm.

During the early 1990s, the university as a whole also experienced some major changes. A new president and a new provost/vice president for academic affairs arrived. The new leadership created a new vision for the whole university and an environment in which various departments and programs were free to challenge some of the old ways. This increased flexibility and autonomy allowed the I/O team the opportunity for self-determination. While the university had been reactive in the past, a new culture that promoted planning was beginning to develop. In addition, a move toward excellence and accountability meant that in the future, programs would be expected to produce measurable results.

Team Development

When the complete eight-person I/O team was in place, they initiated major team development activities. Two core team activities were developing a strategic plan and developing a team performance measurement system, both of which have been used on an ongoing basis and are an integral part of team functioning. The strategic planning consisted of a visioning activity and a fishbone diagram, and the team performance measurement system was designed as a method of performance evaluation.

These planning and evaluation efforts were aligned with the university's new culture and overall direction. Although the new culture allowed self-determination, the I/O team believed that long-term success of the program was dependent on team goals being congruent with the goals of the larger organization. In addition, the team culture (proactive, questioning, quality oriented, planning oriented, quantitative results oriented) was in keeping with the emerging organizational culture.

Vision

A visioning exercise was conducted in which team members closed their eyes and imagined where they wanted the I/O program to be in five years. What would it be like? How would it feel to be a part of it? How would the team know it was there? They voiced their visions and reached a consensus, which was an ambitious, overarching goal: to be the top I/O psychology master's degree program in the United States.

Fishbone

The planning process began with a meeting in which the team developed a fishbone diagram (see figure 1). With the goal as an end point, the team worked backward to identify what needed to happen to get from the starting point (where they currently were) to the end point. They identified seven areas important for success:
1. Enhance student training.
2. Improve student selection.
3. Develop faculty.
4. Increase access to internal resources (within the university—funding for students, student access to computers, faculty research support).
5. Increase access to external resources (outside the university—internships, grants, consulting projects).
6. Develop a positive relationship with the external environment (outside the university—network of alumni, benchmark other programs).
7. Develop a positive internal environment (within the program, department, and university—a more unified program, an exciting climate).

Within each area, the team developed a detailed outline. For example, the following factors were listed for student training:

Figure 1. I/O psychology program fishbone diagram.

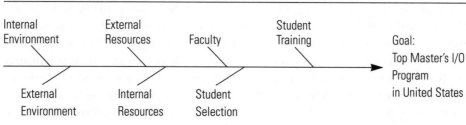

- Make sure students understand the big picture (that is, how separate pieces of their knowledge fit together).
- Develop students' practical skills and experiences.

Then, in the area of developing students' practical skills and experiences, the outline included the following:
- Teach practical skills.
- Conduct class projects in organizations.

Specific actions were identified in all areas. For example, establishing good internships included actions such as staying in contact with alumni and interacting with local professionals. Thus, the fishbone diagram was a detailed, actionable road map to get from the current position to the five-year goal. It provided subgoals to monitor progress toward the large goal.

The next step in the planning process was to set priorities. The team identified two major areas in which actions would have the greatest impact on progress toward the goal. The team decided to focus on student training and student selection since, in an academic program, both the primary customer and the primary product are the students. The team believed that the top I/O psychology master's degree program in the United States would produce excellent, well-trained graduates, and the most direct route to this goal would be through attracting the best students to the program and providing them with the best possible training.

The team marked targeted areas on the fishbone with red dots, used yellow dots for areas where progress was being made, and used green dots for goals that were accomplished. This created a visual summary of where the team stood and gave the team a sense of progress. To maintain its high performance, the team needed both recognition of its accomplishments in order to maintain motivation and clear identification of its shortcomings in order to direct its efforts.

Evaluation

Throughout the strategic planning process, the cohesiveness of the team increased noticeably. The faculty members took pride in being a self-created team, increasingly referred to themselves as team members, and became more and more focused on their shared goals. They recognized, however, that camaraderie aside, only empirical evaluation would decisively indicate how much progress they were making toward their goal. The team wanted and needed objective feedback, because, although planning and goals could tell the team where to go, only objective feedback could tell them where they were.

The team decided that the evaluation process would be open to all of the I/O students, as well as departmental faculty and the university administration. They believe that this decision indicates a central value of the team, namely, that it remain open to the scrutiny and feedback of important customer groups. Complete openness with evaluation results was risky and anxiety provoking, but the team decided that the potential benefits outweighed the costs. With this level of openness, successes would more readily result in rewards, increased resources, and enhanced reputation, both within and outside the university. The risk was that the team could not hide shortcomings, and failure could be embarrassing.

The I/O graduate students were heavily involved in the administration of the evaluation process, which was in keeping with the culture of openness. Ultimately, I/O psychology programs at other universities provided data for comparison, and evaluation results were presented to university administration and to national professional organizations. Thus the team embarked on a very public self-evaluation. One team member said, "We're going to get naked."

The evaluation process was accomplished through benchmarking and the development and validation of a measurement system. Support for development of the team through systematic evaluation also was provided through the development of a skills taxonomy, an identification and classification of I/O psychology skills. These evaluation processes were in keeping with the team value of objective, quantifiable feedback.

Benchmarking

Benchmarking is a commonly used technique for assessing the relative standing or competitiveness of an organization in relation to others that produce a similar product. Of the two major actionable areas from the fishbone diagram, the team decided that measures from the student selection area could be benchmarked easily. In early 1994, three I/O psychology master's degree programs were identified as among the best in the nation; the team members chose those programs as benchmarking partners. Indexes from these programs on three student measures concerning the quality and number of incoming students were collected and compared to MTSU's I/O program indexes. The benchmarking results indicated that the team lagged far behind its benchmarking partners. As a result, the team committed to two courses of action: simultaneously increasing entrance requirements and choosing to admit fewer students to the graduate program each year. These actions have been successful; the team has continued to collect data yearly on the indexes and has noted substantial improvement.

Development of a Performance Measurement System

In keeping with the team's overall vision to become the top I/O master's program in the nation, it became evident that the team would need to quantitatively measure their performance along numerous dimensions. To systematically measure the performance of the team, an established performance measurement system (ProMES: Pritchard, 1990) was adapted for use. As part of a class project, seven graduate students played key roles in facilitating the development of this system.

Team members first determined five dimensions (areas in which the team must do well to meet the overall goal) to represent the domain of the program:
1. students (selecting, training)
2. faculty (research, development, retention)
3. internal processes (communication, decision making)
4. internal resources (monetary support, time)
5. outside activities (consulting, public relations).

Next the team established 16 measures of these dimensions by following specific criteria for practicality, goal relevance, and the extent to which the program has control over the measure. For example, measures for the outside activities dimension included student and faculty involvement in professional organizations. A procedure for deriving a yearly effectiveness score for each measure was established. This process allowed the team to put together an integrated feedback system, with the composite of the 16 measures' effectiveness scores representing the total effectiveness of the team (Hein, Payne, and Jones, 1995).

Periodically the team compares the measurement system to its goals and vision. They have an understanding that if at any time the measurement system no longer appears to match its strategy and priorities, they will make adjustments to the measurement system accordingly.

Although the measurement system was constructed using an established methodology (ProMES), it was based primarily on internal team members' judgments. As such, it was important to verify the external validity of the system (how applicable it was to other similar teams). This information was gathered by relying on the judgments of subject matter experts who were members of I/O psychology master's degree programs at other universities (Hein, Payne, and Jones, 1995). This validation process was similar in concept to the benchmarking process discussed earlier, but broader in scope, as the experts were asked to make the judgments involved in the development of the entire measurement system. Analyses of these judgments indicated strong agreement between the outside experts and the team's system on the dimensions selected and on the measures used to capture those dimensions. The outside experts also agreed, but to a lesser extent, with the relative importance of the measures and with the levels of performance on the measures necessary for effectiveness. These findings provided support for the external validity of the system, while allowing for differences among programs on specific aspects of the system.

Skills Taxonomy

Another evaluation effort is a skills taxonomy, a classification system of I/O psychology skills. The taxonomy was developed for the purposes of evaluating the curriculum and making specific action plans for refinement of student training. The research methodology was based on a participant action research model (French and Bell, 1990). As such, the input of various customers of the I/O program was solicited as part of the research. These customers included students and alumni, practicum supervisors, and potential employers. I/O faculty also were heavily involved in the research process.

Various action plans have resulted from the development of the skills taxonomy. For example, a skills-based evaluation form for internships was developed, and the I/O faculty are developing a standard method for student skill and knowledge assessment and feedback. Course content and process may also change as a result of the development of the taxonomy. That is, new courses may be developed, existing course content may change, and instructional techniques may be altered. Thus decisions about changes in student training do not have to be made simply on judgment or intuition but can be made based on objective data with input from customer groups.

Ongoing Evaluation Efforts

The data for the 16 measures in the performance measurement system are collected yearly through a combination of conscientious record-keeping and survey administration to students and team members. Each year the collected data are fed back to the faculty, students, and administration, and summaries are posted for all to view. The decision for openness has had both positive and negative consequences. For example, the team's visibility and positive reputation within the university community has grown as a result of sharing its progress with members of the university administration. Performance in most areas has been quite high, and the openness has provided the opportunity to advertise these successes.

Publicizing that the team has high expectations for themselves has created high expectations for the team from others, however. For example, the student satisfaction measure decreased slightly due to students' higher expectations. The reaction of team members was to become both more stressed and more challenged. One team member said, "We're in the spotlight," to which another team member responded, "Now we have to dance."

The results of this ongoing evaluation indicate that the team has made substantial progress toward its goal over the period of 1993-1996. The overall effectiveness of the I/O program rose steadily from 1991 to 1996.

Of the 16 measures of effectiveness, two examples with significant improvements were selection ratio, and consulting projects and paid internships. Selection ratio is the percentage of applicants admitted to the program, and smaller values are desirable because they mean that admission is limited to the best applicants. In 1990, the selection ratio was at 100 percent, then dropped to 80 percent in 1993, to 60 percent in 1995, and to 37 percent in 1996. Student selection was one of the priorities set by the team in the fishbone diagram and these results verified rapid progress.

The measure that included the number of consulting projects and paid internships also improved dramatically. As measured on a per-person, per-semester basis, it started at 0 in 1990, went to 24 in 1993, to 74 in 1995, and to 94 in 1996. The results were due largely to efforts to build relationships with the local business community. The relationship with SHRM and other professional organizations provided many contacts, and work on a few consulting projects enhanced the reputation of the I/O program and brought in more consulting projects. These were activities targeted in the fishbone diagram, and again, the measurement system demonstrated the positive results of the strategic planning process.

Although the team found these gains gratifying, results of the evaluation also brought to light an area of weakness. One of the 16 measures of effectiveness, the number of faculty publications, had declined from seven in 1991 to four in 1993, to two and a half in 1995, and to a low point of zero in 1996. This feedback served to focus the team's attention on research productivity, and the team's efforts were quickly directed toward the research problem.

Trouble in Paradise

Following review of the performance measurement system, the team periodically reviews its strategic plan. A review of this type conducted in 1995 led team members to recognize that, although faculty research was one of the measures in the performance measurement system, it was not specifically represented in the fishbone diagram. This was a serious omission, since, although the faculty members operated as a team in many respects, the university reward system (promotion and tenure) was still based to a large extent on individual research productivity. This was a matter of concern to the team, because only two of the eight team members were tenured and at the highest rank, leaving six team members to face tenure and promotion decisions in the near future. This was a threat to the team because the team would lose any members not granted tenure.

Subsequently the team engaged in discussion of why research had been omitted. It appeared likely that the omission had resulted from at least three factors: the team's focus on improving the program through student selection and training, the fact that the junior faculty on the team did not have well-developed research programs, and the perception that research was primarily an individual activity. The team decided that to help ensure its survival, research must become a higher priority. Furthermore the team needed to revise its strategic plan to remedy the omission of research. Thus the process of annual performance measurement helped the team's planning efforts.

The team decided to attack the research productivity problem with the same vigor with which they had overcome other challenges. They enthusiastically outlined barriers to accomplishing research and discussed ways of trying to remove those barriers. They agreed to resist the temptation to continue to fix aspects of the program that weren't broken in order to focus more attention on research productivity. They identified joint research projects that would take advantage of their individual strengths and discussed ways of publishing as many student theses as possible. They began a system of tracking team members' research projects and holding each other accountable for progress.

Their initial energy soon dissipated, however, and it became obvious that the team was doing more planning and analyzing than actually publishing manuscripts. Many team members felt guilty about not being more productive, believing that one senior faculty member was carrying a disproportionate amount of the research load, and they were filled with a sense of dread in advance of research-oriented meetings. At these meetings, a palpable tension filled the air, tempers became short, and much of the meeting time was spent ventilating frustrations about conflicting priorities and heavy workloads. One team member summed up the feelings of other team members by saying, "I feel like it's impossible to do everything well!"

It soon became clear that a large part of the team's frustration was a result of the lack of immediate results from their research efforts. The research process is a lengthy one that includes research design, data collection, data analysis, writing, and submission to an academic journal for review. Manuscripts often receive several rejections before being accepted for publication, and only a subset of submissions are ultimately accepted. In contrast, the team was used to making changes (for example, in course content, administrative policies) that resulted in near-immediate and measurable payoffs. Comments from team members included "We've been picking the low-hanging fruit" and "We've got to stop kicking ourselves."

At that point, the team became more realistic and revised its approach to research productivity. The team members learned to coordinate research efforts, to make better use of resources (for example, graduate assistants), to use short-term goal setting, and to be more patient about seeing results. For example, since the process for publishing research is so long, the team decided to set the subgoal of submitting papers to journals. This was a successful strategy in that seven papers were submitted during the 1995-1996 academic year. The team then set the goal of submitting 16 papers during the 1996-1997 academic year. This is a difficult goal (more than doubling the previous year's performance), but the team finds the short-term subgoal more motivating than the long-term goal represented in the measurement system.

The team continues to approach problems with a willingness to question assumptions and revise strategies. Also, the team has learned that crisis points are a normal part of team functioning and that the team's ability to successfully work through those crisis points is a sign of success. At the present time, the team is working diligently on a number of research projects, seeing results (more submissions to journals, positive reviews from the journals, and some papers accepted for publication), and learning to view the goal of higher research productivity with a longer time horizon. Early in 1997, it is apparent that the faculty publications measure is on its way back up.

From this experience, the team learned that the autonomy and interdependence of a team tends to exaggerate the complexity of dealing with problems. With traditional management styles, plans and goals are handed down from others, and individuals receive more explicit directions about how to respond to problems. In a team environment, the team must solve its own problems and members must coordinate problem solving—a complicated and time-consuming process. Furthermore, when team problem solving occurs in an atmosphere of negative emotions associated with a performance deficit, the group processes (communication, interpersonal relationships, conflict resolution) become more evident.

Current Status of the Team

In 1997, the eight-member team is intact, although the former I/O program director has taken a half-time administrative position and is less involved in the day-to-day functioning of the team. Another team member replaced him as the team coordinator. Team membership seems to be stable in that some team members have gotten tenure and promotion.

As a result of the research issue, the team has been forced to take a closer look at their internal processes. As the team tackles more complex problems, it continues learning and developing new strategies, and it realizes that team development is an ongoing process. The team is benefiting from its earlier efforts and has found maintaining the overall system to be less time-consuming than getting it started.

Another gratifying turn of events is that members of the university administration have been impressed by the system established by the team and view the team's system as a model for effective planning and evaluation. This serves to underscore that the goals of the I/O team and of the university administration (excellence, accountability, quantifiable results, self-determination) are similar. The Psychology Department also has drawn upon the I/O team's experiences during its ongoing long-range planning process.

Lessons Learned

1. Team development is an ongoing process in which there will be mistakes and self-correction.
2. As the initial, obvious problems are addressed, more difficult, complex problems emerge. These bring crisis points in which team members fear failure, but working through these crisis points is a sign of successful team functioning.
3. Planning and a performance feedback mechanism are necessary for high performance, because they continuously guide efforts.
4. Self-created teams are possible and can reach high levels of performance, but they need a source of team expertise.
5. Teams must question assumptions and be willing to break traditional patterns of behavior in order to achieve the exceptional accomplishments of a high-performance team.
6. Teams need a radical goal to stimulate the excitement and urgency necessary for peak performance.

Questions for Discussion

1. What factors may facilitate or hamper a self-created team?

2. Analyze the team's difficulties with research productivity. When a team's morale and productivity are affected by self-defeating thoughts, what actions can team members take to get the team back on track?

3. What are some strategies to maintain high performance when goals become increasingly difficult?

4. Select another team discussed in this book. What are some dimensions that might affect that team's effectiveness? What measures could be used to assess those dimensions?

The Authors

Beverly G. Burke is an associate professor of psychology at Middle Tennessee State University. She received her Ph.D. from Auburn University and is on the faculty of the industrial/organizational psychology master's degree program at MTSU. She teaches courses in psychological testing and work attitudes and motivation. Her applied experience includes work in job analysis, performance appraisal, testing, training, recruiting, attrition, job satisfaction, and organizational surveys. Her main area of research is on response validity in organizational surveys. Her research has been published in several journals and has been presented at national and regional conferences. Burke can be reached by writing to Middle Tennessee State University, Box X-104, Murfreesboro, TN 37132; phone: 615.898.5936; e-mail: bburke@mtsu.edu.

Sharon L. Wagner is an associate professor at Middle Tennessee State University where she teaches and conducts research in the area of industrial/organizational psychology. She received her Ph.D. in 1989 from the University of Tennessee, Knoxville, and her research interests include organizational citizenship behavior, employee motivation, transformational leadership, and organizational culture. As an organizational consultant, she has worked with manufacturing, utilities, transportation, publishing, and government organizations in the areas of employee assessment and selection, performance evaluation, employee attitude surveys, training, and organization development. She can be reached by writing Middle Tennessee State University, Box 87, Murfreesboro, TN 37132; phone: 615.898.5998; e-mail: swagner@mtsu.edu.

Judith L. Van Hein is an associate professor in the Psychology Department at Middle Tennessee State University. She received her Ph.D. in 1992 from the Georgia Institute of Technology. Her specialty area is industrial/organizational psychology, with emphasis in personnel selection, perceptions of fairness, and legal issues in human resources. Her research has been published in several psychology journals. She has consulted with industry on projects concerning employee surveys, selection recommendations, and training needs assessment, and she has conducted seminars on human resource selection. She can be reached at Middle Tennessee State University, Department of Psychology, Box 87, Murfreesboro, TN 37132; phone: 615.898.5752; e-mail: jvanhein@frank.mtsu.edu.

References

Hein, M.B., S.L. Payne, and S.D. Jones. "Effectiveness Measurement of a Knowledge Work Team in an Academic Setting." In *Measurement Issues with Teams*. Symposium conducted at the Annual Meeting of the American Psychological Association, New York, August 1995.

French, W.L., and C.H. Bell. *Organization Development: Behavioral Science Interventions for Organization Improvement* (fourth edition). Englewood Cliffs, NJ: Prentice Hall, 1990.

Pritchard, R.D. *Measuring and Improving Organizational Productivity*. New York: Praeger, 1990.

Reach Out and Touch Your Team: Development of a High-Performing Virtual Team

The Internal Revenue Service

Matthew J. Ferrero and Donna Lewis

Virtual teams are a new phenomena. What does it take to develop a sense of team when the members are geographically dispersed? How is this leader's role different from that of leaders with colocated teams? What kinds of team building activities are effective? How can trust be developed in an organization that is restructuring? These issues and others are addressed in this case.

The Internal Revenue Service (IRS) takes pride in administering a complex tax system that helps support the economic infrastructure of the world's largest democracy. Over the past 40 years, the IRS has accomplished its mission using a typical bureaucratic and hierarchical structure. IRS employees enjoyed a relatively stable work environment, and the informal employment contract was well understood: Do your job well and you will always have a job to do.

In the 1990s, the dramatic downsizing and reorganizations that affected the private sector reached government. The Clinton administration's National Performance Review and the "reinventing government" process promoted and rewarded innovation and smaller, more responsive government. Congress, determined to reduce government's size and privatize or eliminate some services (or even entire agencies), passed budgets that fell far short of the costs of doing business as usual. These and other factors forced government to begin restructuring its operations.

This case was prepared to serve as a basis for discussion rather than to illustrate either effective or ineffective administrative and management practices.

In 1994, the IRS initiated a series of significant structural changes that, by October 1996, would centralize many core business functions and cut approximately 1,000 management positions. The 1994 reorganization plan consolidated the support services (that is, human resources function) and created a formal internal organizational development (OD) function managed through support services with an OD team in each region and one in Washington, D.C. Included was a formal OD intern education process to train 16 people in a program sponsored by National Training Labs at The American University. These interns joined 27 other IRS employees with prior OD training and experience to form the teams. OD's role is to provide assistance to the 114,000 employees and managers to deal with the many challenges facing the IRS.

This study describes how a group of individuals in the Western Region evolved from independent consultants into a high-performing OD work team. Specific topics covered include
- getting underway: team member selection process
- team leader selection and leadership issues
- team formation: values, norms, work processes, and customer service
- communication links in a remote environment
- OD and the business strategy
- feedback and measures
- the road ahead.

Getting Underway

The giant pine tree grows from a tiny sprout. The journey of a thousand miles starts from beneath your feet.—Lao-tzu (1992)

In September 1994, the IRS did not have a formal, coordinated, and managed OD consulting function. Rather, employees who happened to have advanced training in psychology, business administration, or organization development often provided consulting services to managers on an ad hoc basis. Most worked in training or other human resource areas and consulted on the side. Consequently, services were, at best, informally tied to supporting IRS strategic business objectives. To focus consulting expertise on strategic, servicewide issues, the IRS deputy commissioner authorized the formation of OD teams. The next step was to identify team leaders and members with the right mix of skills, temperament, and potential for both short- and long-term success.

Selection of the 10 experienced members of the Western Region team was a straightforward process. Personnel records and performance ratings of interested individuals were reviewed. Previous management experience was desirable but not required. Formal interviews were not conducted because these employees were well known. The Western Region was fortunate to have three people in a district office who had earned master's degrees in OD and had been delivering OD consulting services since 1989. In addition, four other people with OD training and experience from outside the IRS were hired as temporary appointments in 1993 and early 1994. Three other employees with suitable education and backgrounds rounded out the experienced cadre.

Selecting OD interns was a more formal undertaking. The opportunity was announced regionally and applicants were required to submit a résumé and narrative statement regarding their knowledge, skills, and abilities. In addition, interviews were conducted. The Western Region interview panel included two IRS managers, an IRS OD consultant, and an external OD consultant. Two interns were selected and began their course of study at American University in February 1995. Once selections were completed, the Western Region OD team was composed of 12 consultants in five different cities. Obviously issues of remote management and teamwork would soon come into play.

The team leader selection process created a major issue with the more experienced team members, because the leader selected lacked formal training and experience in OD. Thus a major challenge to team formation was dealing with the frustration, suspicion, and anger caused by the team leader selection process. Until these feelings surfaced and the issue was resolved, healthy team formation was not possible.

Leadership and Team Formation

All streams flow to the sea because it is lower than they are. Humility gives it its power. If you want to lead the people, you must learn how to follow them.—Lao-tzu (1992)

October 1994

Team effectiveness is built on trust. In particular, there must be a high degree of trust between the leader and the team members. If trust is lacking, the team's journey is tortuous and high performance is not possible. Trust building within the Western Region OD team took several months and the willingness of all involved to focus primarily on the team and on our customers. Most important, it took willingness to learn about and from one another.

The trust building process was complicated by the significant changes in the overall structure of IRS, including the continuing consolidation of the support services. By October 1994, the number of offices providing support services was cut by 75 percent, and numerous management jobs were abolished. In fact, three of the experienced consultants selected for the OD team, along with the team leader, were managers whose jobs were abolished during the 1994 consolidation.

As mentioned above, Western Region had had a cadre of experienced and active consultants in a district office in northern California since 1989. This cadre had developed relationships with district management and progressed from providing basic team building and facilitation to high-level strategic planning assistance. By 1992-1993, OD was well established in northern California, and services were being provided upon request to three district offices in the San Francisco Bay area as well as to other districts and the regional office. Naturally the senior OD consultant, who managed this operation through the training branch in her district, was quite interested in the regional OD team leader position. She believed her OD skills and management experience made her a logical and highly qualified candidate.

In July 1994, the Western Region support services management decided that the regional OD program would be located and managed in the support services site in southern California. In October 1994, the former chief of the training branch in a southern California district office was named acting leader of the OD team. He had a strong background in total quality and extensive managerial experience; however, he did not have formal OD training or experience. Both the decision to manage OD from southern California and the team leader selection generated extreme distress among the consultants in northern California. Therefore the team was in crisis as it was added to the organization chart. The challenge for all members was to deal effectively with the issue of leadership and move on to team formation.

November 1994

Many of the OD team members did not know each other. Thus a face-to-face meeting was imperative. The two-day initial meeting was held in southern California in November 1995. There were no office distractions, and an ambitious task-focused agenda involving team strategy and processes, such as administrative issues, internal communication, work planning, and marketing services, dominated the discussions. The main goal was to establish processes to serve clients throughout the region efficiently and effectively.

Much was accomplished at the meeting. Team members started to get to know each other and an adviser was selected for the interns. Guidelines for short-term team operations in the new regional structure, customer service issues, and communication links were defined. Also, the team agreed that consensus decision making was the foundation of its ground rules. Most important, the team decided it needed a formal team building and long-term strategic planning meeting. The team agreed this meeting would take place at an off-site location in January or February 1995, and be facilitated by an external OD consultant.

Although the November 1994 meeting was task focused, the shadow of the team leader selection process and the emotions it generated were palpable. On the morning of the meeting's second day, the acting team leader and senior OD consultant who had led the northern California OD cadre had a personal conversation to try and clear the air. This conversation went fairly well. It was clear, however, that the issue remained open, with strong feelings involved. The turning point in team formation occurred at the January-February 1995 meeting. It was there that the leadership issue was resolved.

January 31-February 2, 1995

We must not cease from exploration. And the end of all our exploring will be to arrive where we began and to know the place for the first time.—T.S. Eliot (1966)

During December and January, the acting team leader worked closely with the external consultant and team members to design the January-February meeting. First and foremost in the design was a process to allow all team members to express their hopes and concerns for the OD team, openly and freely in a safe environment. It was expected that the leadership issue would emerge naturally as part of the broader discussion, including such issues as the transition from an OD independent contractor to a team concept of operations; team values, norms, and processes; balancing team v. individual needs; methods for supporting and developing less experienced consultants; obtaining and assigning work; the customer feedback and evaluation process; and, effective internal-external communication links.

The meeting's physical location and the use of a skilled facilitator were critical to achieving the desired outcomes. After extensive research, the team selected a conference facility in central California. The site was beautiful and very reasonably priced. All meals were provided, and the participants were required to serve themselves and to do cleanup. (An excellent built-in team building experience!) Moreover there were no TVs or radios, and only one telephone for emergency use. All in all, the site provided an environment for success.

The external facilitator had consulted to the IRS previously and was familiar with its culture and basic organizational structure. He encouraged feedback on the design from the team and willingly made adjustments both before and during the meeting. In addition, the acting team leader modeled a supportive and participative leadership style in planning the meeting and in dealing with other business issues that arose during December and January. The experienced OD consultants willingly shared information with one another; supported and mentored those with less experience; and provided open, honest, and balanced feedback to the acting team leader. Thus the stage was set for a highly revealing and productive session in central California.

A key group activity designed to help team members learn from and understand one another better occurred in the late afternoon and evening of day one and was scheduled to include a dinner break. Called the "paper bag exercise," it involved the use of brown paper lunch sacks, craft materials, and a variety of old magazines. Participants took a paper bag, scissors, tape, and glue and were asked to describe themselves, using any items from the craft table or pictures from the magazines. The outside of the bag represented their public, professional, or "known" self; the inside represented the more private self—the beliefs, values, feelings, and experiences that affect behavior and communication preferences. Participants constructed their "paper bag story" prior to dinner. After dinner, the external consultant skillfully facilitated a disclosure activity in which participants talked about their paper bag, linking the issues on the outside to those within. The team responded to this exercise with honesty and openness; it became a rich source of understanding and caring for the team, and formed the relationship foundation for the rest of the meeting.

At the end of the paper bag exercise, the team leader and external consultant debriefed the day's events. Both were comfortable with the progress made; however, the external consultant believed the leadership issue was not fully resolved and could impede the meeting's desired outcomes. He suggested engaging the team in a general discussion about that issue the next morning. This general discussion led to a recommendation by the team members that the team leader and senior consultant go offline to again discuss the leadership issue. The goal was for them to become comfortable with each other's roles within the team and better define how they would work together. This meeting lasted about one hour. Due largely to the previous day's activities, the meeting was very open and very successful. Later that morning, both the team leader and senior consultant were able to jointly address the team and state that the leadership issue was resolved.

From this point, the team moved through a variety of rich and revealing exercises that helped in articulating values, norms, and processes (see table 1). For example, one exercise asked all members to describe their values and vision for the team, which were captured through graphic facilitation. The resulting drawings and sketches elicited a lively and positive discussion that helped focus the team's direction. The illustrations depicted the energy of the sun, with the talents of individual team members radiating out from the center. In another exercise called "alien encounter," the team was asked to analyze a space flight scenario and make mission decisions based on the data supplied. This provided information on different styles and approaches to decision making that the team still uses.

Table 1. Western region OD consulting team.

Values	Norms
Integrity	Work as Partners Together.
Trust/Respect	We Own Our Perspectives.
Freedom/Autonomy	Take Personal Responsibility.
Challenging/Stimulating Work	Feedback on Task/Behavior.
Professional/Personal Balance	Respectful Confrontation.
Personal/Team Excellence	Everyone Contributes.
Experiment/Risk Taking	Have Fun!

Process Approach
Collaborative Teamwork
Build on Past Successes
Participative Decision Making
Mutual Agreement and Discussion
About What I Do
Self/Peer Assessment
Learning Organization—On the Leading Edge

These exercises helped the team develop processes for assigning work and obtaining customer feedback. This was crucial because the OD team is a regional asset with a varied and geographically dispersed customer base. To effectively meet customer needs, the team formed a structure of multiple interlocking partnerships between the team leader and the consultants in the five different cities. The consultants focus on the customers in their own geographic area and also are available for travel to other areas when needed. The team developed and flowcharted a process for assigning client work and referring work to other consultants (see figures 1 and 2). In addition, the team successfully refined its customer feedback form and the feedback process. Next, team members assessed their technical strengths, areas of interest, and areas requiring development. This process helped to target some specific training opportunities over the next six months. Finally, the team identified communication issues and potential solutions. These are discussed in some detail under The Remote Leadership Challenge, below. The team left the meeting renewed and energetic, with a clear picture of what they were about and how they would accomplish their work.

The Remote Leadership Challenge

Stewardship is the willingness to be accountable for the well-being of the larger organization by operating in service, rather than in control, of those around us.—Peter Block (1993)

Block's perspective meshes nicely with remote leadership. After all, when most team members are anywhere from 50 to 800 miles away, attempting to exert control not only is ill-advised, it's impossible. Communicating effectively is the salient issue, raising issues like: How do team members know what their colleagues are doing? How does the team leader stay abreast of the team's key activities? How can team members learn from one another when a lean travel budget allows only one or two face-to-face meetings per year? How can you best stay connected with your customers if they are distant?

For the OD team, the answers are within available technology. For example, the team has a 90-minute telephone conference call every other Monday morning. A formal agenda is sent via e-mail to the team two working days prior to the call. Team members rotate the role of facilitator. In addition to phone conferences, the team uses facilitated teleconferences on an electronic bulletin board to share successful and, at

Figure 1. IRS western region OD specialists work flow process.

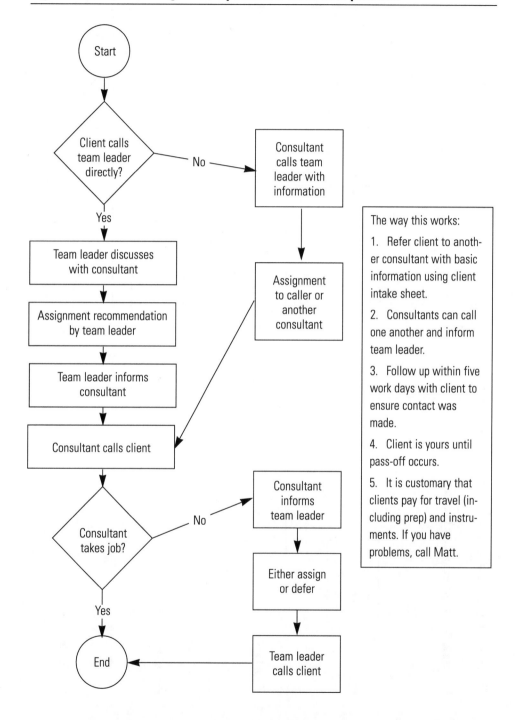

The way this works:

1. Refer client to another consultant with basic information using client intake sheet.

2. Consultants can call one another and inform team leader.

3. Follow up within five work days with client to ensure contact was made.

4. Client is yours until pass-off occurs.

5. It is customary that clients pay for travel (including prep) and instruments. If you have problems, call Matt.

Figure 2. Handoff flow for new client intake process.

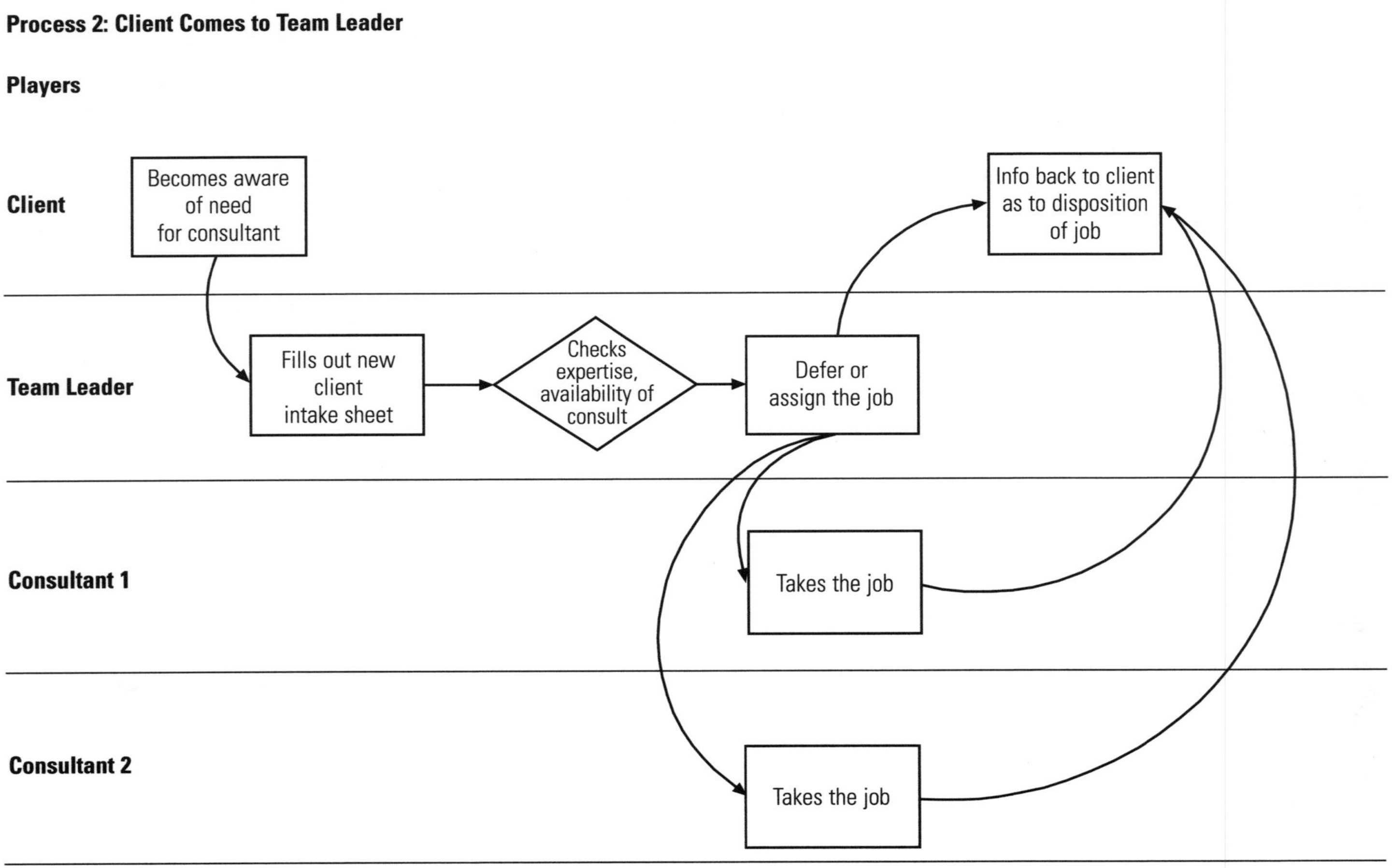

Process 2: Client Comes to Team Leader

Players

times, not so successful interventions. Moreover, team members and clients are connected to e-mail and can also access the Internet. Finally, the IRS voice-mail system can be accessed nationwide via an 800 number. The team and its clients have learned to adapt to these media, and there have been very few significant communication disconnects between team members or with clients.

As the IRS travel budget has declined, the team has experimented with "virtual meetings," using a variety of media. The team recently developed a guide for managers and other consultants called "The Skinny Book on Virtual Conferences." Topics include matching the appropriate medium to the agenda and activities; logistics; preparing participants to use conference media; anticipating and troubleshooting technical difficulties; and evaluating meeting effectiveness.

OD and the Business Strategy: March-November 1995

> *OD has been losing relevance to business executives and organizations seeking changed performance, not just process facilitation...What OD should do is involve itself in the life and death issues that help organizations live, thrive, and survive.*—Christopher Worley (1996)

The book, *Integrated Strategic Change* (Hitchen, Ross, and Worley), describes how OD can help organizations build competitive advantage. Though the IRS made a decision to invest in OD, especially through the intern program, it was up to the teams to demonstrate OD's value and market their services.

As mentioned before, OD has been established in some parts of the Western Region since 1989. These existing relationships helped to validate and promote OD's value. For example, in March 1995, the IRS initiated a national work group to plan and implement a process to reduce the number of regions from seven to four, and districts from 63 to 33. One of the executive leaders, a former client in northern California, invited two of the team's senior consultants to assist this team. This consultation lasted 60 days and had nationwide impact. Based on this success, the national consolidation team recommended that OD consultants participate on the region and district teams responsible for implementing the consolidation over the next 18 months. In the Western Region, for instance, the OD team has consulted to three of the four consolidating districts and to the regional office. This success opened the door for other high-level, strategic work, including implementing the new Field Information Systems Organization; establishing customer service sites; the continuing evolution of the support services structure; and transition sessions for new executives and their work teams. The feedback on these interventions has been very positive, and more calls for assistance have resulted.

In August 1995, the team asked their customers to list their anticipated needs for FY96 (fiscal year 1996, October 1 through September 30). The response was excellent, resulting in a work plan with 118 requests for assistance at all levels of management. Currently the consulting team's calendar is booked an average of five weeks in advance. Nationally, all regional consulting teams have been linked to servicewide initiatives that originate at the national office level in Washington, D.C. Much of this work is in the process reengineering and work systems design area. All regional OD work plans have been consolidated at the national office, so that OD resources can be more closely tied to strategic planning.

As the demand for OD services grows, timely response to customer requests is an issue. An approach to this problem initiated by the Western Region OD team involves partnerships with universities that have masters of science programs in organizational development. For example, the OD team formed a partnership with both Pepperdine University in the Los Angeles area and John F. Kennedy University in the San Francisco area. Graduate students at both schools provided facilitation to managers to complete the IRS's all-employee feedback process. Since November 1995, students in these programs have provided about 140 hours of facilitation assistance. The OD team is also working with JFK University to arrange a graduate course that can be team taught by a JFK faculty member and an IRS OD team member. Overall, this partnership has been very successful and will be showcased at an April 1996 seminar on government-academic partnerships sponsored by the Southern California College Federal Council.

Feedback and Measures

For years, managers have grappled with measuring human resource's impact on the business. Much of the work in training and OD, for example, is not easy to quantify or tie directly to return-on-investment. In the Western Region, the OD team uses a rating scale (one through five, with five being best) that customers complete at the end of an intervention. It asks for feedback on 12 specific items within three major categories: the consulting process, consultant effectiveness, and outcomes. The feedback is provided directly to the consultant, who then forwards it to the team leader for consolidation. A recent roll up of data from the feedback forms revealed customers' overall ratings at 4.6—a tribute to the skills and abilities of the OD team.

Currently uniform measures for OD are being developed by a national task team. These measures will be more detailed and will specifically differentiate between results and process. In addition, costing formulas are being reviewed in an attempt to better capture return-on-investment.

The Road Ahead: March 1996

Each team creates its own story line... The collective memory of where you have been can reveal a great deal about where you should go.
—The Fifth Discipline Field Book (1994)

As this paper is being written, the IRS is reassessing its business vision and objectives in light of current and anticipated budget cuts. FY 96 has seen the agency take extraordinary cost-cutting steps to help reduce the possibility of an all-employee furlough (nonwork days) late in the fiscal year. In addition, the agency plans to cut its workforce by 8,000 employees over the next year. For the first time in the agency's history, a reduction in force is possible.

In this environment, every human resource operation must continually demonstrate its value to IRS's core business objectives: increasing voluntary compliance, reducing taxpayer burden, and increasing quality-driven productivity. The Western Region OD team, fully aware that its survival is not guaranteed, already has experienced the sting of downsizing. This year the consultants on temporary appointments were released, not to be replaced. Still the team remains focused on the future and how it can continue to add value. Aside from providing high-quality consulting services, the team has produced an issues paper on downsizing and best practices that was well received by management. The virtual conference guide will be issued very soon, and a guide to reengineering at the work team level is also being developed. In addition, shadow consulting relationships with other consultants in total quality management and in diversity are being explored. The goal is to create synergy and increase productivity.

In conclusion, the support and investment by management at both the national and regional levels provided an opportunity for the team to excel. The team members took full advantage of that opportunity and plan to be a vital component of IRS's strategic fabric in the years to come.

Questions for Discussion

1. What specific factors affected the federal government's structure in the 1990s? How was the IRS affected, and what was its response?

2. Why did the IRS decide to commit to an internal OD consulting structure in 1994? What are the advantages and potential drawbacks of an internal consulting function?

3. What were the organizational factors in human resources that helped complicate the leadership issue for the OD team?

4. Describe the dynamics of the November meeting. What else could the team leader have done either before or during the meeting?

5. What were the important elements in preparing for the January-February meeting? How did these elements set the stage for an effective meeting?

6. Describe the activity at the meeting that helped pave the way for resolving the leadership issue. Do you consider it a high-risk activity? If so, why?

7. Review the OD team's values, norms, and work processes in table 1. What do they say about the team's current level of formation?

8. How did the OD team communicate "remotely"? Discuss some of the major challenges in the techniques described?

9. How did the OD team obtain entry into important, high-level projects? Also, describe the benefits you see in partnering on OD work, both for the IRS and universities.

10. Are there other approaches for effectively measuring human resource activities, especially OD?

11. How can high-performing work teams continue to grow and improve? How is complacency avoided?

The Authors

The members of the OD consulting team bring nearly 175 years of cumulative IRS experience to their work. Members have previously worked in a variety of IRS divisions, including examination, collection, taxpayer service and resources management. Several were frontline and mid-level managers. Their expertise and, most important, their ability to effectively share that expertise by creating a learning environment for clients, adds value to the organization. They hope the lessons in this case study are valuable to those who read it. Questions and comments are welcome and may be directed to Matthew J. Ferrero, Team Leader, Internal Revenue Service, 24000 Avila Road, Laguna Niguel, CA 92677; phone: 714.360.2384; fax: 714.360.2497; e-mail: Mathew_Ferrero@ccmail.wr.irs.gov.

References

Block, P. *Stewardship: Choosing Service Over Self-Interest.* San Francisco: Berrett-Koehler, 1993.

Eliot, T.S. *Collected Poems.* London: Oxford University Press, 1966.

Hitchen, D.E., W.L. Ross, and C.G. Worley. *Integrated Strategic Change: How OD Builds Competitive Advantage.* New York: Addison-Wesley, 1996.

Kliener, A., C. Roberts, R.B. Ross, B.J. Smith, and P.M. Senge. *The Fifth Discipline Field Book.* New York: Doubleday, 1994.

Lao-tzu. *Tao Te Ching.* New York: HarperPerennial, 1992.

Developing an Empowered Work Team

Sapphire Electronics

Bob Carroll

This case demonstrates the use of management interventions in developing empowered work teams. It accomplishes this by describing the actual management interventions that were used at critical times during the five-year development of a cross-functional production team. These interventions are shown in the context of the major improvements that were made by the team itself to turn their troubled project into a model project—a project whose success surpassed everyone's expectations, including their manager's. The case ends with a list of lessons learned, derived from this project and subsequently used by the manager in developing other teams.

Case Study

Sapphire Electronics had about 3,000 employees in a matrix organizational structure. The employees reported to a functional department (engineering, operations, finance, and so forth) and were assigned to a cross-functional project that was managed by a program manager. Each project consisted of 10 to 50 members, all of whom were responsible for the success of that project.

The development of this empowered team began in the spring of 1987. One operations section manager had a program in trouble. The program had always been successful, but because of a part testing failure, it had serious schedule and cost problems requiring special attention. To correct the schedule problem, the project doubled the number

This case was prepared to serve as a basis for discussion rather than to illustrate either effective or ineffective administrative and management practices. All names, dates, places, and organizations have been disguised at the request of the organization involved or the case author.

of assemblers. This did not help; it actually made matters worse. The additional people created bad feelings and increased conflicts, which resulted in greater schedule loss and a significant increase in cost. The project leader came to his section manager several times asking how to correct the situation. The manager had attended a number of sessions on using team empowerment to reduce cost by reducing manufacturing cycle time. He had been looking for a program to experiment with these techniques. Since this approach to improve productivity was new to the organization, he wanted to find a project that would benefit from empowerment and had enough history to measure its effects.

The program selected seemed perfect. It had excellent leadership, and its five-year duration was long enough to allow a slow introduction of empowerment, as well as sufficient time to reap the benefit of team development. It had a mature product design requiring very few changes, and a long history with a good database to provide before and after comparisons relative to quality, cost, and schedule. Most important, the program was in serious trouble and needed some kind of major management intervention to get it back on track.

As it turned out, short-cycle manufacturing is an excellent methodology for team development. It is a clearly defined process that focuses the entire team on jointly accomplishing measurable improvements in cycle time. The process is simple but powerful. Each reduction in cycle time exposes obstructions to that reduction. These obstructions range from design and process deficiencies to nonvalue steps throughout the process. Correcting the deficiencies results in a more reliable product. Removing the nonvalue steps results in fewer hours per unit. As each obstruction is identified, the team must decide how to remove it. In the beginning this is relatively easy, but as the process continues, it becomes increasingly more difficult. Significant reductions in cycle time cannot occur without a cohesive, cooperative team willing to share tasks and responsibilities.

When the empowerment process was started, the program was organized in the traditional method of project management. There was a project leader whose primary tasks were customer interface and overall project planning and responsibility. He had a production task leader to manage the production effort. This person had a supervisor, three group leaders, and two production control people to give direction and to track hardware. The project was divided into three sections. Each section had a group leader and a separate part of the project. The operators built the product in batches, as directed by the group leaders. Each person built one type of board. While it was recognized that this project organization and method of operation would not be needed when an empowered team was in place, it was important that all changes be evolutionary and fit the needs of the team at each stage of team development. Since this was the first program to be empowered, it was essential to ensure that the process of implementing empowerment did not adversely effect this project's performance. The implementation process required small, carefully thought-through steps, taking the time necessary to make sure each step was contributing to the program's success or was, at a minimum, neutral.

Baseline Data

Since the use of empowerment to increase productivity was new to the organization and to the section manager, he wanted to be able to measure whether the empowerment did improve productivity. To accomplish this, he needed good baseline data. He assigned an industrial engineering aide to gather data on monthly output, cycle time, and quality. She generated flow diagrams on each of the modules that showed all operations with delays, movement, and distance moved. Next she generated cycle-time data on every module. From this information, she developed a flow diagram of the entire system, showing best, worst, and average times. This task was performed offline so that the project was not disturbed. It was completed before starting the process to ensure good before-and-after data. The data was used by the team in their cycle-time reduction effort, as well as to measure progress.

Train the Coaches

The next step was to send the project leadership team (future coaches) through cycle-time training before the rest of the team. The manager (hereafter called the coach, since that is the primary role he played in developing this team) wanted to ensure that future coaches had a clear understanding of what needed to be accomplished. They would need a thorough grasp of the empowerment and short-cycle manufacturing concepts before the start of the team development process.

Continuous Improvement Meetings

Continuous improvement meetings were then put in place to support team formation. These meetings were attended weekly by all those individuals directly involved in the production phase of the program: assemblers, inspectors, test technicians, engineers, team leaders, and the coach. These meetings served many purposes: showing and reviewing cycle-time data, communicating program issues, and resolving conflicts or misunderstandings. The primary activity, however, was team building.

In the beginning, the production task leader chaired the meetings, maintained the minutes, and assigned actions. The minutes were distributed to each member of the team describing the action required, the person responsible for completing the action, the date it was expected to be accomplished, and the current status of this action. While each action was usually small, cumulatively they had a significant impact on improving productivity. More than 800 actions were identified and were either completed or, with the consensus of the team, closed with no action taken. The coach attended the meetings to provide guidance, mentor the production task leader, encourage the participants to voice their concerns and ideas, ensure the actions identified were completed, and champion the development of an empowered work team.

Progress Data

There was a weekly posting of the updated cycle-time and quality data: defects per million operations, Pareto charts, output charts, and cycle-time reduction updates. This data was used in the workplace and in the continuous improvement meetings to further cycle-time reduction efforts.

First Cross-Functional Problem-Solving Team

Early in the process, one of the operators made a recommendation on how manufacturing cycle time could be reduced if the procedure for parts traceability was changed. The procedure stated that if operators found an error on the traceability sheet, they were to make a correction on the sheet; then initial and date the correction; then get that correction approved by an inspector or a production control person, who would also initial and date it. The procedure required that the operators obtain this approval before they could continue building the hardware. The operator recommended that operators be allowed to make the correction, initial and date it, then complete the assembly and send it to inspection. The first thing inspectors did when they conducted their inspection was to check the traceability sheet to ensure it was correct. The inspector at that point could approve the correction. That way operators would not have to stop and find one of these people to sign the paper.

This sounded good to the coach, but he wanted to use this to start developing the team's ability to solve problems. He formed a small cross-functional problem-solving team composed of the operator who made the recommendation, an inspector, and a production control person. He then instructed them to meet during the next week to review the procedure and make a recommendation at next week's meeting as to whether the procedure should be changed. The product quality engineer jumped up, very agitated, and said that the procedures had to be followed. They could not be changed. The coach asked him who wrote the procedures. He did not respond, so the coach answered his own question. He said we did, and we could change them as long as we followed the systems rules for changing procedures. He then requested the team to do as he asked. He had high hopes that this would be the start of the doers solving their problems as a team. He had no idea, at this point, how difficult this process was going to be to get started.

During the week before the next continuous improvement meeting, the coach asked the production task leader how the small team was doing. He answered that the operator asked him to go to the meeting with her, since the other two people invited their managers. The managers took over that meeting and decided there was no need to change anything. The coach then intervened again by holding a meeting with these managers to tell them in the future to stay out of the small team meetings until that team had a chance to reach a conclusion and make a recommendation to the whole team. They could object at that time, but their objections had to be based on what was the best way to accomplish the task. They could not raise objections just to maintain the status quo or protect their turf, and if the new way was the best way, the coach expected these managers to show the team how to change the procedure within the system. This intervention demonstrates that the manager who is first championing empowered team development should have a position in the organization to allow him to shield the process, have access to all the required resources, and be able to remove the barriers and obstructions that the team will identify or encounter.

Project Stockroom Established

The team determined that obtaining kits from the central stockroom contributed to the overall cycle time to manufacture a system. To correct this, the team's material manager (one of the future coaches) established a project stockroom in the project area. This significantly cut down the cycle time associated with obtaining kits and material. The project stockroom filled kanbans (a device, usually an empty container, to automatically signal the need for new material) in place of working to a preset kitting schedule. As each system was assembled, the empty tote bins (kanbans) were returned to the project stockroom and refilled, automatically keeping the kitting in balance with assembly. This eliminated one of the schedules. A single individual was assigned the responsibility for all kitting. Where there was no contact in the past, there was now a positive interaction between the assemblers and this person. Many good ideas passed back and forth between them. During peak needs, the assemblers were cross-trained to perform kitting tasks, and the stock person was cross-trained to do assembly tasks.

Formal Training of Entire Program Team

After the team was about six months into the cycle-time reduction process, they hit one of the many walls they would encounter on their road to becoming a fully empowered team. The coach started to notice at the continuous improvement meetings that the team was starting to come apart. They had fixed all the easy things, and they were getting restless. They started to lash out at one another over trivial things and were starting to drift back to their old habits of blaming one another for not improving the process. The intervention that the coach chose to break through this impasse was training. He had the Training Department train the whole team in short-cycle manufacturing. Working together over three days of very intense interactive training, the team broke through their interpersonal barriers and started to function as a team again. The net result of this training, in addition to bringing the team together, was expansion of the team's knowledge of cycle-time reduction. It also reinforced the theme that was developed in the continuous improvement meetings, that significant improvements in cycle time would have to come from the individuals best equipped to accomplish them—the team itself. While many people contributed to the ultimate success of this project, it was, in retrospect, the improvements that were originated and implemented by the team itself that contributed the most to that success. The major improvements that the team made are outlined below.

Batch Construction Replaced by Linear Build

After the entire team went through cycle-time reduction training, the assemblers requested that instead of building the same circuit board all the time, each operator be allowed to build a system of circuit boards (all the circuit boards required to build a single system). This was agreed to, since it had a number of advantages: greater satisfaction and interest, cross-training, no batching, quality improvement from faster feedback, and ownership of that system. The disadvantages were that it took two to four weeks to complete a system, and boards were not always available in the types and quantities needed to build the required four systems per week.

The coach knew that whatever the solution was, it would involve a closer interaction of the team as well as their buy-in. He raised the issue a number of times at the weekly productivity meeting, explaining the problem and suggesting that maybe they could form two-person teams that would build a system together. While he knew it was difficult to match people up who would be willing to share work, he had no other ideas. He hoped the team would be willing to try the two-person team approach or, if not that, come up with a different approach that would accomplish the same thing. They did. After a couple of months working on their own, they found a way to produce four systems per week. They set up four systems' worth of boards on a shelf and made a list of the boards in the order they should be built. Then each operator, who was now cross-trained to build all the boards, took the next board on the list from the shelf, signed it out, and built it. This was done until the four systems were complete. The advantages of this approach were a full complement of boards for four systems were completed each week, the assemblers felt an ownership for the whole program, and the previous benefits remained.

Over time, this concept of organizing and building four systems per week was refined so the systems were built linearly (one system at a time) and later was expanded to the rest of the program. Four work centers were put in place: board assembly, board test, system assembly, and system test. Each center had a weekly requirements sheet showing what had to be produced during that week. Each center was self-regulating as to how they organized their work in order to accomplish the weekly goal. If a center did not have what it needed, it went to the previous center to pull it.

Interventions to Remove Organizational Obstructions

The linear build required a significant amount of cross-functional sharing of tasks. This brought the team to the next serious impediment to cycle-time reduction and empowerment: job descriptions. As the need for cross-functional sharing increased, the team kept encountering reasons why people could not do tasks outside their job description. The team kept hearing "It's not my job" or "My job description does not let me do that." The coach remembered he had read about other companies, who were developing teams, creating cross-functional positions called "worker one," "two," and "three" where there was no job description. The person just did whatever was required to complete the task. He talked to the local human development person about changing the job descriptions. She recommended that the two of them set up a meeting with compensation and propose changing the job descriptions. Compensation accepted the idea and said that if the coach could convince his director of operation of the merits of the idea, he would develop it and then institute it. The coach did so. Compensation then created five operation association positions that replaced 106 job descriptions. The assemblers, inspectors, and production control personnel now all had a common title. This common title eliminated functional barriers, promoted team cohesion, and removed the organizational restrictions on performing cross-functional tasks. This was a major contributor to the feeling that they were all one team with a common purpose. When the coach started this effort, he thought it was going to be an almost impossible task. It was in actuality surprisingly easy.

To give just one example of how these new job titles improved the project's productivity, before this change there was a separate production control function. This group had the sole responsibility for the moving and tracking of all project hardware. The assembler would build the hardware and put it on the assembly out-shelf. One of the production control people would log the hardware in their book and move it to the inspector's in-shelf. The inspector would inspect the hardware and put it on the inspection out-shelf. The production control person would then log the hardware in their book and move it to the next in-shelf. This process repeated itself many times before that hardware completed its cycle.

With the change in the job descriptions, production control as a separate function was eliminated. Employees moved their own hardware to the next work center and logged it on that work cell's weekly requirement sheet. These sheets recorded the status of the program and provided all the cycle-time data. All out-shelves were removed. The program's words for this were "Your out-shelf is the next person's in-shelf." The flow of hardware was controlled by the weekly requirement sheets and the system test schedule. This eliminated the large inventory that used to fill many shelves and significantly reduced the floor space required to produce the same amount of product from 8,000 to 3,500 square feet. Most important, it allowed everyone on the project to know the location of the hardware.

Improved Test Cycle Time

The requirement sheets eliminated three of the four detail schedules. The only detail schedule that remained was for system test. The four sets of automated system test equipment along with the environmental test equipment were the critical capacity resources. Each set of equipment tested four systems at a time, 24 hours a day, for three weeks. This three-week test cycle required each unit to be vibrated, burned in, and thermal cycled. Since there was only one burn-in oven, one thermal vacuum chamber, and one shake table, the utilization of this equipment had to be planned in great detail to maximize its use. How well it was utilized determined how many systems could be shipped each month.

Working this equipment to what used to seem its capacity allowed the testing of 16 systems in four weeks. Accordingly, the system test detail schedule was laid out to reflect this capacity. When 16 systems were tested in a month, it was considered to have been a very successful month. As it turned out, that goal was seldom met. More typically, they tested 16 systems in five or six weeks. There were a number of reasons for this. In the beginning, it was not a major concern because the test team very seldom had the four systems per month to test. It only became an issue when the assembly team started to consistently produce four systems per week. At this point, the only way to improve cycle time was to either purchase very expensive environmental test equipment or find ways to test more units with the same equipment.

Because the purchase of new equipment was not justified from a return-on-investment analysis, the project leadership team, including the coach, accepted the proposition that the test limitation meant that cycle time had been reduced to its minimum level. Fortunately not everyone on the team accepted this proposition. Once the team had been imbued with the cycle-time reduction spirit, they started to question all the dogmatic statements of why something could not be improved: "It cannot be changed"; "This is the only way it can be done"; "This is the way it has always be done"; or in this case, "We cannot test more than 16 systems per month with the equipment we have, and we probably cannot do that consistently."

Very often in this type of situation, it is a person who has no expertise in the area being examined who comes up with a new way of looking at the problem. In this case, it was the person who generated and maintained all the schedules and tracked all the cycle-time data. This person noticed that occasionally they tested 16 systems in three weeks. Armed with this data, she set up a meeting with the project leader and the senior technician. She presented the data and inquired why they could not test 16 systems in three weeks. The idea of being able to test only 16 in four weeks was so ingrained that it was difficult to get the project leader and the senior technician to look at this data objectively, especially when the idea came from a person who did not know anything about testing. To them it had to be some kind of fluke, an aberration; someone must have recorded the wrong dates. They came up with numerous other reasons why it might have happened, always coming to the conclusion that it was irrelevant; there was no way that 16 systems could be consistently tested in three weeks. Fortunately, the scheduler was not dissuaded. Convinced that their reasons did not stand up, she went back to her area to make a new schedule showing how it could be done. The project leader was finally persuaded that it might be possible; the senior technician was not. The project leader decided that the best way to resolve the issue was to form a small team composed of the three of them to examine the issue in depth. They met daily and brainstormed each impediment to being able to test 16 systems in three weeks. After several weeks, they came up with a way to accomplish the task by slightly modifying the equipment, upgrading some support equipment, and alternating the order in which certain tests were performed.

The scheduler then made a new detail schedule that reflected these changes. This new schedule showed by system serial number when each system had to start and complete each test. This test cycle-time improvement team explained to the rest of the project team what they had done and then showed the team the new schedule. They said they would need the help of everyone to make it work. They had to have the systems on the dates shown in the test schedule, or they would not be able to test 16 systems every three weeks. It required a lot of hard work, but the team consistently made those dates, and the project was able to ship 16 systems every three weeks. This was a gain of more than 60 systems per year using the same equipment.

Team Charter

The team had been working hard for almost three years. They were functioning almost perfectly together and making a significant effort to ensure the project was successful, but developmentally, they were standing still. They were on a plateau and seemed to find it difficult to take the final step toward full empowerment. They seemed contented with the way things were and almost afraid to change anything for fear that everything would unravel. This could not last, since all things change. The change in this case was the necessity to add people to the project to replace those who left, and to meet the requirement for increased output.

The addition of new people did not go well; they were a disruption to the old team. Each person on the old team knew exactly what was expected of him or her and met these expectations. The new team was still functioning as if they were in a traditional organization. The conflict between the two groups started to manifest itself. The new team members thought the old team members were too pushy. The old team members thought the new team members were not committed enough. By this time, the team was very sensitive about solving their own problems. They did not like to admit they could not resolve these interpersonal conflicts as a team. So the coach resisted doing anything; he just watched the team from a distance as they thrashed around, forming little groups, making remarks to one another. People from both sides would come into his office to tell him how bad the other group was, hoping he would step in and fix the problem. It was always the other group that was causing all the problems. Morale and productivity were declining, but the coach did not want to step in until they as a team either came up with a solution or realized they were at an impasse. If he had inserted himself without the team realizing they were at an impasse, it would have set the process back. The team would have thought that he did not have faith in them—that as soon as they encountered a significant problem, he would step in without giving them a chance to resolve it.

After two or three weeks of turmoil, the team acknowledged the problem and their frustration at the weekly continuous improvement meeting. They asked the coach for ideas on how they could resolve their problem. His recommendation was that they write a charter for new team members that described what the team stood for and what was expected of each member. They agreed. They had covered chartering in earlier training sessions, but at that time, they were not interested in it because they had no need for it. The coach was not sure this would work, but it was at least a good vehicle for getting everything out in the open in a nonthreatening way.

He had been in the middle of teaching the team analytical problem-solving techniques and suggested that they take the next three to four continuous improvement meetings and use the brainstorming techniques they had learned in order to generate a list of ideas about what should be in the charter. He made it clear that his role was only to facilitate the brainstorming, not to contribute ideas; all the ideas had to be theirs if they were going to resolve their problem and learn how to use these analytical tools to solve future problems. The primary objective was to get everything out on the table. The team could list anything they wanted on the brainstorming sheets, since these ideas were, as he kept reminding them, to be treated nonjudgmentally. After they completed the brainstorming sessions, they reduced the list to a charter.

The output of this effort far exceeded the coach's expectations. Along with producing a charter they were all quite proud of, they came to appreciate one another's perspective, developed a common vision and direction, acquired an increased knowledge of what a self-directed team should be, and learned how to use analytical problem-solving skills to systematically resolve real work problems. Most important, this activity bonded the team together and gave them an increased feeling of competence that allowed them to start growing again.

Quality Board

After about four years of continuous improvement and growth, the team was self-managed, functioning without a supervisor, group leader, production task leader, material manager, quality engineer, or test engineer. All the activities that had been performed by the aforementioned people were now performed by this high-commitment team, consisting of the project leader, quality product engineer, operation associates, and test technicians. The members of the team took turns every two weeks attending the project leader's morning meeting, chairing the continuous improvement meeting, and doing the tasks previously performed by the production task leader, supervisor, and group leader.

The assembly member whose turn it was to attend the 15-minute, 8 a.m. test status meeting would join the project leader along with the test member to determine what had to be accomplished that day in order to meet the test equipment schedule. That person would then return to the assembly center and identify what had to be pulled forward to make the scheduled test start dates. The team would develop a quick plan to accomplish this within the constraints of having the required hardware into customer inspection by 3 p.m., so it would be ready for staking, masking, and conformal coating by 3:30 p.m., to allow an overnight cure. The team would then adhere to that plan and accomplish all the tasks required. The test member would do the same. Test and assembly kept each other informed of any changes that had to be made to the morning plan.

The inspector, who was an integral part of the team, kept a running status of the assemblies required to complete each system in the order needed. She used this status to prioritize her work, so the assemblies were inspected in the order that would meet the test schedule. As the team reviewed this running status each day to see if they could put systems together, they noticed that sometimes boards that were needed to complete a system were held up because of quality problems. They came to realize that they must improve their quality if they were going to consistently meet the system test schedule. As the team explored how they could improve the quality, they concluded that the quality data they were receiving was not timely, and what they did receive was not formatted so people could use it to improve their individual quality. If each person did not know how to improve his or her own quality, there was no way the project could improve the total quality.

Historically, as the quality data were identified, they were entered into the Quality Information System. From this system, quality reports were generated weekly, providing information such as total project defects, project progress relative to goal, and Pareto charts of major defects. The assemblers also received quality data when they received assemblies back for rework. But they did not believe this data was timely or complete enough. To rectify this, they developed their quality board. The way it worked was simple: A large white board was modified by adding columns to it to enter the information they needed. As operators completed their work, they would record on the white board the assembly number, the operation step, and the number of opportunities for defects that assembly had at that point in the process. When inspectors completed the inspection of that assembly, they would record whether that assembly had any defects and if it had, the quantity of defects and a description of each one. From this information, the operators would calculate their own and the team's quality level. By providing team members with hourly feedback on their quality, the system alerted the individual and the other teammates to errors and thereby prevented these errors from being repeated.

Over time, team members came to realize that their defects interrupted the product flow and increased the total cycle time, making it more difficult for the team to achieve its cycle-time reduction objectives. This changed the team's approach to the quality board. This board went from being just a tool to provide quick quality information to individuals so they could improve their individual quality to being a tool to provide timely quality information to everyone on the team, so all the team members could help one another improve their quality.

One of the tools the team used to accomplish this was a meeting held every morning at 7:30 for fifteen minutes. The team members called these meetings "ownership meetings," because at them they would state the defect or problem they caused or encountered the previous day, why they thought it occurred, and what they thought could be done to eliminate it. The purpose was to alert the other team members to potential problems, involve the rest of the team in developing permanent solutions to the problems encountered, and heighten each person's sensitivity about the importance of doing zero-defect work. This required a change in thinking. Instead of team members only worrying about, and being responsible for, their individual quality, they now took responsibility for the effect their quality had on the total process. These meetings demonstrated how far the team had come. It requires a lot of mutual trust to stand up before your peers, admit that you made errors, and ask for suggestions from those peers on how to avoid those errors in the future.

Inspection Award—Dinner for Two

The last example of the team's improvements demonstrated how elegant some of these improvements can be. A program was established within the division by the operation section managers to improve quality by rewarding defect-free work. Quality calculations were derived by dividing actual defects by opportunities for defects. For example, a lap soldered axial resistor would have three opportunities for defects: one for forming the resistor and one for each of the lap solder joints. When an assembler achieved no defects for 5,000 opportunities for defects, he received a Number One pin and a certificate. When he received three pins, he received a dinner for two at a local restaurant. Since this defect-free program was established at the same time the assemblers were working to improve their individual quality, all the assemblers ended up very quickly receiving a dinner for two. After a while, it bothered them that they had received a reward while the other members of the team, the inspector and the test technician, were not eligible, since there was no quality measurement for them.

They asked the coach if there was some way these people could qualify for a dinner for two. The coach told them that if they could devise a way to measure these individuals' quality as value added to the project and product, he would get it approved. But it could not be a sham; it had to be real. He explained to them the difficulty of coming up with a system that was real. The problem was that most of the inspection criteria were somewhat subjective: shiny, disturbed, insufficient, or excess solder on solder joints. For that reason, he did not want to base the reward on the amount of defects found by the inspector because he feared that that might encourage the inspector, consciously or unconsciously, to find defects that might not normally be found. Since the coach could not think of any other way of measuring the inspector's quality other than counting how many defects they found and could not even conceive of a way to measure the technician, he thought the team had taken on an impossible task. He never expected to hear anything again on the subject. He was wrong. They came up with a measurement that more than met his conditions for approval.

The measurement was based on the inspector or the technician finding defects during the configuration check that would have resulted in a test failure: miswire, wrong component, missing component, component in backwards. When they found four of these defects, they would receive a Number One pin and a certificate. When they received three pins, they received a dinner for two. This measurement was powerful; it shifted the emphasis from finding minor, subjective defects to finding major defects that could cause significant delays in the testing of the hardware. The coach got the plan approved, and although it took longer than it did for the assemblers, both the inspector and the technician received a certificate for a dinner for two.

High-Performance Empowered Team in Place

The team now had the same project leader who did essentially what he had done before: customer interface and overall project planning and responsibility. The rest of the team tracked their own defects, participated in the daily planning, gave and accepted direct feedback on their performance from fellow team members, and took responsibility for making sure the project goals were met.

The above-outlined improvements enabled the team to be aware of every piece of hardware through its production cycle. They knew where it was, where it should be, and what had to happen next. They knew why each delay occurred and took measures to prevent it in the future. This continuous, constant feedback resulted in a continuous, constant improvement in the product and process. This total team focus on quality and product flow produced significant improvements in the project's performance.

Outstanding Results

Cycle times were reduced fourfold; quality improved more than 30-fold; total hours per unit were significantly reduced; the project's space needs were reduced from 8,000 square feet to 3,500 square feet while producing more product; and the contract was completed a year ahead of the original contract schedule. These results reflect the team's sense of purpose, competence, and commitment. The project's success became their success. It was their planning, doing, checking, and improvements that made it happen.

Continuous improvement necessitates continuous creativity from those individuals who are closest to the process being improved. This requires a very different organization from the traditional command and control organization. In those organizations, creativity, by necessity, has been throttled down so a single individual can direct and control the daily activities of a group of individuals—the span of control. Creativity requires an organization in which information and decision making are driven down to the people accomplishing the task—an organization in which these people are empowered to identify and improve the product, process, or service for which they are now responsible.

Getting Started
Team Selection

The team should be composed of individuals who have a common task and who must interact with one another to accomplish this task. If the project is large, organize it into subsets of 10 to 20 individuals who have a common focus, goals, and objectives. In the beginning, select teams that have the highest probability of becoming empowered—those with a whole, clear, self-contained task: building a complete product, performing a well-bounded service such as a payroll department, or designing a particular product or subset of a product. Once these teams are empowered, the process can be gradually expanded to include progressively more difficult segments of the organization. Remember this is a long-term process; management and these teams are both learning a new method of management.

Coaches' Training

Train the coaches in empowered team concepts before the start of the team development process. For this process to work, the coaches must be believers and have a clear understanding of what you are trying to accomplish. These individuals must be trained to empower, energize, and enable instead of direct people. In the beginning, select people who already use this style of leadership. If possible, assign the coaches to teams other than the teams they are presently managing. That way they and the team will both be starting a new way of managing together. If they coach the team they are presently managing, it will be more difficult to get out of the old patterns of behavior. The coach is accustomed to directing the team, and the team is accustomed to being directed by this coach. Under these circumstances, it is very hard for the team to start managing itself.

Kickoff/Overview Meeting

Start the team development process with a meeting attended by the entire team and the coach, the champion, and the senior managers who are ultimately responsible for that team's success. Each manager gives a short presentation on why teams are important and what they expect the benefit to be to the organization. Then the champion describes the developmental process and how a self-directed empowered team should be operating at an advanced stage of the process. This gives the team a clear vision of what is expected of them. Since upper management is present, it is understood as an organizational expectation. The champion then opens the meeting to questions about the process, expectation, and organizational interest. This process helps the champion gain insight into the team's concerns and ensures that the managers, champion, coach, and team all have a common expectation and vision.

Continuous Improvement Meeting

A week after the overview meeting, start holding weekly meetings to support team formation on a continuous basis. These meetings should be held offline (preferably in a conference room), last about an hour, and be attended by all the team members. These meetings serve many purposes: showing and reviewing data, communicating team issues, and resolving conflicts or misunderstandings. The primary activity, however, is continuous improvement and team building.

In the beginning, since the team does not have the necessary problem-solving or meeting management skills, the coach chairs the meetings, maintains the minutes, and assigns actions. The minutes are distributed to each member of the team describing the action required, the person responsible for completing the action, the date it is expected to be accomplished, and the current status of this action. Working together in a controlled, supportive setting and watching the continuous improvement process, the team learns how changes are made in an orderly fashion. While each action is usually small, cumulatively they have a significant impact on the team's performance and development. As the team develops, they progressively take over the management of these meetings.

The champion attends the meetings to provide guidance, mentor the future coaches, encourage the participants to voice their concerns and ideas, and ensure the actions identified are carried out. Over time the champion becomes just an observer and gets back into the process only when it stalls or appears to be regressing.

A few cautions should be noted. First, the objective is to encourage the people to come up with solutions, to voice their ideas, and to find better ways to do things. This has to be nurtured, and it cannot be nurtured if their ideas are repeatedly rejected. If the idea is not costly, and does not have a negative impact, do it! Do not measure it against payback. The process of these people finding solutions to the problems they understand best will provide payback many times over. Be supportive of every recommendation that is possible, and if it has to be turned down, discuss it with the team.

Second, these meetings are a powerful tool, but they must be managed. The meetings can become very tense, almost disruptive, especially during the early stages of team development. Continuous improvement, by its very nature, is disruptive. It forces examination of everything, exposes weaknesses, and demands change. This can be very troubling for many people, including the champion and the coach. Be patient; it is all part of the growth process. If everyone's position and feelings are taken into consideration, they will become less sensitive over time. The important point is not to overreact. Recognize this as part of the normal team development process and use it for that purpose. Always keep the team focused on continuous improvement, and do not let it wander off to personalities, personnel issues, or company policies that are not related to continuous improvement.

Setting Team Objectives and Constraints

During the first three or four meetings, the team must be given a very clear set of tasks to accomplish and information on all their constraints: legal, organizational, contractual, and managerial. It is important that this information be given up front. Nothing is more destructive to the team development process than for the team to repeatedly work up improvements only to be told it violates some rule, requires some management approvals they did not know about, or does not meet some management expectation.

Constraints and Boundaries

There should be a lengthy discussion with the team on each constraint, accompanied by a detailed explanation of why it is there. While it is very important that team members understand that there are constraints they must work within, it is equally important that the champion be open and ready to work closely with the team to change or remove those constraints that can be changed and are currently impeding the team development process.

Constraints are often a very difficult problem for the champion. Their removal tends to make the champion and the organization very uncomfortable. Restraints are viewed as essential to prevent the team from getting out of control, but the team cannot progressively take on more responsibility while those constraints are in place. Boundaries are not to prevent mistakes; mistakes are the way we learn. Boundaries are to keep those mistakes within acceptable limits. The champion must walk the delicate line of removing or lessening constraints while ensuring the team stays within the legal and organizational boundaries required at each stage of development. There is a natural temptation to keep all the constraints in place to avoid the risk of removing some constraint and having the team make a bad call. While this strategy may appear safe, it will not result in a self-directed empowered team.

A well-informed team typically makes better tactical decisions than the manager. They are closer to the problem and have a better understanding of what is required, and the decision is derived from a collective seeing and knowing that far exceeds the seeing and knowing of the individual manager.

Team Objectives and Goals

The assigned tasks and goals must be measurable. Do not overly constrain. The tasks should be in weekly or monthly increments to allow the team enough room and flexibility to improve the way those tasks are to be accomplished. Make sure the tasks and goals are clearly understood and agreed upon by the entire team. Allow the team to work out how to achieve and measure the achievement of these goals. Have the team collect and post the data that measure the team's progress. As the team evolves, they should be setting more difficult goals. The champion can challenge the team to accept reach-out goals, but the champion must be sure the team has really accepted them. If these goals are seen as management goals that they do not believe they can meet, they will not make the same effort to achieve them that they would if they had buy-in. Ownership is important.

Baseline and Ongoing Data

It is essential to have sound data, both baseline and ongoing—units per week, cycle time, quality, cost, and customer satisfaction—against which all progress will be measured. The data must be posted in an area where people can see and react to it. The effectiveness of the data is significantly enhanced if the team is responsible for collecting, reducing, analyzing, and displaying this data. The process of someone performing a task and then measuring the effect of their actions gives them an insight into the relationship between that action and the effect of that action that is an absolute necessity for constant, continuous improvement.

Job Enlargement and Whole Tasks

One of the more subtle results of empowered teams is the drive away from specialization of both skills and locality. If the project requires a portion of some specialist's time, the organization either pays that individual when they are not fully engaged or suffers delays while they wait in line for their time. Empowered teams force job enlargement. When the team members are cross-trained to do all the required tasks, they eliminate the need for part-time support personnel. Where specialists are required, such as in a concurrent design team, cross-train the team so they can share the portion of each other's task that does not require specialized knowledge, such as administrative tasks, researching information, or contacting outside experts. Expand the team's activities so their responsibilities are for whole products, tasks, or processes. This gives the team the control and ownership it needs to achieve its assigned objectives.

Team Development and Training

A note of caution before starting out; teams cannot be trained into existence any more than a manager can be trained to be a successful manager. In both cases, a developmental process is required in which training is strategically combined with increasingly more responsible tasks and a manager who will mentor and guide the team through the process.

While empowered teams cannot be trained into existence, training is still an essential element in team development. It can bring the team together at critical times, motivate the team when they need a lift, and provide them with the interactive, problem-solving, and managerial skills required to manage their activities. Since the objective of the training is skill acquisition and team building, not knowledge conveyance, it should be delivered over an extended period of time in one- or two-hour sessions once a week, with breaks to ensure the training does not get ahead of the team development. The objective of training should be to give the team the skills it needs when it needs them, not before. If the team wants to start running the continuous improvement meetings, train them at that time in meeting management. If the training is given at the moment it is needed, it will be much more effective.

Start the team development process by teaching the team the basic interactive and analytical problem-solving skills they will need to start working together on their assigned tasks. After the team has a good understanding of these foundation skills, the developmental process, including training, must be tailored to fit the dynamics of each team. No two teams are alike.

Focus Activity

Find an activity that is important to the team and requires the participation of all the members to accomplish. This can be reducing cycle time, planning how the team will accomplish the objectives that have been assigned, improving a process, or working together to resolve a problem that they have identified as a major obstruction to achieving their assigned objectives. This activity is used as a catalyst for team development. The activity can be part of a training session or part of the weekly continuous improvement meetings, but it is best done in a controlled setting where the champion can promote group participation and encourage the participants to use the foundation skills they receive in training. Whatever the activity is, it is important that the champion stay close to the process and use it to bring the team together.

Have a number of training modules ready at all times. Choose the training that is appropriate for a particular stage of development. Do not train every week if it is not appropriate. Do not let the training get ahead of the team development.

Intervention

Teams, like managers, require a developmental process in which training is strategically combined with increasingly more responsible tasks and a supervisor who will oversee that developmental process. This process is simply a series of interventions initiated by the champion to keep the team moving toward self-management at the rate and in the direction that is appropriate for that team. The intervention may be the necessity to remove some organizational barrier, help the team acquire some new skill they need to achieve their objectives, get them to face some interpersonal conflicts, or challenge them to take on some new responsibilities. Whatever the intervention, its primary purpose must be to move the team forward. The team can grow only by developing the ability to solve its own problems, make its own decisions, and manage its own activities.

Stages of the Champion's Activities

The role of the champion changes over time. The activity ranges from intense involvement in the daily process in the beginning to occasionally looking in on the team to ensure they are still growing. For descriptive purposes, this activity can be broken into four phases. The initial phase is explaining the vision: What is an empowered team? How does it work? Why is the organization going to these teams? What do they expect from them? The next phase is intense involvement with team members to help them acquire the management, problem solving, decision making, and team skills that will be required to become an empowered team. The third phase is to take on the role of the team adviser, facilitator, and enabler. The fourth and last phase is to step back and allow the team to manage the day-to-day activities. The champion then starts to develop new teams or starts to work strategic and future growth issues.

Explaining the Vision

Most teams are skeptical at this phase. They do not believe management will ever allow them to make decisions. It is very important that the champion address each issue raised and close it quickly. The champion must always be straight with the team. When asked a question, always answer it truthfully. If it cannot be answered, tell them that; do not try to side step it or give a vague response. Trust between the champion and the team is essential for team development, and it takes a long time to build that trust. Trust is hard to establish, but easy to destroy. Nothing erodes trust faster than inconsistencies between what is said and what is done—in the team development jargon you have to "walk the talk."

During the development process, the champion should continually come back to the vision in order to keep the team focused, ensure there is common understanding of what you are trying to accomplish, surface any organizational obstructions, and update the vision and plan to meet reality. Since the team has no way of comparing where they are in the process relative to where they should be, they always think they are farther along in the process than they are and usually see no need to change. By coming back to the original vision, the champion can show the team what a fully empowered team looks like, so the team can figure out what they have to do to get there.

Direct Involvement

This phase requires a significant effort from the manager. The champion must work closely with the team to help them acquire the skills that will be necessary to manage their activities: interpersonal, problem solving, planning, setting goals, devising measurement to measure those goals, and data collecting and analysis. In other words, all the skills the champion had to acquire to be an effective manager, and all the skills the champion would help a new manager acquire. While this effort is similar to developing a new manager, it is much more. It is developing a group of people to interact in such a fashion that they can collectively manage these activities. The champion cannot direct a group of individuals to function as a team. The champion has to create an environment and a group dynamic whereby these individuals want to do it. This is much more difficult than directing someone to do something. It requires a commitment of time and energy to a group of people that far exceeds anything that the champion has experienced in the past. As the team develops and starts to take on more and more responsibility, however, the commitment usually results in a personal satisfaction that also far exceeds anything that has been experienced.

Team Adviser

As the team develops, the champion takes on the role of adviser, facilitator, and enabler. Champions now become involved in the process only when asked to by the team or when they sense that the team is getting into trouble or going in the wrong direction. At this stage of development, the team often realizes that if they are going to continue to grow, they must make decisions on their own and not involve the champion. This phase can and should be very rewarding for the champion, but for some managers it is a difficult, almost troubling period. They have gone from being the most important player on the team, to one who is now viewed by the team almost as an impediment to their further development.

This is particularly troubling for the managers, because they think that they could solve the problems with very little effort. They are accustomed to solving problems and making decisions; it is easy for them, they enjoy it, and it gives them a feeling of competence. It is difficult, almost painful, to allow the team to thrash around going in the wrong direction and making mistakes, but it has to be done. The only way the team can learn to make decisions is to make them. This means the champion must allow the team to make decisions even though those decisions might be wrong. This is the same way the champion learned to solve problems.

The type and extent of the decisions the team can make should be bounded by the champion, so they are commensurate with the developmental level of the team. In addition, the champion must become involved in the process whenever he or she feels the consequences of the team decision or indecision exceed the level of disruption or cost that is organizationally acceptable. There will be times when the champion must make a decision that runs counter to the decision of the team, but these should be rare. The best way to correct the situation is to explain to the team why their proposed action or solution would not be acceptable, and then work with them so they can come up with a solution that will be acceptable. With this method, the team learns the process of problem solving and decision making by repeatedly doing it.

Stepping Back

In the fourth and last phase, the champion fades into the background, takes on the role of observer, and allows the team to manage its activities. At this stage of development, the champion monitors the progress of the team by mutually agreed-upon measurements that the team has developed. The champion then builds on this team development experience to develop new teams, cascading the team development process throughout the organization.

Summary

From the above it can be seen that the role of the manager is essential in developing empowered work teams; empowerment cannot occur without a significant committed effort from management. The reward for this effort will be the creation of an organization that maximizes the ability of all employees to contribute their full potential to the success of that enterprise. The important point to remember is that this is a long-term process—a culture is being changed. There will always be managers, even in a lean, empowering organization, but they will be a different type of a manager. The managers of the future will be measured not on how well they manage the teams, but on how well their teams manage themselves.

Questions for Discussion

1. What were the most important factors contributing to this team's success?
2. Discuss the improvements the team members themselves made to improve their team's performance. Do you feel these could have been done in a traditional organization setting?
3. How did the manager change the way he intervened in the empowerment process over the developmental history of this team?
4. Which lessons learned in this case were most important to you and why?

The Author

Bob Carroll graduated from Harvard University in 1972 and has an extensive background in manufacturing management. He has written numerous papers on technology issues and empowered production and design teams. He is a member of the New York Academy of Sciences and the American Association for the Advancement of Science, and as a professional artist (sculptor), he is a member of the Copley Society of Boston, Massachusetts, and the Arizona Artist Guild. He can be contacted at 5983 North 83rd Street, Scottsdale, AZ 85250; phone: 602.998.4119.

Cross-Functional Support Teams in a Manufacturing Environment

Imperial Manufacturing

Diane Hertel and Suzan Schober Murray

The near collapse of this company because of restrictive union agreements, hierarchical management structure, and obsolete equipment and systems spawned a sense of emergency. Cross-functional support teams became part of the solution when the company relocated. We can learn from those teams that succeeded in making the transition as well as from those that failed.

Organization Background

With no end in sight to a recent history of sustained and significant operating losses, Imperial Manufacturing needed to make some dramatic changes to justify retention in the parent company's portfolio. Along with executive management from the parent company, the general manager decided to take some bold steps to turn the company around. This U.S.-based company had been in operation in the province of Quebec, Canada, for 30 years. The aging industrial facility built in the late 1930s employed 350-plus hourly union employees, including machinists, mill wrights, electrical/mechanical maintenance personnel, machine operators, assemblers and fabricators, purchasing agents, and others. Their core work was to build and repair heavy equipment for the Canadian paper industry. Engineering, sales, and customer service were located in another facility 60 miles from the plant. Approximately 200 administrative personnel spread across both sites provided support to the core business.

This case was prepared to serve as a basis for discussion rather than to illustrate either effective or ineffective administrative and management practices. All names, dates, places, and organizations have been disguised at the request of the organization involved or the case author.

As is typical in a case like this, the operating losses were the result of a combination of problems. The factors that the design team had to reduce or eliminate included

- work standards and policies that encouraged inefficiency and eroded productivity
- disproportionate, indirect labor costs
- poor communication and disruptive status issues due to geographic separation and a hierarchical structure
- higher than usual inventory losses
- expense due to age and condition of the plant and equipment
- work methods and procedures that were not standardized
- information systems that were outdated and cumbersome
- adversarial labor-management relations and a stifling labor contract that prevented flexibility
- duplicated personnel required on tasks.

This case focuses on the implementation of cross-functional support teams, one component of the new team system design that was instituted to address many of these problems in varying degrees.

Design

The parent company recognized that nothing short of a new beginning would turn the tide. Therefore they committed themselves to shutting down the existing operation and reopening a new, more innovative version of the former company. While the shutdown plans were under way, the general manager contracted Hertel & Murray Human Resource Consultants in Green Bay, Wisconsin, to guide the organization through the redesign effort and assist them with the implementation and start-up of the new operation. The design team consisted of the general manager and eight handpicked existing managers from all functional areas who would be relocating with the operation. With this team, the consultants began a six-month process of education in innovative work systems, team building, and organization redesign as a strategy to deliver the turnaround objectives of leadership.

The new operation opened six months later in the English-speaking province of Ontario, with much of the old equipment now refurbished and reinstalled in a new, but existing, facility. The eight-member management team was assigned to lead eight primary work teams that would eventually be filled by 120 salaried, nonunion employees. Except for these managers and the general manager, there were no other layers of management. All employees were on functional area teams (that is, manufacturing, materials management, customer service, engineering) and structurally at the same level. There is minimal deference in the system for seniority, but instead people are encouraged to accumulate and maintain skill blocks to earn increases in pay. Within and across the teams, all members share the same rights and status. There are no rankings of teams or individuals within teams. Seniority would factor in only in the event of a layoff, and even then, a higher value would be placed on diversity of acquired skills, teamwork, and attitude.

Support Teams Defined

Design parameters required that the organization keep indirect labor costs to a minimum. Therefore much of the work performed by middle managers in the old system would have to be covered in another way. Rather than viewing this as an obstacle, the design team saw it as an opportunity to meet another design parameter, that of involving the employees as much as possible in more aspects of the operation than strictly tasks in their functional areas. The objective of this parameter was to encourage a sense of ownership and better decision making by all employees through increased awareness of the total operation.

The design includes several cross-functional support teams with members from functional area teams who collaboratively solve problems concerning a specific topic area affecting the entire organization. Each support team has a management sponsor, who may or may not attend all meetings, and a rotating team leader, who is selected from among the regular team members. Everyone in the organization is expected to serve on at least one support team during their employment. Most employees serve for one year, and on only one support team at a time. While on a support team, they maintain their team status on their "home" or functional area team and also are responsible for their daily core work.

The areas initially identified as having potential to be handled by cross-functional support teams were: total quality; information systems; waste management; health and safety; hiring and selection; training and education; employee events; public relations; process and technical improvement; cycle time; team system support; and 911 (an emergency customer response team). Under the old system, many of these areas had one or more specific managers who were accountable for tasks and performance. Where allowable in the new system, the support teams are even accountable for government-regulated policies and reports. In other instances, a specific manager is the contact person accountable for regulatory or legal reasons, but the support team does much of the leg work, development, and decision making.

All of the support teams meet on a regular basis, from once a week to quarterly. The most common frequency is monthly, and the duration is usually one hour. All teams have a system for establishing an agenda and keeping minutes (these tasks are usually rotated among the membership). Minutes are posted on a bulletin board and also filed in the company library for anyone in the organization to read. The consultants facilitated each team's initiation through a formal process to establish their mission statement and define the team's roles and responsibilities. Team size varies, but the majority of them have eight members. One team consists of three, while the two largest have 10 members. Size is determined by the topic area and work load or extent of impact of that area on other parts of the organization.

The sponsor role has evolved over time to come to mean that person who helps to maintain the communication link to the management leadership team and provides guidance and perspective in decision making and assistance when the support team needs resources. Initially, sponsors were seen as educators and directors of activity.

Case Example

One early example of the success of the support team structure was the IS (information systems) support team. In addition to moving all the machines and equipment, and starting up the operation in a new province in a new facility with new employees, the company replaced the old IS operation with a new and, at the time, untested integrated manufacturing software system. As was to be expected, the system had a tremendous number of bugs and adjustments that needed to be worked out before the value of integration could be realized. Problems arose almost immediately because employees had knowledge of the system only from their own limited functional area viewpoint. And even that knowledge was minimal, because as new hires, they had only limited exposure to the entire Imperial Manufacturing system.

While the software supplier was of some help, it was clear that this would not be sufficient on an ongoing basis. The supplier did not have extensive knowledge of all the intricacies of the work flow, and had not been able to bring employees along as the system was installed because the employees hadn't been hired yet. Also, the supplier was more accustomed to working in an environment where there was an IS manager or director and was not attuned to working with teams of people who wanted to learn and adapt a system to their own specific needs. Early on, it became clear that a more innovative and effective approach was needed. Key information fell through the cracks, was never generated, or was discovered too late. Deliveries and quality were at stake. Frustration was threatening the functioning of the whole operation.

The IS support team was formed with nine members from all areas of the organization: managers, engineers, machine technicians, administrative members, customer service representatives—shop and office employees alike, professional and technical side by side. Their first task was to define their mission: "To ensure the integrated software system meets the operating needs of the business with accurate and consistent information and reports." They then identified roles and responsibilities and performance optimization elements (see table 1).

The team then clarified the objectives they would measure against (some were already set by urgency of business needs) and developed a list of tasks to accomplish in order to meet these objectives and deliver on the mission. The first task they identified served a dual purpose: (1) educating everyone on the process flow from start to finish; and (2) developing a master map of the process with the corresponding IS interfaces using "sticky notes." Once this was complete, they were able to see where system bugs, outages, and overlaps were corrupting their information. A side benefit was that all team members had a better appreciation for how their work affected others in the organization, and they let go of some of their own personal agendas. All team decisions are made by consensus. Therefore the team thought that the quality of their decisions was exceptional. Over time and with practice, the team was able to make decisions efficiently and see results coming from a quality process.

The team then went about addressing specific problems with the system, sometimes in smaller task groups, and within two months, they had addressed most of the troublesome issues that had been causing delays in deliveries and inefficiencies in production. Team members reported great satisfaction with the process and the speed at which they were able to resolve problems that had appeared insurmountable initially, when they were not yet commissioned to tackle them and when they were viewed from an individual perspective. The element of control over their own work life was tremendously gratifying. They believed that they were able to resolve their IS problems better, quicker, and to a higher level of satisfaction than the supplier would have.

Once the initial work was done, team members were charged to return to their functional teams to train other team members by providing a system overview and giving them specifics on how to use the system to meet their day-to-day needs. The ongoing efforts of this support team are now focused on system enhancements, improvements, and corrective action.

Table 1. IS support team: roles, responsibilities, and performance optimization.

Team Mission Statement:

To ensure the integrated software system meets the operating needs of the business with accurate and consistent information and reports.

Roles and Responsibilities:

- Review the needs of the business.
- Evaluate system capabilities.
- Review and define procedures.
- Identify reports needed.
- Identify training needs.
- Train all team members on IS procedures and maintain team awareness in the event of procedure revisions.
- Maintain cross-team communications.
- Identify and investigate problems; recommend and evaluate corrective action.
- Optimize the use of the system.
- Provide feedback to management on team activities.

Performance Optimization:

- Meetings: monthly
- Location: training room
- Duration: one hour
- Agenda items will be published prior to meeting.
- Each team member will be assigned tasks or action items to perform and report on at meetings.
- Minutes of meetings will be published promptly and action items will be forwarded to appropriate manager or team for processing and feedback.

It is debatable that this approach is less costly than traditional decision-making approaches in terms of the people-hours spent to resolve the problem. The benefit in terms of learning, acceptance, and the quality of decisions affecting multiple functional areas is immeasurable, however. Very few organizations can say that most people understand or support the IS decisions that have been forced upon them by the IS director or staff. The payback in terms of employee gratification and satisfaction is evident, although not highly measurable. In addition, the overall process understanding and perspective that people developed while on the team has born fruit even when they are back on their home teams, allowing them to be more empathetic to other teams and their needs. The freedom and sense of independence of having a knowledgeable person on the home team as a resource helps people to ask questions and learn when the time is right. These teams are moving significantly toward a real understanding of their system, as opposed to being chained to a system and merely executing memorized steps without meaning. This approach allowed them to sidestep an organizational dependency on either the supplier or the IS staff that will save money in the long run and allow for more ongoing, continuous improvement, learning, and commitment.

Implementation of Cross-Functional Support Teams

At start-up the plant was minimally staffed, and that meant that some employees had to do double duty on multiple support teams. Also in the beginning, some of the support teams were not launched because a need had not yet been identified for them, they were not a high priority, or the timing was not right. One such example was the team system support team, which was designed to take over aspects of the consultants' roles once the operation was fully staffed and running. This team was not launched until the spring of 1996 even though the operation began in May 1994. The delay was strategic because nearly all employees were too new to the system, the facility was not yet fully staffed, and the kinks in the design needed to be worked out. In addition, there was an accountability to system integrity that was best left in the hands of the consultants for the interim, until the employees were acclimated to the system and ready to take on this responsibility.

As employee numbers increased, the support teams were staffed to support the system design. Employees were asked to submit their names for those teams they had an interest in or where they had relevant experience. Management then made the initial assignments to the support teams. Generally the number of support team members matched the number of functional teams in the organization because the issues they addressed affected the entire organization. Where this was not the case, however, team numbers were lower (for example, the public relations support team has three members.) Employees serve on only one support team at a time, and their terms are established at one year of service. Individual employee development plans reflect future cross-functional support team involvement. The teams are designed to become more self-sufficient in their selection process and general functioning.

The consultants guided each support team through a formal formation process in which they

- developed a mission/purpose statement and boundaries
- established team objectives and measurements
- defined team roles and responsibilities
- identified team procedures/practices including decision processes; meeting frequency, length, and times; behaviors; and communication methods (minutes, agendas)
- assigned priorities and accountabilities
- clarified interfaces with others in the organization
- identified resources needed including training for team members.

Teams sought out opportunities for inexpensive or free training in their topical area such as books, videos, publications, seminars, in-house management experts, and supplier assistance. Some cross-functional teams received training subsidies from the Canadian government for technical-, safety-, and human resources-related topics. The consultants also were tapped as training resources for effective meetings, decision making, problem solving, and constructive team behaviors.

Cross-Functional Support Teams in Operation

As support teams started up, most held regular meetings and kept track of their progress in minutes that were posted and placed in a binder in the company resource library for all to reference. Members also provided regular updates in their functional area team meeting and solicited input for the issues at hand on the support team. They tracked their progress by the number of objectives they were able to meet. Support teams turned in mixed performance records. It is not surprising that those teams with the most pressing business-related tasks generally turned in the best performance records, because the organization readily dedicated time and resources to those tasks that met an impending business need.

As a result of typical start-up pressures, those support teams with fewer immediate tasks related to production lost momentum, as their sponsors allowed meeting schedules to fall victim to time and energy demands. These teams in particular became very disenchanted with and cynical about the cross-functional support team structure. The training and education, and selection and hiring teams experienced this the most. Unfortunately they also had the same sponsor who took over the teams' tasks in the "interest of efficiency" and assumed the team was not able to tackle problems from a knowledge or judgment perspective. Some of this thinking was simply a rationale for the sponsor's inability to relinquish control. The consultants intervened as much as possible to provide specific coaching to the sponsor regarding his role.

The consultants also provided operational feedback to the cross-functional support teams during routine consultant visits to monitor the system and made suggestions for improvement. Initially these visits were held once a quarter and then spread out to once every six months.

A Backward Glance—Problems and Learnings

Several other support teams were started up at the same time as the IS support team with varying results. Total quality; waste management; health and safety; employee events; process and technical improvement; and 911 teams had some success. The features common to these teams were a fire-fighting, or problem-solving, stance and a task orientation or purpose that had some vestige in the old system (for example, safety committees or task forces). Those teams with management problems (present management needed to give up some control or increase trust of their employees) got off to a slow start. It is probably significant to the IS support team's success that the organization did not bring the former IS manager along, nor did they bring any former IS employees on permanently.

Managers seemed to have the most difficulty allowing teams to take charge in their area of expertise. For example, two teams that had a rocky start were the training and education and the selection and hiring support teams. This was partly because the sponsor had a background in human resources and industrial relations and insisted on doing much of the team's work under the premise that they were not up to handling the responsibility yet. This objection could have been launched against any of the teams, but where the teams were allowed to, they rose to the task and learned what they needed to know. This resistance to give up the reins is not uncommon, since managers frequently slip back to tasks they are comfortable with in times of stress.

In addition to management control, time and training also were obstacles. Because of the urgency to get up and running, and the fact that all the employees were new to the business (with the exception of the eight transferred managers), time was a valuable commodity, and the training focus was justifiably on the technical aspects of the operation. The system has survived the post-start-up blues by staying focused on their vision, mission, values, and the culture they were trying to create. Cross-functional support teams were implemented and became operational as the work system matured. Those that were still struggling got a much-needed face lift in the spring of 1996, as the consultants and general manager reinitiated all support teams, launched the team system support team, clarified the sponsor roles and duties, and adjusted team membership now that the plant was nearly fully staffed. Now the cross-functional support teams are instrumental in the organization's success and continuing ability to undertake increasing challenges of new product lines with great flexibility, speed, and responsiveness.

Conclusion

In general, employees and managers alike conclude that the advantages of cross-functional support teams have outweighed the disadvantages. Expanded learning about the business, additional team learning opportunities, and better business decisions are apparent on a daily basis. The increased commitment to and involvement in the operation have allowed the organization to achieve performance numbers ahead of schedule and, in many cases, beyond expectations. The result impressed corporate leadership so much that it inspired the organization to undertake team initiatives in its other plants. The operation now posts a profit. The number of indirect employees has dropped from almost 60 percent to 40 percent. The original intention of the redesign effort and the design team has been well served by the cross-functional support teams that are now an integral part of this dynamic organization.

Questions for Discussion

1. How could this organization have avoided having sponsors take over the duties of the support team and not sacrifice results?
2. For which types of organizations would this type of support team design be suitable? Can you think of any other applications for these concepts?
3. What issues would arise if an established organization attempted to adopt this support team design?
4. What implications would you predict as this design evolves into its fifth year?
5. How would you design the process for changing support team members at the 12-month point?

The Authors

Diane Hertel has been in consulting since 1983. Her focus is a systems perspective of human resources and organizational effectiveness. Her prior professional experience includes 12 years in various business and academic settings. She holds a master's degree from the University of Washington-Seattle and a bachelor's degree from Marquette University, both in English and education, with additional coursework in the M.B.A. program at the University of Wisconsin-Oshkosh.

Suzan Schober Murray has been a human resource consultant since 1989. Her background is in facilitating organizational change and assisting in the transition management process. She held various management positions for more than 12 years with Procter & Gamble. Her educational credentials include an M.S. in organizational development from the University of Wisconsin-Green Bay, and a B.S. in industrial sociology from Iowa State University.

Diane Hertel and Suzan Murray can be reached at Hertel & Murray Human Resource Consultants, Inc., 414 East Walnut Street, Suite 220, PO Box 367, Green Bay, WI 54305-0367; phone: 414.436.4686; fax: 414.436.4696; e-mail: hmiinc@aol.com.

High-Performance Teams in the Construction Industry

BE&K Construction

Kathleen Chapman and Gigi Gerson

Construction companies have to deal with two major problems, turnover and safety. Many of the problems they face are part of the industry: various crews work side by side and never communicate; plans are changed but only the supervisor knows. This case study focuses on one construction company that decided to test high-performance work teams. Team members need to feel they have the support of management in order to succeed. This case focuses on work teams that passed through four stages: Form, Storm, Norm, and Perform.

BE&K Construction, an international firm headquartered in Birmingham, Alabama, has developed a pilot program to use a high-performance work team approach on construction projects, the first program of its kind in the construction industry. In its initial trial, both the performance and attitudes displayed by the team members gave cause to be optimistic about its future value. Although the results of the pilot project were better than expected, and confirm the success of the program, further scientific analysis is needed to confirm the effects of high-performance work teams on project results. Only preliminary assessments are currently available, but the processes and procedures for future measurement plans are in place to calculate the program's future return.

Industry Background

Traditional construction projects are usually planned, scheduled, and completed using a single craft, or specific job skill, approach. This

This case was prepared to serve as a basis for discussion rather than to illustrate either effective or ineffective administrative and management practices.

approach involves workers from each craft operating at the same time, each person moving from one area to another on the project completing work only for his or her specific craft. Each group of individual craft workers is monitored by a supervisor, who also makes decisions and performs administrative duties. This approach functions much like a factory assembly line, where workers repeatedly perform a single task as a product travels down the line.

Like factory workers, single-craft construction workers rarely have the opportunity to follow a job through to its completion, nor do they have much input into project development. The construction industry traditionally has had multiple layers of supervision and most hourly construction workers have not been required to think through problems and provide solutions on their own. Today, however, because of fewer workers on the job and increased competition, they must be able to do so.

This change is not the result of intentional downsizing but of a shortage of qualified employees. One of the key concerns of the industry today is the lack of good workers. According to recent studies and industry experience, today's construction industry is in crisis. Construction companies are getting worried that there won't be enough skilled tradespeople available to meet their needs in the next few years.

About 71 percent of the 401 respondents to a national survey of general contractors, subcontractors, and design firms said they expect a "dearth of skilled people in the industry." In addition, 53 percent of contractors polled believe construction activity in the private sector will increase, and 42 percent see an increase in construction for the public sector as well. Construction increases, coupled with fewer workers entering the construction field, will make finding qualified and certified workers more and more difficult.

According to an ENR (Engineering News Reporter) survey of the top 400 U.S. general contractors and the top 600 specialty contractors, construction companies in some areas are "knee deep in labor shortages." Shortages were reported in more than half of the 18 crafts examined. The 217 firms responding to the survey reported that 58 percent of the crafts they use have some degree of labor shortages, and nonunion contractors are being hit the hardest with worker shortages. Fifty-three percent of these firms believe the spreading craft labor shortages are adding to the cost of projects, and 13 percent are now offering bonuses and incentives to attract the skilled labor they need (*ENR*, December 25, 1995).

The construction industry also struggles with trying to train and develop a workforce that is largely transient. Craft superintendents and above are the only true salaried BE&K employees; all other supervision is drawn from hourly personnel who are temporarily employed for specific projects and are often hired at the current job location. One of the challenges of developing high-performance work teams for these workers is that they are not a continuous presence in the company; instead, they are hired only for the duration of a project, which may be anywhere from six to 24 months.

In addition to a transient workforce, the construction industry is plagued with high rates of turnover and absenteeism; therefore, workforce retention has become a key industry concern. Companies have a problem getting good hourly people to stay with the company long enough to become salaried employees. Young people are not coming into the construction field, and if they do come, they don't stay. A number of studies asking young people what careers they wanted to pursue put construction near the bottom and report that young people's perceptions of construction work is that it is "not full time" and "not lucrative" (*ENR*, July 31, 1995).

To address these issues, BE&K decided to design a high-performance work teams model and training program specifically for BE&K Construction. They planned to implement the process on one small pilot project, determine its effectiveness, modify it as needed, and then implement it on a larger project.

Organization Profile

BE&K Construction is one of the nation's largest industrial construction firms, specializing in the pulp and paper, petrochemical, and other process-oriented industries. Consistently ranked by *ENR* in the top 20 construction companies in the United States, BE&K also has been ranked by two publications as one of the top 100 best companies to work for in America. Since BE&K is a privately held company, all details concerning company size and financial status are proprietary.

In an effort to improve workforce retention and employee loyalty, BE&K decided to implement high-performance work teams on selected sites to improve communications and help employees gain a feeling of ownership in their work, as well as to ensure the highest level of commitment and productivity available to workers. The vice president of BE&K Construction observed, "BE&K is constantly searching for ways to be more cost effective and to pass that cost savings on to our clients." BE&K believes that a high-performance work team approach is one solution to that search.

High-performance work teams allow individuals to develop new skills. Rather than being a single cog in a vast wheel, the individuals in the team join together to become a hub, and as such, become stronger and more valuable to the project. High-performance work teams contain multitalented people willing to do whatever it takes to get the job done.

In 1994, BE&K experimented with a small, controlled high-performance work team effort on a project in South Carolina. BE&K decided to try the job with a group of about 30 workers as a high-performance work team. Since it was a small job in a controlled situation (a subjob of a big job), the company was prepared to take a risk with a new work process— one that turned out to be highly successful. The teams had some high-performance work team training. All the numbers (cost, safety, and schedule) on this project were good. The project came in under budget and ahead of schedule with almost no turnover or absenteeism. Even more amazing, however, was the exceptional commitment the workers themselves displayed—to their teams, to BE&K, and to one another. One of the supervisors said that he thought it was his best work experience in his 10+ years in construction. This is a remarkable comment, especially since he was not even a salaried BE&K employee. Everyone left that project with a great deal of commitment to BE&K.

In early 1995, the company decided to try high-performance work teams on a slightly larger scale. BE&K was awarded a lump-sum contract by a Monroe, Georgia, mill to install the equipment for a new process in the wood-products industry. They decided to accomplish this work using a high-performance work teams approach, seeking to develop a higher level of teamwork among workers by giving them more decision-making and some multicraft responsibilities. The project superintendent on this job also had experienced this approach at the South Carolina project.

To develop the program, a training consultant from Performance Productions worked under the guidance of the director of professional development and education (PD&E) at BE&K, who had come with a wealth of experience in total quality management and quality teams from her work with other large companies, one of which received the Demming Prize. Combining their areas of expertise, they formed the design team that would develop the model and training for the work team initiative.

Key Success Components for High-Performance Work Teams

To develop a successful high-performance work teams program, key components must be included in the process. Neglecting any of these essential elements will lessen the chances of developing a successful program (see figure 1).

Figure 1. Key high-performance work team success components.

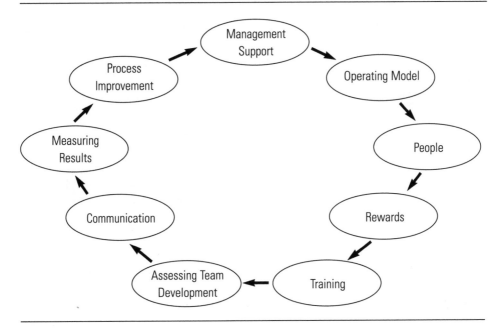

Management Support

Much of the success of high-performance work teams depends on the project management's willingness to share decision making, information, and possibly some of the project's profit with the team members. As BE&K began to develop this new approach, management took strong positive action to communicate the "big project picture" to all personnel. They also solicited ideas from team members and discussed suggestions for carrying out the work. For high-performance work teams to succeed, team members must feel confident that management will keep their promises, and management must trust that team members want to perform well and will not take advantage.

Ultimately hoping to improve worker retention and employee loyalty, BE&K's vice president of construction also was committed to high-performance work teams because "it makes the workers feel better about working at BE&K." To confirm management's commitment to high-performance work teams, he had the letter presented in table 1 sent to each team member.

Developing the Operating Model

Converting to work teams is different from other training initiatives because more is involved than simply developing a training pro-

Table 1. Management letter to team members.

Thank you for joining this unique effort on this project for BE&K at Monroe, Georgia. BE&K has decided to use the high-performance work team concept for implementation on this project. We all hear a great deal today about safety, employee involvement, productivity, and competitiveness, all of which are driving this project.

This concept is based on the idea that five heads are better than one, and that five people working together as a team will find a safer, more efficient, and quicker way of getting things done than one person working alone. It embraces the belief that if team members are part of the decision-making process on how something should be done, they will claim ownership and be self-motivated to support that decision and will project a greater success.

This concept empowers teams to take correction actions and resolve day-to-day conflicts. It will capitalize each member's skills and leadership abilities and will foster open and honest communication between all team members.

We have created a reward system that we feel will produce a safer project, increase productivity, optimize the schedule, and produce a winning team for everyone involved.

I will stay involved with this project and will closely monitor the feedback on its progress. We are all looking forward to a very successful project using this concept, and I feel confident that when we finish, we will declare it a success.

gram. Developing the model for a work teams approach is just as important as the training that is done later. Because construction is by nature supervisor driven, with the supervisor often being the only constant throughout the project, the design team knew that the teams would need to be led, not self-directed, so they focused their needs analysis on the supervisor.

The design team developed the BE&K model by asking what skills or competencies would be needed in the team leader and team coordinator (and all supervision) to make this work? Because no one in construction had implemented work teams, it was first necessary to develop a model for the initiative. This took several steps: (1) research other companies and programs; (2) conduct a needs analysis, including task analysis and a focus group; (3) develop a generic model; and (4) apply the model to a current project.

Research Other Companies and Training Programs

The design team went first to academic literature to learn as much as possible about work teams. Then they researched other generic work team programs, such as Blanchard and Zenger Miller. They talked with a Zenger Miller master trainer to see if their existing material could be adapted for BE&K's use, but found it didn't adequately fit BE&K's situation because it needed the look and feel of the BE&K culture.

Since there was no one in the construction industry to benchmark from (BE&K was a pioneer then, and still is), the design team researched other paper company practices, conducting minimal research, mostly in the form of telephone interviews with a company facilitator who had set up a team's program. They researched practices of large paper companies that would be likely clients and benchmarked against them because they had used work teams. Since a paper mill is a continuous process industry and construction isn't, however, the design team concluded that no similarities existed between the two situations, so their model could not be used. After failing to find a model in literature, the design team decided to apply the research and use it to create their own model.

Conduct a Needs Analysis

Since both the model and the training are critical components of successful teams, the initial development began with an extensive needs analysis, asking "How does a typical construction group work now?" or "What is the current way work is being performed?" The consultant decided to visit other project sites to learn what a supervisor traditionally does; work with a focus group of five supervisors from various crafts; and work with project supervisors to design a program to help them function successfully in a team environment.

TASK ANALYSIS. The first step in this process was to visit and analyze an ongoing project to accomplish the following objectives:
- Define the responsibilities of the supervisor.
- Define the responsibilities of the crew members.
- Discuss the technical or direct construction-related responsibilities of the supervisor within each craft.
- Observe supervisor and crew working in the field.
- Outline possible craft "matches" for multicraft work team members.

The consultant shadowed a civil (carpenter) supervisor, beginning with the daily morning meeting with the project superintendent, going on to the daily planning and safety meeting, and finally, going into the field to oversee work, look at blueprints, and do paperwork. She concluded that "basically, the supervisor gives the instructions for the daily tasks and then closely monitors the work."

FOCUS GROUP. To get a feel for how the supervisors would react to working in teams, a focus group was assembled, made up of five supervisors from a variety of crafts. After explaining to them the work team concept and asking for their input, four out of five of the focus group members indicated that they saw an advantage to working this way, particularly in the area of utilizing personnel—being able to use workers who were not busy at that particular time. They emphasized, however, that to work properly, significant attention to planning would be vital.

While on this trip, the consultant also interviewed three superintendents for their ideas about which crafts complement one another well enough to support cross-training of craft workers. Some suggested combinations included

- millwright and instrumentation (both crafts require precision work)
- iron and rebar or riggers (in other companies are one craft)
- millwright and pipe fitters (both require attention to detail)
- electrical and instrumentation (both crafts require math skills)
- iron workers and any craft (they are already accustomed to working with other crafts, as are carpenters).

While observing the supervisor and his crew, the consultant also observed several key situations that supported the initiative to move to work teams:

- Various crews of different crafts were working in the same area, but did not communicate very much.
- A client representative walked by, and the supervisor didn't know who he was.
- An inexperienced helper committed a safety violation, and a journeyworker in his crew was standing right there and did not say anything. The supervisor had to point out the violation and correct it, even though this procedure had been specifically discussed in the safety meeting that morning.
- A field engineer was required to complete a task, and communication between the crew and the engineer was stifled.
- Crew members frequently came to the supervisor for assurance that they were doing the right thing.
- A superintendent notified the supervisor of an unsafe condition created by one of his crew members.
- Only the supervisor knew when blueprints were updated.

All the information gathered was then used to develop the model and the training design by asking "What skills do the team leaders need?" and "How does the project need to be organized to make the teams work?"

Develop a Generic Model

The design team created the structure and approach for the BE&K specific work team model as follows:

- A work team is one whose members actively focus their skills, knowledge, and abilities on the team's performance.
- Team members hold one another jointly responsible for the entire team's results.
- A work team contains team members from all levels of construction workers, from third-class helper to master craftsperson, with one supervisor serving as the team leader.
- The team members are chosen from different crafts and combine their individual skills, knowledge, and capabilities to reach the goals of the work team, as well as the goals of the entire construction project.
- The teams encourage problem solving and innovation and share in decision making.
- In a work team environment, the role of the leader is a bit different from that in a traditional work environment.
- Team leaders share the figures from cost reports with their teams and help them to discover new ways to do things. They also meet with the craft superintendents and schedulers, which is not typical in traditional construction.

The team leader in a work team plays a different role from the supervisor in the traditional construction environment. Traditionally, the supervisor is responsible for many day-to-day administrative and managerial tasks. In the work team environment, team leaders expand their roles to include team and individual goal setting, coaching or facilitating decision making, providing information, removing barriers, and planning.

To be successful, the team leader must hand off some of those day-to-day responsibilities in order to have the time needed to plan and facilitate. Some responsibilities, however, the team leader must keep; so he or she must delegate part of the old day-to-day responsibilities to have time to assume these new roles, and the team members must assume some new responsibilities as well. With training, a work team can eventually

- select, develop, and train its members
- define team goals and maintain accountability for those goals
- establish a code of conduct or behavior
- monitor performance
- recognize individual and team milestones
- communicate effectively with the team
- perform day-to-day administrative duties.

The model places the team leader at the hub of the team, communicating vital information to the team members and involving them in planning and decision making. The model and roles must evolve from the old thought process toward the new model as members learn to become a team. Amazingly, in the Monroe pilot, when the first steps were made toward empowering employees, some teams progressed farther and faster toward the model goal than anyone had anticipated, exhibiting team skills not expected at this phase.

Apply the Model to a Current Project

The facility being built at Monroe was designed to produce a wood product using a relatively new process and was only the second such facility that ACME Paper had built. The project was expected to last 12 months. Because the process was so new, the engineering drawings were continually being modified as the facility was being built.

BE&K's project scope for the ACME facility in Monroe was mechanical equipment erection of the nine major pieces of equipment. Early in the preconstruction phase of the project, the superintendent worked enthusiastically to structure this project to fit the work team model, consulting the PD&E director to determine how this larger project could be set up to support multicraft teams. The project superintendent had worked on the South Carolina job and believed in the power of the team approach. He was empowered by the project manager, who also was familiar with work teams, to develop the plan to make it work. Accordingly, the superintendent divided the project into six areas, based on the following:
- crafts that were necessary to the work and were complementary
- work-hours needed to erect each piece of equipment
- flow of the engineering and construction schedule
- installation sequence of major pieces.

Structure of Teams

With these criteria in mind, the project superintendent recruited the expertise of the two craft superintendents assigned to the project (millwright and structural crafts) to define the make-up of each area team. They decided that each team should include one team leader; eight to 16 team members; levels—helper to journeyworker; and a blend of millwright, structural, instrumentation, and electrical crafts.

Since the work being performed by BE&K was primarily erecting and setting equipment, the crafts needed would be mostly structural and millwright; therefore, the teams contained mostly those two crafts with one or two electricians per team. One area concentrated on pipe, so it was not multicraft. All members of that team were pipe craft workers.

People

Since people in work teams were expected to work differently and have different behaviors, they needed different job titles to reflect this and to send a message to the team leaders and members (see table 2).

Rewards and Incentives

Rewards and incentives were seen as essential to the project's success and necessary to attract and keep quality workers. At the beginning of the project, a formal incentive plan was set up, with incentives to be awarded at the end of project giving workers a piece of the profits for the project's successful completion, as defined by two criteria: safety and work-hours. The process for calculating the incentive was shared with the team members as they hired on, so they knew from the beginning how their success would be measured.

The incentives were not as effective as planned in attracting and retaining quality workers. Workers were reluctant to believe that the

Table 2. Job titles.

	Traditional Title	Team Role
Management team:	VP construction	Corporate sponsor
	ACME mill manager	ACME Paper sponsor
	Project manager/	Project team manager
	BE&K home office	Project team leader
	Project superintendent	
Project team:	Craft superintendent (2)	Team coordinators
	Supervisor (5); one per area	Team leaders
	Craft workers: journeyworkers and helpers	Team members
Training and performance team:	Director of professional development and education	Training adviser/ assistant facilitator
	Trainer	Facilitator
	Internal consultant (formerly project manager)	Multicraft adviser
	Trainer	Assistant facilitator

bonuses would actually be given because they had seen other construction companies make similar promises and not follow through; therefore, the workers first had to develop trust in management's promises. Then, when situations beyond the teams' control caused work-hour overruns, team members became upset, figuring that their bonuses would be lost as a result.

At the end of the project, BE&K rewarded team members with a dinner to recognize the teams and award prizes. Although the project had gone over budget in work-hours, management unanimously voted to give the workers an incentive in the form of a per diem award, since the factors that caused the overruns were beyond the control of the workers who had performed exceptionally well in spite of everything. The teams' safety performance also had been exceptional and played a part in the per diem awarded. In addition, BE&K's management knew that earning the trust of the team members was critical if the workers were to go on to the next work team project.

Training—Design and Development

To develop the training, a needs analysis was done based on the criteria used to develop the model: focus on the team leaders, and look at the gap between a supervisor's current skills and the skills required to be a team leader. The design team then developed a customized curriculum designed initially to train supervisors and superintendents to be team leaders and team coordinators. The overall training design was divided into four segments: (1) orientation; (2) team launch; (3) team leader development; and (4) team development for group decision making.

The home office made the initial commitment to the training, but then money and time got tight, so the facilitators were not able to design the additional training that was supposed to be offered as the project progressed. The initial training was conducted as in the following manner.

Orientation: Conducted by the Project Team Leader

As a person was hired on the job site, the project team leader, the team leader, and the worker meet for a one-on-one orientation to decide where the new worker would best be assigned. During the orientation, the project team leader would explain BE&K's work team; tell the new employee what was expected of him or her; ask what the employee's expectations were; and ask the employee up front, "Could you work in this environment?"

Team Launch: Conducted by Facilitators, Training Adviser, and Multicraft Adviser

After enough people had been hired to provide all teams at least part of their members, the training effort began with a team launch, which involved team leaders, team members, management from BE&K's home office in Birmingham, and representatives from ACME Paper. Workers from ACME who had already been through team training attended the team launch and spoke to the group during lunch. Support from ACME was instrumental to the overall success of the project. More than 100 people participated in this fully paid, 8-hour kick off.

During the team launch, participants learned the introductory skills required to begin the "forming" process out in the field. Included were the following objectives:

- Identify different types of teams.
- Define work team on this project.
- Identify team member skills and abilities.
- Define who is accountable for what and how to let other people be accountable.
- Describe the differences between an effective team and individual performance.
- Identify factors contributing to team effectiveness.
- Describe different team roles and how they fit into the big picture.
- Define the role of team leader v. a team member.
- Define the project goals and how their team helps achieve those goals.
- Identify the stages of team development, as well as what stage a team is in.
- Increase personal effectiveness by being able to use the personal DIS-Cernment inventory to identify the DISC style of each team member.

Team Leader Development: Conducted by the Principal Facilitator

One week after the team launch, all team leaders attended a team leader development workshop that was designed to equip them with the foundation skills needed to lead their teams in the forming process. They learned how to

- assess their performance as team leaders and use that information to improve
- solve problems and implement solutions as a team
- share information (for example, construction schedule and cost report) with team members
- reward and recognize team accomplishments

- establish team representatives in their own teams to be responsible for specific team maintenance duties
- understand the need for self-assessment, and use a self-assessment tool for monitoring their progress and development needs.

During this workshop, the facilitator conducted a problem-solving session, in which they discussed a scheduling issue that resulted from equipment not being delivered on time. The team leaders brainstormed about what they could do to fix the problem. They then took action by proposing their ideas for solutions to the project team leader, who then took one of the team leaders to the next client meeting to present several of their options for solutions. The client implemented one of their suggestions, which helped but did not completely solve the initial problem. The team leaders also brainstormed ideas for informal rewards and set up the office supervisor to serve as the training facilitator's on-site contact to report the team leaders' progress.

Team Development for Group Decision Making: Conducted by the Principal Facilitator

Several weeks after the team leader training, each team participated in individual team development sessions that were cofacilitated by the team leader. These sessions taught team decision making and trained the team leader to become a facilitator for his team. Consensual decision making was facilitated by the team leader. The principal facilitator stayed on site for two days, rotating the teams in and out. During this training, each team practiced skills designed to develop the following competencies:
- Define four methods of making decisions and the advantages and disadvantages of each.
- Use team agreement as a decision-making method and be aware of what team members must do to reach team agreement.
- Identify three factors that influence decision-making methods and explain which method to use with which factor.

Follow-up and assessment of the team leaders to see if and how they were using the skills learned in training was incomplete. Some assessment was done over the phone with an on-site facilitator, and one visit was made in which the facilitator coached team coordinators on how to deal with problems. But the off-site facilitators were not able to travel to the job site as much as needed.

Assessing Team Performance

As work teams progress in working together, they usually pass through four stages before beginning to work as a high performance team. Those stages are: (1) form, (2) storm, (3) norm, and (4) perform—F-S-N-P.

Form—July 1995

After the training, the teams, the team leaders and the management team all began to form, a team stage that traditionally exhibits the following characteristics:

- Team members begin getting to know one another.
- They feel the need to protect themselves by not revealing too much personal information.
- On the surface, team members are polite and a bit restrained.
- Beneath the surface, they feel a variety of emotions: excitement, enthusiasm, concern, anxiety.
- The team's task during this phase is to define roles, clarify its mission, set goals, and establish ground rules.

The team leaders began forming as a leadership group as well. As planned from the team leader workshop, the group of five leaders met once a week to solve problems concerning such things as staying within the budgeted work-hours and meeting the aggressive schedule.

Each team also met each week, and the team leader guided his crew as they learned to read and understand the cost report and use it to come up with new and innovative ways to beat the budget. Safety also was a priority for the weekly team meetings, and team leaders helped their crews learn to plan safety into each task. As the Level 3 (on-the-job behavior) evaluation discovered, however, these meetings were not consistent. The management team was forming at this time too, with the project team leader beginning to work closely with the client, making him part of the process.

Norm

The model is F-S-N-P; however, our teams "normed" before they "stormed." This is probably because the managers and team leaders were still somewhat in control, so the teams were not empowered to storm yet. By late August, working as a team in geographical areas instead of by crafts was becoming more familiar. Some multicraft work was being done.

Storm and Perform

By September, factors outside the teams' control were causing problems. This created a unique situation for the work teams and resulted in periods of storming and performing almost simultaneously. Fabrication errors and late equipment deliveries became such a problem that exceeding budgeted work-hours was inevitable. This caused the teams to become depressed, fearing that they would not get their incentive, and most of all, that the project would look like a failure. These desperate situations also had another effect, however—the teams began to become "super human." A team member described the situation:

The schedule was greatly affected by late deliveries, as well as fabrication errors, to the point that an overrun of work-hours was inevitable. To our credit, when the late items did arrive, they were promptly and safely put into place. For example, the dryers were approximately two months late. Though they were shipped in reverse order, the team was able to install them in only an hour and 45 minutes. Quite an accomplishment, considering each dryer weighed 170,000 pounds.

The project also was plagued with safety situations that were beyond the control of the BE&K teams. There were an enormous number of subcontractors on this project (42)—many with inferior safety programs. (Note: BE&K is the leader in safety in the construction industry.) There were times when the BE&K teams were working practically on top of other contractors. In addition, a disastrous accident occurred involving one of the other contractors: a fall that resulted in death. Again the BE&K teams performed beyond expectation at the time of the accident. They went to the rescue of the other contractor using every emergency response technique. The accident affected everyone on the project. BE&K persevered to win three safety awards, however, and the owner recognized the Monroe teams for their exceptional safety record on the project.

Highest Performing Team

As the project progressed, only one team reached true team performance. Their team leader was extraordinary, demonstrating most of the team leader competencies: information sharing, shared decision making, use of multicraft, and empowerment. Members of his team also exhibited more pride and ownership in their work, as exemplified by the following situation: One member of the team witnessed another using a hammer to install a bearing. He promptly told his team leader, who informed the man using the hammer that it would damage the bearing and suggested another way of doing the installation. Later that day, another team member saw the same man using the hammer again. The team leader then took that man off the assignment and took him to the tool room. He then got his team together and made them aware of what was happening. He told them he had already given the man a verbal warning and wanted their opinion on his next course of action. The team decided the man had been given enough chances, and rather than run the risk of him doing something else that would jeopardize the integrity of their work, they unanimously agreed he should be terminated.

The teams performed at times as multicraft teams. Considerable skepticism remained on the part of some craftsmen about multicraft work, however, with welding being the most reluctant.

Communication

Once the model was developed and put into place and the initial training was finished, the teams and team leaders were basically left to make their successes or failures on their own. As stated before, the model called for the team leaders to have weekly team leader meetings to do problem solving. Each team also was to have weekly meetings to go over the cost report and schedule in order to check their progress against cost, schedule, and safety standards.

Written communication was sent to the project managers periodically to update the teams' progress. All these processes helped to meet the teams' most important need: developing trust among all involved— team members, team leaders, management, and the client. The training adviser checked in occasionally and had an office staff person set up a register of how the teams were doing. She also occasionally did one-on-one coaching with the team leaders and the team coordinators. Communication was the weakest component on this pilot. An adequate communication plan was set up, but it was not carried out consistently by on-site team members or off-site (home office) facilitators and managers.

Measuring Results

Although the results of the project were better than expected, scientifically, they cannot be attributed to the work teams. Why? Because (1) they did not collect predata or set up a control group; (2) Level 2 training evaluation (learning) was not formally gathered; (3) Level 3 training evaluation (behavior change) was incomplete; and (4) the effects of the work team model or training were not isolated.

Level 3: On-the-Job Behaviors

Level 3 measurements were collected through interviews with team leaders and observation of team leaders and teams. A weak component of the Level 3 measurement was that no interviews were conducted with team members.

Interviews

Many comments were made by team leaders to show that behaviors and attitudes on the Monroe job were different. When asked in an interview to discuss the difference in his role on this project, a team leader whose team most fully embraced the work team model, responded: "My role was different, because I involved the team members instead of dictating the work. Even if I had my own way of doing things, I would let the team decide what to do, and if I didn't see anything wrong with their ideas, I would let them do it their way. I was pleased with the results."

In addition, the attitude expressed by a manager of ACME Paper indicated his positive reaction to the work and interest in working with BE&K again: "Of all our contractors, none came close to BE&K. The project superintendent did an excellent job, as did his team leaders, in setting up the project under the team concept and achieving their goals. The key to any successful team is the quality of the supervision, and I saw quality in the BE&K teams and their organization."

Another team leader said he watched as employees "took pride in completing their tasks. They enjoyed their work and showed interest in all activities." A third team leader added, "Everyone had a job to do, and each did it well."

Observations

During the on-site visit, the facilitator observed and recorded examples of on-the-job use of work team behaviors:

- Helpers and journeyworkers acted together as teammates to solve a problem.
- Team leaders and journeyworkers collaborated with engineers.
- A cost report was displayed in a team leader's shed for team member's reference.
- Job and construction plans were displayed in the personnel trailer for all to reference.

One display of how much this project meant to the workers themselves can be seen in the attendance at the awards dinner. BE&K observed almost full attendance by team members, even though more than one-third of the workers had already finished their work and left the job site. Many workers traveled long distances to attend this special awards dinner.

Level 4: Business Results
Success Indicators

The project's key safety indicators showed very favorable results in safety, exceeding project goals. Personnel turnover was 34 percent below budget (what was expected), and absenteeism was 68 percent below budget. Work-hours exceeded the budget by approximately 5 percent, but as stated earlier, this was attributed to factors outside the teams' control. Profitability of the job exceeded that budgeted, in spite of all the equipment delivery delays and the morale-debilitating rework on equipment. As impressive as these figures are, however, since the effects of the work teams were not isolated, it is impossible to guarantee a relationship between the results and work teams.

An additional confirmation of the successful team environment can be seen in the feelings of the team members themselves. Workers from the Monroe project overwhelmingly expressed a desire to go to another high-performance team work site. Given such encouraging initial results, BE&K is continuing to train for team performance and plans to use work teams on their next project.

Costs

The cost of the training-direct expenses was $17,000. The per diem incentive was $70,000. Training costs do not include paid time off the job for employees while training. The return-on-investment was not calculated. BE&K did express, however, that "this job more than repaid the training costs and per diem incentive."

Implementing on Another Project

An indication of the success of this pilot effort is that BE&K is now implementing work teams on another, larger construction project and making improvements to the model.

Process Improvement. Lessons learned (see table 3) were compiled from a contribution of observations and analysis by facilitators, designer, project team leaders, a team member, and an internal consultant. All lessons learned were part of the needs analysis for the future work team implementations. Some solutions were incorporated into the January 1997 work team (Pilot #2) construction project. Others will be part of the next generation.

Conclusion

Work teams present a significant change from the traditional way construction work and supervision has been handled. Because the hierarchy of supervision has been so deeply ingrained in the traditions of the construction industry, many in the industry have predicted that the change to work teams would not be readily accepted.

Although change is often difficult, even painful for some, the construction industry itself is changing, and to survive, companies must

Table 3. Learnings.

Lessons Learned	Solution
Since BE&K was not the primary contractor, they were not in control of all aspects of the project; therefore, the teams were unable to control certain factors.	Use work teams only on projects where BE&K is the primary contractor. **Pilot #2: BE&K is primary construction contractor.**
Training—team leaders and members did not get the work team training needed to see profound and universal behavior change, and new hires were left out of initial training.	Commit to and implement comprehensive work team curriculum and continue throughout project. **Pilot #2: All team leaders and members are required to complete curriculum.**
There was a lack of ongoing, continuous communication and feedback since facilitators were not able to travel to the job site frequently enough.	Commit to on-site work team facilitator/coordinator and consultant for duration of project. **Pilot #2: On-site facilitator identified and being trained. Consultant and PD&E facilitator assigned to project for duration.**
An end-of-project incentive is not enough to attract the best workers.	Offer travel/lodging per diem, or higher pay scale.
Not every worker is suited to work in a work team environment.	Use work team selection process. **Pilot #2: Developing behavioral selection process.**

change as well. When the work team concept was begun at BE&K, the process was designed as an evolutionary one, from current practices to true team performance in order to be more readily embraced by those in the industry.

One only has to read a sampling of the many stories or examples from the job site, telling how the workers themselves reacted to being even slightly empowered and of the ways many of them pushed themselves to make the project a success, to realize that in spite of the construction industry not fitting exactly into the models or stages of work teams, the spirit of teams—the spirit that exhibits the real essence of teamwork—was embraced overwhelmingly by those to whom it was introduced.

Table 3. Learnings (continued).

Lessons Learned	Solution
More extensive use of multicraft approach will improve productivity even more.	Set up multicraft training plan and wage scale.
Need more input from team leaders and team members in job planning.	Bring salaried and hourly supervisors in prior to start-up of construction to plan job using work teams. **Pilot #2: Craft superintendents and general supervisors are participating in preconstruction planning using work team concept.**
Couldn't show as much value as wanted to.	Employ extensive measurement system including predata. **Pilot #2: Data collected prior to beginning. Work teams using information gathered in phase 1 of project—completed December 1996. Results: Plan developed to measure throughout project.**

Questions for Discussion

1. How can work team methods and concepts from other models be applied to this construction model?
2. How is this model different from other models in other industries?
3. How could this model make better use of predata for measurement?
4. How was the changing role of the supervisor critical to the success of this project?
5. How did the lack of formality of BE&K enable the transition to teams?

The Authors

Kathleen Chapman, owner of Communications Excellence, is a writer, instructional designer, and business communications specialist. Since founding her company in 1994, she has developed training, marketing, proposals, and executive reports for organizations such as SCI, Monsanto Chemical, Performance Productions/BE&K, University of Alabama-Huntsville

(UAH), American Society on Aging, ABWA, and The Executive Speaker. She specializes in technical writing, business communications, and training design. Her background includes developing materials for all educational levels from adult nonreaders to courses taught as a UAH faculty member. She can be reached at Communications Excellence, 73 Paradise Lane, Hartselle, AL 35640; phone: 205.773.8147; e-mail: kechap@aol.com.

Gigi Gerson, founder and president of Performance Productions, is an instructional designer and performance improvement consultant. Her company has provided total training design for AmSouth Bank, JBEK Engineering, The Executive Speaker, SONAT, and Baptist Health Systems, as well as a safety training program for BE&K that won top awards from ISPI and ASTD. She also has an extensive background in writing, directing, and producing training videos. She has developed more than 50 training videos for business, industry, and education for companies such as GenCorp and Wal-Mart, and an award-winning video for AmSouth. She can be reached at 205.871.0711; e-mail: perfpro@ix.netcom.com.

References

"Craft Shortages Creeping In." *Engineering News Reporter,* 34, December 25, 1995.
"Shortfall of Workers Seen." *Engineering News Reporter,* 21, July 31, 1995.

TwinStar, an International Joint Venture

Hitachi and Texas Instruments

Ronald Shenberger

Imagine meshing Japanese and American corporate cultures for a new plant start-up in the volatile semiconductor industry. Need more challenge? Add team implementation, hiring in a tight labor market, and community concerns about new plant construction to up the ante. This new company bet millions on the old-fashioned principles of trust and relationships alongside high-tech manufacturing.

Background

Consider what it takes to bring a new manufacturing business on line. Factor in that it is a cyclical, high-tech industry. Add to the situation multinational and multicultural dimensions. Build the plant next to an affluent, residential neighborhood. Employ a relatively young, inexperienced workforce. Establish expectations that the business will be operational within a year.

In January 1995, two leading companies in the semiconductor industry joined resources with 13 international investment banks to create a new joint venture company, TwinStar Semiconductor. The two companies, Hitachi, a Japanese company, and Texas Instruments, a Texas-based company, hold a 27.5 percent interest each in the joint venture, and 12 banks hold the remaining 45 percent interest. TwinStar's vision evolved from the expectations of its two parent customers: "To be recognized by our shareholders as the lowest-cost, highest-productivity producer of reliable, high-quality sub-half micron memory products."

This case was prepared to serve as a basis for discussion rather than to illustrate either effective or ineffective administrative and management practices.

Organizational Profile

TwinStar manufactures DRAM memory for the two parent companies. It uses Hitachi and Texas Instruments manufacturing technology to create its product. Hitachi and Texas Instruments buy all of TwinStar's output. The company's mission is "to combine the strengths of Hitachi and Texas Instruments with the commitment and innovation of TwinStar people and the support of the local community to create a safe and profitable company for the production of memory products." The mission is expressed in the motto "1+1=3."

While Hitachi and Texas Instruments have participated in previous collaborative ventures, this is the first joint venture involving the construction of a wafer manufacturing/fabrication facility (fab) in the United States. TwinStar's plant, located in Richardson, Texas, occupies 450,000 square feet of which 50,000 is clean room manufacturing space. The plan was to employ 600 people during start-up from January 1995 to December 1996. Of that number, about half the employees were to be involved in direct production and the remainder in professional and technical support. TwinStar moved into its facility in January 1996 and began manufacturing qualification in May of the same year.

Industry Profile

Historically the semiconductor industry has been volatile. Not only is there continuous competition to stay on top of the technology, but the industry also is characterized by cycles of over and under capacity. The industry is currently experiencing a worldwide expansion of manufacturing capacity at a time when the 16 megabit DRAM memory product is selling at commodity prices. The expansion in manufacturing capacity is explained through an optimistic forecast for semiconductor products as new electronic applications are developed for the market. Both Texas Instruments and Hitachi are expanding their manufacturing capacity internally for other product lines as well as participating in other joint ventures.

The nature of work in a fab involves extreme levels of cleanliness. The manufacturing process requires people to work safely with highly toxic chemicals and gases in a controlled environment. All equipment is computer controlled and operates on scientific and technological principles. The manufacturing process is continuous and requires monitoring seven days a week, 24 hours a day. TwinStar employees work 12-hour shifts from midnight to noon and noon to midnight. Shifts rotate three days on, two days off, two days on, three days off, two days on, and two days off over a two-week period.

The industry is challenged to find an adequate supply of qualified candidates at all levels. Few schools have programs dedicated to the preparation of engineering and technical people for this industry. Most high schools and community colleges do not address the industry's needs unless they happen to reside in communities that already have a dominant semiconductor presence.

Case Description

Presently TwinStar is a case under development. This case describes a brief history of the company's formation, the goals during start-up, and how the initial workforce was recruited, selected, and trained. A review of where the company is in its evolution toward a steady state provides a measure of predictable, reliable, consistent performance. Each leader responded to interview questions about significant accomplishments they were most proud of and their most challenging experience during start-up. The results of the interviews describe the nature of the support received during start-up. Much success can be attributed to the support from the parent companies. That support is a story of merging four cultures: Japanese, American, Hitachi, and Texas Instruments. TwinStars revealed some of the challenges the company is currently experiencing, anticipated its future, and shared some lessons learned on the journey. This case is a synthesis and summarization of their responses to interviews.

Key Issues and Events
Cultural Merging

The most significant accomplishment in the successful creation of Twin-Star is the integration of four very strong cultures to create a fifth distinct culture. The most obvious integration is American culture (with its action orientation and pragmatic style with little concern for form and ritual) with Japanese culture. Japanese culture by contrast is oriented toward establishing trust before initiating business relationships. This need involves time that most American managers are not accustomed to committing before conducting business. The second cultural integration is between Hitachi and Texas Instruments. Hitachi is a very large and formal Japanese company with a tradition of stability and continuity. Communication avoids criticism and recognizes formal social rank. In contrast, Texas Instruments is a very dynamic company that responds rapidly to market changes. There is less concern with tradition, form, social rank, and relationships.

There has been high-level commitment from both companies in the creation of TwinStar. The product that TwinStar will make is the result of an ongoing collaboration between Texas Instruments and Hitachi in the design of the 64 megabit DRAM chip. When it was decided to build the plant in Richardson, TwinStar purchased the land from Texas Instruments. Texas Instruments managed the construction of the facility according to a master schedule. The plant design, while state of the art in technical specifications, is essentially the same as previous plant designs. Texas Instruments provides the manufacturing operating systems. Hitachi is the owner of the manufacturing processes and technology. They specify the manufacturing equipment, processes, and specifications. The company chairman of the board is a Hitachi executive. The chief engineer and quality leaders are Hitachi managers on assignment.

Leadership

The TwinStar culture has been created in part by the cooperative efforts of its two major stakeholders. It seeks to assert itself as a unique autonomous culture that serves its customers without being a subsidiary. TwinStar's management team realized early in its forming stage that additional time was necessary to work through both language and cultural differences in understanding. Composed of former managers from Texas Instruments and Hitachi, TwinStar leadership has learned to allow time for discussion during meetings to achieve full understanding before decision making. Early in its forming, the TwinStar Leadership Team created its vision, mission, and values statements that have become a part of orientation for all TwinStars.

According to TwinStar's president, a retired Texas Instruments executive, each leader is a strong personality. They were chosen because they possessed technical capability and talent, and the ability to work collaboratively to achieve TwinStar's goal. There has been a concerted effort among its leadership to become participative in leadership practices. Some admit to being challenged to conduct business in ways that are not familiar to them. The Japanese managers almost assume unity as a cultural way of doing business. American managers, because they are much more autonomous, must work at team building to achieve unity.

Plant Construction

One of the first significant challenges was building the plant next to an affluent residential community. TwinStar leaders worked closely with local government to minimize any adverse impact on the community. Initially some local residents objected to construction of a manufacturing facility adjacent to their homes. TwinStar leadership met monthly with residents to hear and address their issues and concerns, thus establishing a trusting relationship as a good neighbor and citizen in the community. Construction took one year from ground breaking in January 1995 to occupancy in January 1996. The streets were cleaned daily during construction. The building is architecturally appealing with a minimum of industrial appearance from the two intersecting streets. A high, grass-covered earthen berm shields the view of the parking area. TwinStar leaders continue to meet with community members and encourage employees to participate in community activities.

Recruitment, Selection, and Orientation

The first people hired at TwinStar in early 1996 were technical, professional, and administrative people. Many of them came from Texas Instruments and brought experience in the Texas Instruments semiconductor manufacturing systems. Of the 600 TwinStar employees, 30 are former Texas Instruments people and three are former Hitachi employees. In addition, representatives of Texas Instruments and Hitachi served as technical advisers during start-up. TwinStar managers began the process of recruiting and selecting a new workforce in January 1995.

Human resources was challenged to find a pool of qualified candidates in the Dallas employment market. The state unemployment figures under 6 percent suggest full employment. TwinStar competes with Texas Instruments and other semiconductor manufacturers as well as other high-tech manufacturers in the Dallas and Texas market for the same pool of people. TwinStar managers recruited nationally from technical universities for professionals and first-line supervisors. New hires generally had less then 10 years of experience, depending on the specific technical needs.

It was necessary to hire people capable of learning complex technical operations and train them to TwinStar's specifications. New Twin-Stars started their employment with a three-week orientation program. Working with representatives from the continuing education division of Collin County Community College, TwinStar's People and Organizational Development Team designed, developed, and implemented an orientation program that prepares people with little knowledge and experience to work in the semiconductor industry. The first two days include an introduction by plant leadership to TwinStar's vision, mission, and values and to the organizational design, followed by two days of safety overview. Eight days of team-based culture and total quality management follow. The last week is devoted to technical information about semiconductor technology and product manufacturing methods and processes. The orientation is a leveling experience that brings all new TwinStars to a foundation level upon which to build.

Training

TwinStar calls on the technical expertise of Texas Instruments and Hitachi to continue the training process. Its technical and professional employees were deployed to plants in Asia, Europe, and the United States throughout 1995 to learn the specific technical skills they would need to do their work. This training was a formidable task in logistically coordinating and communicating with people around the world. People new to the company and industry were placed in foreign cultures and asked to learn technical processes. There were some cultural and language difficulties during this period; some of the people in these plants did not appreciate their role as trainers, but most people received adequate training to begin their assignments. They had an opportunity to bond with their colleagues during their time together in a foreign country.

TwinStar recruited the operations production and operations support workforce regionally through a local employment agency that conducted preemployment screening. The initial waves of people were hired in part for their previous experience. It was expected that they would become instrumental in training those people who would follow. Production operators and support people go through the same three-week orientation process. The initial two waves of people were then trained locally in Dallas at a Texas Instruments fab until TwinStar's plant was ready for occupancy. Again managers had to deal with the issue of TwinStar people intruding into the normal operations of a manufacturing facility. The People and Organizational Development Team provided concurrent training in skills that facilitated people working collaboratively together. Leaders recognized that they can hire and train technically competent people, but if they cannot or will not work together, TwinStar cannot benefit from their knowledge. The training also provided an opportunity for TwinStar people to process their experiences of working at the Texas Instruments fab.

Workforce Development

The current challenge is to train and certify operation specialists to perform their tasks effectively. There is a six-step plan under development to train and advance people through their technical area. TwinStar leadership is working with community colleges and universities to provide education and training in semiconductor technology. This training and education will provide avenues for specialists to advance into technician and, potentially, engineering positions.

TwinStar's technical and professional people receive training in their areas of responsibility. The People and Organizational Development Team has initiated training in leadership, team development, and personal effectiveness. Local contractors are used to provide computer skills training. Texas Instruments's training center provides technical training. Contractors are used to provide specific technical training through the Alliance for Higher Education, a local consortium of higher education institutions in the Metroplex.

TwinStar's leaders have expressed satisfaction with the level of training available to its people. The real learning occurs as TwinStar's technical and professional people begin to apply their training on the job. They need to leverage their training experience with their colleagues. The challenge now is to mature TwinStar's workforce as quickly as possible.

Hitachi's and Texas Instruments's philosophies are somewhat different as to how maturity is achieved. Japanese engineering education is more theoretical. Graduates begin their careers working as operations specialists or technicians and develop into engineers in two to three years. American engineering education includes internships and work-study experiences. The expectation is that graduates will assume engineering responsibilities at initial employment. TwinStar leadership expects its technical and professional people to achieve an understanding and broad knowledge of all processes in their area of responsibility. They also expect strong team leadership.

Total Quality Management

TwinStar has adopted a unique way of managing its production operations. Most plants operate with a general manager who oversees the operations, engineering, and quality functions. TwinStar chose to forego the general manager role and operate through a factory steering team composed of three managers, one from each function. Total quality management provides a common language and thought process that includes managing by fact, getting the data, and involving employees in decisions. These managers meet regularly to discuss issues and concerns affecting production operations. There is a strong emphasis on defining and managing processes. This begins with the suppliers and the customers who receive the final product. The challenge is to merge the customer's various systems specifications and standardize processes.

The members of the factory steering team report to and are members of the TwinStar Leadership Team. This team includes members from administration, community affairs, human resources, and plant operations. Each leader has autonomy in how he or she chooses to manage operations. Some managers have chosen to operate under more traditional management practices in which they oversee individuals with specific assignments and personal accountability. Other managers are making a transition toward a more team-based approach that shares leadership responsibilities and accountability. They prefer to manage the process and permit team members to manage themselves. The TwinStar leaders have struggled with their own management practices, both as a team and as individual members of that team. There is no easy solution, and the best way has not surfaced to date.

Key Measures of Success

In order to bring TwinStar online over the 20 months since start-up, the company has adhered to a very demanding master schedule. Ultimately the best measure of success is the ability to deliver quality products at an acceptable cost in the long term. To accomplish that, each leader had to commit to achieving deadlines. This meant occupying the building by January, installing and qualifying equipment, and certifying operators by May. As of August 1996, manufacturing and quality systems were operating at or above a 95 percent machine utilization target. The systems availability target is at or above 99.5 percent. The focus was on achieving output and yield targets, and the goal was to achieve a steady state by the end of 1996, at which time reliable, consistent, and predictable performance was to be the standard.

Organizational Design

At this writing, the organizational design could be described as a mixture of functional design with some attempts at teaming. As previously stated, each leader maintains autonomy in how they choose to manage their organization. To paraphrase the president's position: As the workforce matures and develops skills, and the business achieves steady state, the challenge will be for people to adapt to a more participative way of managing. The company may lose some people along the way, but it is important to employ people motivated by the concept of team success rather than individual gain. Leaders must demonstrate less desire to control and more desire to lead through influence and participation, which creates fewer barriers for moving across the boundaries of the organization. By providing opportunities for people to grow in both depth and breath, the organization will stay flat.

Attrition Retention

The company is experiencing problems with turnover; the current experience is 11.7 percent. Some attrition is due to selection errors, the result of a mismatch in expectations and the demanding work schedule of a new plant start-up.

Lessons Learned and Recommendations

When asked about the lessons learned and what recommendations they would make to managers who take on similar projects, TwinStar's leadership responded with the following comments:

Cross-Cultural Communications
- I did not fully understand the language barrier. The Japanese seem capable of hearing and comprehending English, but still must think through the discussion in Japanese.
- Never, never assume the Japanese understand what you are saying just because they are nodding *yes*. Repeat, repeat, and if possible, write out what you are trying to communicate.
- We need to slow down the process. When the situation calls for it, we permit our Japanese colleagues to discuss the topic under consideration among themselves. They accomplish a deeper understanding and are capable of moving forward with a decision.
- It was difficult forming a team with people all over the world. Our team was able to get together off site for an extended period of time and plan. We took training together and were able to bond. We were able to build a plan and commit to it.

Process Management
- We need to define the process in the same way (referring to Texas Instruments/Hitachi process definition).
- It is important to define our in-process customers and who needs to be involved early, including suppliers.
- We need to do source inspections with all suppliers and especially on high-risk equipment.
- We need to define our requirement to our suppliers and expect self-inspection, self-governance, and audits.
- Stay on schedule. Try to do tasks as soon as possible.
- Learn about equipment early.
- Define the major objectives up front and understand the expectations. Negotiate those expectations.
- Spend more time up front and adjust staffing to meet expectations. Hire quality people and give good training.
- If we do not all work together all the time and gain agreement, or at least a consensus, concerning an issue or problems, much time and hard work can be lost.
- Set high goals, even at the risk of failing. It is often surprising what can be attained if you place the bar high enough. At least you will

have tried to do your best, gotten more done, and taken a broader view of what can be accomplished.

- Learn to listen to others. You learn from this, even if their area is outside your area of interest.
- Have good leadership with experience.
- I learned to adapt my management style. I thought that I had developed in my team management beliefs. I learned that I still needed to have control of some decisions.

The Future

TwinStar is on target in accomplishing its goals. They are currently qualifying the 16 megabit DRAM, a fully developed product, with their customers. This product is intended to be a learning product and to prove capability. The next step, the 64 megabit DRAM, is a product jointly designed by Texas Instruments and Hitachi. TwinStar will begin manufacturing this product in 1997.

Summary

The creation of TwinStar has been an ambitious undertaking to merge the strengths of the two parent companies and yet establish its own identity. TwinStar is beginning the transition into steady state, which is the foundation on which to build continuous improvement. Benchmarks compared to other joint ventures are being met and reset. It is fair to say that the mission of making 1+1=3 is well on its way to being achieved. This case is the opening chapter of an ongoing record of TwinStar's evolution.

Questions for Discussion

You have been selected to participate in a new plant start-up team. The manufacturing facility, to be built in your community, is the result of a collaboration between a highly respected international company in your industry and your company. Normally your two businesses would be competitors.

1. What are the major issues and concerns that immediately come to mind as you consider the magnitude of the task before you?

2. What values seem most important in the creation of this new enterprise?

3. What are the priorities for this project, as you see them?

4. How would you discuss these issues with your foreign colleagues?

The Author

Ronald Shenberger is a member of TwinStar's People and Organizational Development Team. His experience includes 17 years in the training and OD field working for several *Fortune* 200 companies. He writes and speaks occasionally about his experiences in new plant start-ups, team-based organizations, and assessment-based selection, assessment, and development. Current interests include creating workplace communities and socially responsible business practices. He can be reached at TwinStar Semiconductor, 500 West Renner Road, Richardson, TX 75080; phone: 972.994.3600; e-mail: 2rgs@gte.net. Shenberger can also be reached at Well Formed Outcomes, 1516 Windsor Drive, Denton, TX 76201; phone: 940.320.4267.

Reading List

James, J. *Thinking in the Future Tense, Leadership Skills for a New Age.* New York: Simon & Schuster, 1996.

Lewis, R.D. *When Cultures Collide: Managing Successfully Across Cultures.* London: Nicholas Brealey, 1996.

Mohrman, S.A., S.G. Cohen, and A.M. Mohrman Jr. *Designing Team-Based Organizations: New Forms for Knowledge Work.* San Francisco: Jossey-Bass, 1995.

About the Editors

Steven D. Jones is an associate professor at Middle Tennessee State University and a member of a self-directed team with the Industrial/Organizational Psychology program. He holds a Ph.D. from the University of Houston (1986). He teaches graduate courses in team performance measurement and training and has published 22 articles and book chapters in his field.

Since 1983, Jones has measured team performance in a wide variety of client organizations including manufacturing, health care, retail, insurance, military installations, as well as his own university. He conducts several workshops each year on team performance measurement at national and international conferences and is currently writing a book on the topic.

He is certified as a Zenger Miller trainer and also certified in Return-on-Investment Training Evaluation by Jack Phillips. The majority of his training over the years has been conducted for managers and team leaders.

Steven D. Jones can be reached at the following address: Industrial Organizational Psychology program, Middle Tennessee State University, Murfreesboro, TN 37129; phone: 615.898.5937; fax: 615.898.5027; e-mail: sdjones @acadi.mtsu.edu.

Michael M. Beyerlein is director and cofounder of the Center for the Study of Work Teams, program director for the International Conference on Self-Managed Work Teams, and associate professor of industrial/organizational psychology at the University of North Texas.

He graduated in philosophy from the University of Oregon in 1969, earned a master's degree in counseling and guidance from Oregon College of Education in 1976, and completed a Ph.D. in industrial/organizational psychology at Colorado State in 1986. He taught industrial/organizational psychology at Fort Hays State University in Kansas for three years. Since then, Beyerlein has taught and supervised graduate students in industrial/organizational psychology at the University of North Texas.

His research focuses on improving performance in creative knowledge work. Within that field of inquiry, his research interests include all aspects of work teams: organizational change and design, cognitive styles and decision making, job stress, creativity, knowledge management, the learning organization, complex adaptive systems, and measurement. Lately, his work has involved the relationship of leadership and work environment to work team failure and success.

Beyerlein's research includes both qualitative and quantitative methodologies with an emphasis on how the two can be used to support each other and be designed for more effective application in work settings. Recent work has expanded in scope to include the following multiple levels of the work system: intraindividual, interindividual, intrateam, interteam, and organizational. He has published in a number of research journals, is a member of the editorial boards for *TEAM* magazine and *Quality Management Journal,* edits *Team Performance Management Journal,* and is senior editor of the JAI Press annual series of books, *Interdisciplinary Studies of Work Teams.* Currently, he is editing a series of case books on high-performing teams with Steven D. Jones, as well as a history of work teams with Susan Beyerlein.

Michael M. Beyerlein can be reached at the following address: Research Office Center for Study of Work Teams, University of North Texas, Terrill Hall, Room 346, Box 311280, Denton, TX 76203-1280; phone: 940.565.4551; fax: 940.565.4806.

About the Series Editor

Jack Phillips has more than 27 years of professional experience in human resources and management, and has served as training and development manager at two *Fortune* 500 firms. In 1992, Phillips founded Performance Resources Organization, an international consulting firm specializing in human resources accountability programs. Phillips consults with his clients in the United States, Canada, England, South Africa, Mexico, Venezuela, Malaysia, Indonesia, Australia, and Singapore on issues ranging from measurement and evaluation to productivity and quality enhancement.

A frequent contributor to management literature, Phillips has authored or edited *Accountability in Human Resource Management* (1996), *Handbook of Training Evaluation and Measurement Methods* (2d edition, 1991), *Measuring Return on Investment* (Vol. 1, 1994), *Conducting Needs Assessment* (1995), *The Development of a Human Resource Effectiveness Index* (1988), *Recruiting, Training and Retaining New Employees* (1987), and *Improving Supervisors' Effectiveness* (1985), which won an award from the Society for Human Resource Management. Phillips has written more than 75 articles for professional, business, and trade publications.

Phillips has earned undergraduate degrees in electrical engineering, physics, and mathematics from Southern College of Technology and Oglethorpe University; a master's in decision sciences from Georgia State University; and a doctorate in human resource management from the University of Alabama. In 1987, he won the Yoder-Heneman Personnel Creative Application Award from the Society for Human Resource Management. He is an active member of several professional organizations.

Jack Phillips can be reached at the following address: Performance Resources Organization, Box 380637, Birmingham, AL 35238-0637; phone: 205.678.9700; fax: 205.678.8070; e-mail: roipro@wwisp.com.